The Innovative School

The Innovative School

Organization and Instruction

Shlomo Sharan, Hanna Shachar,
and Tamar Levine

Foreword by Seymour Sarason

BERGIN & GARVEY
Westport, Connecticut • London

Library of Congress Cataloging-in-Publication Data

Sharan, Shlomo, 1932–
    The innovative school : organization and instruction / Shlomo
Sharan, Hanna Shachar, and Tamar Levine ; foreword by Seymour
Sarason.
        p.   cm.
    Includes bibliographical references and indexes.
    ISBN 0–89789–630–0 (alk. paper)
    1. School management and organization—United States.
    2. Educational change—United States.   I. Shachar, Hanna.
    II. Levine, Tamar.   III. Title.
    LB2805.S546   1999
    371.2'00973—dc21   98–35503

British Library Cataloguing in Publication Data is available.

Library of Congress Catalog Card Number: 98–35503
ISBN: 0–89789–630–0

First published in 1999

Bergin & Garvey, 88 Post Road West, Westport, CT 06881
An imprint of Greenwood Publishing Group, Inc.

Printed in the United States of America

The paper used in this book complies with the
Permanent Paper Standard issued by the National
Information Standards Organization (Z39.48–1984).

10 9 8 7 6 5 4 3 2 1

Copyright Acknowledgments

The authors and publisher are grateful for permission to reprint the following copyrighted material:

Chapter 4: Originally appeared as Hannah Shachar, "Developing New Traditions in Secondary Schools: A Working Model for Organizational and Instructional Change," *Teachers College Record*, Vol. 97, No. 4 (1996), pp. 549–568. Reprinted by permission of Teachers College, Columbia University.

Figure 8.1: Reprinted from R. Canaday and M. Rettig, *Block Scheduling: A Catalyst for Change in High Schools* (Princeton, NJ: Eye on Education, 1995). Eye on Education, 6 Depot Way West, Larchmont, NY, 10538, (914) 833-0551.

Figures 8.3–8.5: Reprinted from *Horace's School,* copyright © 1992 by Theodore R. Sizer, by permission of Houghton Mifflin Co. All rights reserved.

Figure 8.6: Reprinted with permission from "Using Time Well: Schedules in Essential Schools," by Kathleen Cushman, *Horace* 12:2 (November 1995). Providence, Rhode Island, Coalition of Essential Schools, Inc.

Every reasonable effort has been made to trace the owners of copyright materials in this book, but in some instances this has proven impossible. The authors and publisher will be glad to receive information leading to more complete acknowledgments in subsequent printings of the book, and in the meantime extend their apologies for any omissions.

Contents

Figures and Tables

FIGURES

TABLES

Foreword

This is a book we should welcome for several reasons. For one thing, it contains a very reasoned, non-polemical analysis of the major types of efforts to change and improve schools. At the same time, it indicates why most of these efforts have produced meager results. The reasons are many but among the most important are those that have to do with matters of scope, implementation, substantive focus, a shallow conception of the culture of the school, and the purposes of schooling. The authors know whereof they speak because for decades they have been involved in school change efforts which were not only truly heroic but rigorously conducted and commendably analyzed, with impressive results. Professors Sharan, Shachar, and Levine are deservedly recognized for their studies of what is required to incorporate cooperative learning in real classrooms in real schools where problems abound. I said their efforts were heroic, and by that I meant that they took the culture of the school seriously: they adapted a realistic perspective, they did not underestimate what teachers had to unlearn and learn, and they dealt with the daily realities and complexities of schools. If you trace the development of their thinking over the decades, it becomes clear why they had to write this book.

This book is about far more than cooperative learning. It is about the organization of schools and how it impacts negatively on teachers and students despite the good intentions of everyone in the schools. The authors do not engage in the game of blame assignment; there are no villains. There is a historically determined organizational structure which is at cross purposes to creating and sustaining contexts of productive learning both for teachers and students. No one who reads this book will conclude that you can improve student learning without improving the conditions which at present do not provide the contexts of productive learning. It is a distinguishing feature of this book that the point is so persuasively put forward. School change is about more than changing attitudes or practice because both, if they are to be sustained, require radical organizational change, not tinkering.

This book is about educational philosophy and theory, educational practice and action; it is grounded in the behavioral, programmatic, organizational realities of schools. This is not only a "how-to-do-it" book but a "how-to-think-it" book. And this book will cause the reader to think. H. L. Mencken said that for every complicated problem there is a simple answer that is wrong. What we are treated to in this book is an incisive analysis of a complexity to which we are not given a simple answer, but rather one that takes that complexity seriously.

Seymour Sarason
Yale University

Acknowledgments

The authors wish to express their profound gratitude to Dr. Pasi Sahlberg of Helsinki, Finland, who first suggested the idea for this volume. His extraordinary assistance and friendship made possible a sabbatical semester in Helsinki where work on the book was begun. We are grateful to Professor Irving Sigel (Senior Investigator, Emeritus, Educational Testing Service, Princeton, New Jersey) for his insightful and sophisticated critique of an earlier version of the book. We cannot express the depth of our debt to Professor Seymour Sarason (Professor of Psychology, Emeritus, Yale University) for his amazingly endless reservoir of inspiration and support.

Introduction

Educators interested in designing schools for tomorrow's world are likely to approach that task after completing two prior stages of preparatory work. The first is a critique of existing patterns of schooling. Much of creative thinking about schools of the future is based explicitly on an enlightened critique of the current situation. Whoever wishes to change schools must decide which features in the existing situation must be exchanged for others if the school is to improve and progress. However radical may be our critique of existing schools, some features can be retained without being totally replaced, while others require just that. The second preparatory stage entails the selection of one or several models or images to guide thinking and planning of schools of the future. Chapter 1 discusses the three prevailing types of organizational models that influence how we think about schools. A critique of schools today appears in Chapter 2. Chapters 1 and 2 lay the groundwork for Chapter 3, which presents the guidelines we wish to emphasize for the design of tomorrow's schools.

Genuine progress requires that we overcome the impediments existing in the present system. The prevailing organization of schools, the patterns of behavior they require of the people working and learning there, and the kinds of skills people must cultivate and employ in these settings (such as teachers giving lectures to students and marking large numbers of tests and students taking many written examinations) present a formidable barrier to redesigning and restructuring the schools of today in a manner commensurate with our vision of the school of tomorrow.

Chapters 4 to 6 describe methods for changing the organizational structure of present-day schools, providing some replies to the question of how to produce genuine change in schools. Chapter 4 maps the stages on a road by which schools can move toward adopting features of the restructured school. The process may seem long and complicated, but shortcuts have proven inadequate to the task. Although many educators prefer to pin their hopes for school renewal on new schools, any new schools will inevitably constitute a minority in a school system; the majority of schools will follow the very patterns we seek to exchange for new ones. The latter schools will continue to determine the patterns of behavior considered normative for any given school system. New schools will either have to mount a fierce battle to preserve their unique identity or succumb to the status quo. The latter outcome is almost a foregone conclusion in most cases (Sarason, 1971, 1982, 1996c, 1997). Consequently, changing existing schools is really the only option open to those who seek to improve public education.

Chapters 7 and 8 are concerned with the question of what to change, namely, how to organize the content of instruction in light of the pedagogical and organizational goals of the restructured school. Our treatment of the content of instruction is restricted to references to domains of knowledge. We do not undertake to suggest to educators the specific contents, topics, or problems to be employed as study materials.

Readers will notice immediately that this book is not partner to the forecast that schools will or should close down. That outlook has been, in its post-Ilichian version, repeated by devotees of the technological revolution, to the effect that computers will replace schools; students will study by means of the information media. Such a scenario is not a total fantasy. Moreover, although schools foster both cognitive learning and social interaction with peers, that may not be sufficient to save them. If schools continue to cling to outdated and unproductive patterns of organization and instruction and if it becomes apparent that *they cannot learn and change as organizations* (Sarason, 1997; Senge, 1990), the public will circumvent the schools in any and every way it can. Courts in some states have already ruled that parents legally can provide their children with reasonable substitutes for attending school, private or public.

Applications of information technology in the schools, which many people associate with visions of schools in the future, are not discussed here. We do not ignore the significant contribution of technology to teaching and learning in schools. However, we feel that the organizational and instructional aspects of schooling are ignored when educators' enthusiasm is aroused by the dazzling feats of computers, including CD-ROMs, the Internet, and virtual reality. Often an assumption seems implicit in this wonderment that technology, unaided, can extricate the schools from their current predicament. We suggest that is not even possible. The creative use of technologies in schools and education can be realized only if school organization at all levels (curriculum, scheduling, teachers' work patterns, methods of teaching and learning) is restructured to accommodate technology and to utilize it optimally. Large investments in equipment will otherwise fail to yield proportionate improvements in teaching and learning, a phenomenon that has occurred time and again in the history of modern education.

This book focuses on the organization of the restructured school as we envision it. We rely on our professional experience to infuse our thinking with a sense of reality, and we cannot avoid molding our thoughts in light of our personal experience. Nevertheless, the goals and methods presented here for tomorrow's schools are based largely on what we know of the current professional and research literature.

Tomorrow's school is already emerging out of existing schools, although the new one differs in essential ways from its predecessor. The restructured school can yield superior effects on the social, emotional, and intellectual lives of its inhabitants. A large investment in human professional resources will be needed to reach a high enough level of organizational and pedagogical sophistication to maintain the new school. Just how schools will locate and engage these personnel remains a matter of debate among educators concerned with the preparation of educators (Goodlad, 1990; Leithwood, 1989; Sarason, 1993). A discussion of that issue must await another opportunity.

Chapter 1

Images of School Organization

Most theory and research about schools is anchored in some model or image of what a social organization is or should be. Gareth Morgan (1986) made creative use of images and metaphors applied to understanding organizations. Rather than selecting one image to explain the nature of organizations, Morgan asserted that "organizational analysis must start from the premise that organizations can be many things at one and the same time" (Morgan, 1986, 321). Different models can be applied to the same organizations to explain different features of their structure and functioning or to shed light on the same features from different points of view (Griffiths, 1988). The images used to symbolize the nature of organizations have both theoretical and practical implications for our decisions about the design and organization of schools.

In recent years, two theoretical orientations regarding the nature of schools have attracted considerable attention, alongside the still-dominant model of the school as a bureaucracy. One sees the school as a social system; the other sees the school as a community. Both images contribute unique elements to our conception of how school organization and processes should operate and which goals they should seek to achieve. The school as a bureaucracy is the oldest of the three models (Abbot and Caracheo, 1988). After World War II, the model of the school as a social system developed (Banathy, 1971, 1991, 1992). The notion of the school as a community, though it has older roots, is the latest of the models or images of school organization to generate some remarkable and convincing research (Bryk and Driscoll, 1988; Bryk, Lee and Smith, 1990; Newman and Oliver, 1967). Despite these developments in the organizational model or image of school organization and despite what some authors have called "the paradigm shift" (Lincoln, 1985), concepts from each of these models coexist in present-day thinking about school organization. More pointedly, all three models exist simultaneously in the theory and practice of school organization, albeit in different proportions depending upon the particular theorist and school. None of these orientations has been totally abandoned or replaced. As developmental psychology has argued, advance to a new stage of development does not necessarily entail the eradication of the behavioral, emotional, or intellectual qualities of the earlier stage. Schemas or patterns typical of earlier stages survive in many guises and play a role in later stages of existence. No single model of school organization, in and of itself, reflects the complexity of school organization. Rather, some combination of all three models, images, or theoretical orientations can provide a more effective model of the kind of school sought by the movement for school restructuring. In many ways, this combination of images also reflects the development of organizational theory in the realm of education.

Consequently, following Morgan's example, we will claim that no one model (bureaucracy, social systems, or community) is best for explaining how schools are or should be organized. Our understanding of schools, as they are or as they could be, can profit from the use of several images employed simultaneously (Griffiths, 1988). Even if our efforts to reform and restructure schools were to succeed beyond our expectations, the ultimate products of reform will embody elements from all three models—bureaucratic, systemic, and communal. A criterion for identifying the *failure* of a restructuring effort might be that a client school retains the bureaucratic model as its primary pattern of organization and operation instead of incorporating features of the systems and communitarian models, even after consultation and retraining.

Many distinguished authors of the theory and history of organization have presented one or another of these three models in detail. Having emerged in the late nineteenth century, the bureaucratic model is the oldest yet still most prevalent of the three. Theorists who took a systems view of organization generally were unaware of the communitarian approach, which had not yet been formulated or was only beginning to appear. Theorists of the communitarian school frequently disregarded systems theory and did not feel any need to understand the relationship between the two approaches. Representatives of both newer schools of thought were, and are, unable to disregard the prominent position of the bureaucratic theory of organization, which is regularly cited as the "traditional" or standard model. In comparison, a systems or communitarian model is considered to be an alternative approach (Lee and Smith, 1995; Shachar and Sharan, 1995). Since the discussion here requires some acquaintance with the basic notions of all three models, a brief summary of these ideas follows:

THE BUREAUCRATIC MODEL

Two Fredericks made major contributions to bureaucratic management theory—Frederick the Great of Prussia (died 1786), who concentrated on developing military organization, and Frederick Taylor (died 1915), whose "principles of scientific management provided the cornerstone for work design throughout the first half of this century" (Morgan, 1986, 30). Bureaucracy as a model of organization was presented in the monumental works of Max Weber at the beginning of the twentieth century. (For bibliographical guidance and a succinct summary of Weber's thought on this subject, refer to Abbot and Caracheo, 1988; Hoy and Miskel, 1987, ch. 4). Among the critical features of bureaucratic/rational management theory, to which both Fredericks contributed, are the principles of (1) the hierarchy of authority, (2) the division and specialization of labor, (3) rules and regulations to govern behavior in the organization, (4) monitoring/control of performance to ensure that appropriate procedures are followed, (5) a nonpersonal (or impersonal) attitude toward work and toward the people related to work (including the customers), and (6) expertise in carrying out the relevant task (Hall, 1962).

An extensive study carried out by Sousa and Hoy (1981) identified the widespread presence of four basic dimensions of bureaucracy in schools: (1) organizational control, consisting of a hierarchical authority structure, rules and regulations, specification of procedures, and standardization of behavior; (2) rational specialization, whose components are technical expertise and specialization; (3) system centralization, consisting of the concentration of decision-making power in the hands of the principal or an expanded management team; and (4) formal definition of roles and their implementation. Moreover, these investigators found that many other features of school life also followed the bureaucratic model. All in all, it seems patently justifiable to characterize school organization as largely bureaucratic in nature.

Another aspect of bureaucracy in schools is the schools' dependence on directives from district offices and officers. Such directives subordinate the behavior of school personnel to sets of rules and regulations in addition to those found within the school itself. Often these regulations impinge directly and in manifold ways on teachers' instructional behavior, restricting the exercise of their professional judgment and behavior, much to the detriment of their students (Chubb and Moe, 1990; McNeil, 1986). Some examples of these rules and regulations are (Janowitz, 1969):

1. uniform structure of school scheduling in terms of the accepted length of an instructional period,

2. the number of periods per day teachers are to be in class with students,

3. the number of periods students are to study each day,

4. the number of periods of a given subject to be taught each week,

5. the kinds of tests to be given to students, not to speak of the fact of testing itself as a procedure often made mandatory by school authorities,

6. the kind of grading system to be employed,

7. the topics to be taught in each class/discipline, and

8. the amount of time (hours, weeks, months) to be devoted to instruction for each topic in each discipline (i.e., rate of instruction).

Such regulations are frequently imposed on schools without regard for the needs of specific students, except when an ethnic majority demands that particular cultural topics be included in the curriculum. Many educators support the uniformity of district or state educational requirements as indicative of "equity" for all groups in the district. For these educators, equity requires standardization of criteria for achievement, which they do not perceive as an arbitrary application of the same criteria to all students as if they were equal in interests and skills. This mechanistic application of uniformity, typical of bureaucratic organizations, actually ignores peoples' backgrounds, abilities, and interests. Hence, the bureaucratic nature of schools derives as much from control by external agencies as from schools' internal structure.

It is not reasonable to expect that schools will be able to develop organizational patterns essentially different from those embodied in and employed by the central agencies of the educational enterprise. Administrative centers of public education might evolve nonbureaucratic forms of relationships with the public schools. That would certainly provide powerful motivation and legitimation and be an example to the schools to adopt alternative forms of organization. Astute observers and researchers of education are skeptical, to say the least, that such a transformation will or can occur (Chubb and Moe, 1990; Sarason, 1997).

In some countries, educational authorities have moved toward decentralizing authority in the school system, as in transferring decision-making power from the central government to district supervisors or superintendents, as occurred in Israel, for example. But regrettably, the movement for decentralization stopped short of empowering the schools themselves. By relocating the center of decision-making power from one office to many offices (six in Israel), the bureaucracy was merely elongated and made more complex, rather than simplifying matters by placing power in the hands of school personnel, including principals. Now, the troops in the field (including their officers) will have a harder time determining to whom to turn for their orders. Clearly, such half-hearted and misdirected steps taken in the name of decentralization cannot exert a positive effect on the organization and operation of the schools.

The ramifications of the top-down direction of bureaucratic organization in schools do not end at the classroom door, but extend into each and every class. The teaching methods used by most teachers and the nature of human relations in the classroom are profoundly influenced by the organizational patterns current at the level of the administration and teaching staff. Teaching by the presentation-recitation, frontal method is still probably the most widespread style of instruction in the world, and certainly in secondary schools almost everywhere. This pedagogical approach, part and parcel of the bureaucratic system, prevails despite decades of criticism by philosophers, psychologists, and pedagogues. Herbert Thelen dubbed the frontal form of teaching the "guardian angel" of the traditional form of schooling in general, part of the "cultural archetype" powerfully resistant to change (Thelen, 1981). The ability of frontal teaching to outlive its critics and competitors may stem from the essential relationship between frontal teaching in the classroom and the bureaucratic organization of the school. The structure of the institution and its fundamental patterns of behavior sustain this form of teaching because it is a direct extension of bureaucratic organizational logic into the process of teaching: The teacher as authority figure decides on all major matters of instruction and behavior in the classroom (content, quantity, pace, evaluation, and grading), as well as occupying center stage, distributing speaking privileges, and regulating the length of interactions. Perhaps that is the primary reason that all attempts at instructional reform not accompanied by reform at the school's organizational level ultimately have proved inadequate. No particular feature of the frontal method has been demonstrated to be so effective or felicitous in its effects on students as to explain its remarkable longevity (Shachar and Sharan, 1994, 1995; Sharan and Shachar, 1994). A powerful connection exists between organizational patterns at the school and those at the classroom level, far greater than what most educators appear to be aware of during their daily work. Behavioral patterns at each level of the school reinforce and complement each other. Change in one set of patterns in pursuit of more effective means of operation requires similar change in the other set.

Scholars have debated the extent to which schools are or are not typical bureaucracies (Abbot and Caracheo, 1988; Bidwell, 1965; Campbell, Fleming, Newell, and Bennion, 1987). Whether or not schools constitute a "pure type" of bureaucracy, they do display many features that lie at the heart of bureaucratic theory as a model of organization. Indeed, subject-matter specialization with the virtual insulation of one subject from another during instruction, a clear derivative of the bureaucratic model, has been the hallmark of secondary education in this century. It forms the substructure of school organization to this day.

Centralized control over schooling through complex regulations, mandated curricular requirements, standardized testing, and the like are also part of the bureaucratic approach, as we noted. These practices continue to enjoy widespread popularity among administrators at many levels of the school system, despite their frequently negative effects on the behavior of teachers, on the content and process of instruction, and on students' learning (Chubb and Moe, 1990). Hence, the power hierarchy of decision making and control remains largely intact in secondary education, along with the compartmentalization of knowledge and instruction. Teacher participation in policy setting, with problem-solving and decision-making teams invested with authority to design and carry out programs, are organizational innovations derived from a systems perspective on organization that stresses the free flow of information among the system's members. Yet, these innovations are still primarily in the talking stage despite two decades of academic research and debate and despite their successful adoption by large sectors of the business and industrial world.

We do not wish to claim that the separation of instruction into distinct disciplines is solely the consequence of direct influence of the bureaucratic model on education. More than likely the prevailing division of knowledge current in the universities affected the structure of knowledge as presented in high schools. The latter are profoundly influenced by the universities through a variety of channels, not the least of which is that they prepare the teachers. Be this as it may, the division of subject matter into separate courses taught by subject specialists, with little or no connection with the subjects taught to the same students by other specialists on the same day or during the same week, became the bedrock foundation of secondary education and has remained so to this day. This manner of organizing schools certainly is highly consistent with the bureaucratic model, along with the hierarchy of decision-making authority, and continues to determine a wide range of behavior, that of teachers as well as that of students, during the hours of schooling.

These patterns of organization also have far-reaching influence on the schools' proverbial resistance to change. Countless efforts to change school organization and teaching methods have been launched over the past few decades, though relatively fewer were directed at secondary schools than at elementary schools until the recent advent of two or three nationwide projects, about which the data are not yet in. Many observers agree that bureaucratic organization inevitably produces organizational rigidity and marked conservatism regarding steps toward renewal that could make schools more responsive to their environments (Abbot and Caracheo, 1988).

Changes in school structure and processes sought by the restructuring movement require, first of all, the adoption of a completely different organizational model as a basis and guide for organizational and pedagogical renewal (Sarason, 1997; Sizer, 1993). Admittedly, it is not possible at this time to predict how successfully the bureaucratic model can be replaced or sidestepped to permit the introduction of new models and methods of the kind described later in this book. By all accounts that is a formidable task. It seems more likely that change efforts could succeed in limiting the number of operations in the school that are dominated by the bureaucratic model to those functions only for which that model is still efficient and for which no superior substitute has been found.

THE SOCIAL SYSTEMS MODEL

The application of systems theory to social organizations was given considerable impetus by the publication (1966) of the classic work *The Social Psychology of Organizations* by David Katz and Robert Kahn (revised edition, 1978). During the three decades from 1960 to the early 1990s, theorists and researchers spelled out many of the features and implications of systems theory for the organization and conduct of schooling (Banathy, 1971, 1991, 1992; Bidwell, 1965; Clark, 1985; Getzels and Guba, 1957; Getzels, Lipham, and Campbell, 1968; Griffiths, 1964; Hoy and Miskel, 1987; Kaufman, 1972; Litterer, 1969; Miles, 1967; Milstein and Belasco, 1973; Schmuck and Runkel, 1972).

Systems can be defined as a complex of elements that are related to and interact with one another over time. All systems—within the limits of human knowledge thus far—both have smaller subsystems embedded within them and are part of larger systems that form their environment. This definition emphasizes the mutual relationship or interconnection between the parts of the system. This conception differs considerably from the top-down, hierarchical structure of the bureaucratic organization. Important, too, is the attention to the environment of the system, which may be conceived of as a larger system, with its own set or sets of interacting elements. Again, bureaucratic theory pays little or no attention to the nature of the environment when conceiving of the manner in which the organization operates. Nor does it focus on the horizontal (rather than vertical) relationships and interaction in the organization, the exchanges and information flow between colleagues, which comprise another fundamental feature of systems theory. Bureaucracies divide and specialize, systems combine!

Systems share a number of distinct properties: They exchange matter, energy, and information with their environment, that is, they have *inputs* and *outputs*. The system performs work on the inputs to transform them (*throughput*) in some way in order to yield a product (output). Systems are self-regulating and maintain a steady balance of inputs, throughputs, and outputs through the constant monitoring of their functioning by means of *feedback*, which is the information relayed back into the system from its throughput and from its output in order to adjust future operation on the basis of past performance. (The thermostat that signals the refrigerator's motor when the temperature in the box rises to a specified point is a particularly well-known example of a feedback loop). The processes of input, throughput, output, and feedback repeat in cyclical fashion as long as the system continues to operate. However, the universal *law of entropy* (paradoxically called "positive entropy") predicts that all forms of organization become increasingly disorganized (parts wear out or break) and ultimately cease to function, or die. The importation of energy from the environment in many types of organizations (new skills, alternative modes of operation, new ideas, spare parts, new resources) can prolong the life of the system and postpone its ultimate demise ("negative entropy"). The extent to which disintegration can be withstood or counteracted by the system depends upon the limits set by a host of factors, including the goals of the system (religious organizations have different life expectancies than commercial ones, for example), the structure of the system (rocks take longer to disintegrate than organic bodies), various environmental conditions (dripping water takes longer to wear away rocks than does the constant pounding of huge waves and fierce winds), and the effectiveness with which the organization generates, receives, and learns from feedback. Organizations that demonstrate an ability to benefit from feedback, learn from their mistakes, and redirect or redesign their activities to be more effective and creative have been called "learning organizations" (Sarason, 1997; Senge, 1990).

Finally, we will mention the principle of *equifinality*, which means that a system can reach the same goal by a variety of ways: No one solution to a problem is the only and best solution. Systems have different options open to them to solve the complex problems they face (Banathy, 1992, 14–15; Griffiths, 1964; Hoy and Miskel, 1987, 63–73; Katz and Kahn, 1978, 23–30). Therefore, systems must survey their options in any given situation and choose one, not arbitrarily because one or another person likes that solution or because it is the easiest to implement, but on the basis of relevant information. This process entails systematic problem solving and decision making by those who have experience with and information about the given situation, instead of anticipating that all major decisions are to be made by the upper echelons of the authority hierarchy. By emphasizing the role of feedback as a major source of information in the problem-solving and decision-making process, systems seek to ensure a reasonable degree of rationality in this process. This entire approach to systems management entails the establishment and maintenance of differentiated organizational components, such as teams of teachers who will employ rational problem-solving methods to identify, analyze, and solve problems and who will engage in the cycle of planning, implementation, evaluation, feedback, and re-planning presented in coming chapters. Such forms of organization remain relatively unknown in today's schools, where almost all teachers continue to view their role in one way only, and that as being to "teach," which often does not mean to plan, to solve problems, to gather data for feedback purposes, and to perform other similar tasks. These features of the teacher's role are critical for the fulfillment of the vision of the restructured school. To this extent, tomorrow's school as presented here owes much of its substance to systems theory.

Another basic component of systems theory that has deeply influenced the vision of tomorrow's schools is the notion of the interdependence of parts of the system, instead of the state of compartmentalization typical of bureaucratic theory. Some theorists of school organization became so impressed with the relative absence of connection between different parts of the school's operation that they evolved what is known as "loose coupling theory" (Meyer and Rowan, 1977; Weick, 1976). Schools may be social systems, says this theory, but unlike systems in general, the parts are not so interdependent as one might expect. In fact, they are so loosely connected that much that transpires within one part of the system does not really affect anything of great importance in some other part of the system. Therefore, schools are a rather strange kind of system, unlike other well-known examples of social systems. For example, students take many subjects at the same time, but there is little or no relationship between them, either in the minds of the teachers or in the way the subject is studied by students. Thus, the components of the curriculum are basically disconnected, as are the classrooms in which these subjects are taught and the teachers who teach these classes, and so on down the line.

Change agents, school reformers, and educators with a vision of tomorrow's schools have learned to view schools in a systems fashion, holistically, as far as possible. Efforts at instructional change are known to depend for their success on efforts at broader organizational restructuring, such as rescheduling classes to facilitate teaching methods more sophisticated than merely a transfer of information from teachers, textbooks, or even computers to students. The sectorial view of the school as consisting of discrete disciplines displays no awareness of this holistic interdependence of parts. A noteworthy example, quite ironic in some ways, emerged when a new theory of second-language acquisition, termed the "communicative theory," drew teachers' attention to the need for emphasizing interpersonal communication as a central means for cultivating the knowledge and use of a second language. Educators tried to inject the new emphasis into classroom teaching, especially in high schools; these efforts were conducted without reference to the method of instruction common in the other subjects students were studying. Nor did these efforts at instructional change seek to alter procedures at the schoolwide organizational level, as if second-language instruction could be switched from frontal teaching to an interactive form of learning without a similar change in any other discipline. (The "irony," of course, is that the "communicative" approach to teaching failed to understand the importance of communication). The results of this effort were far from remarkable, hardly commensurate with the investment of time and money in the change effort. This project is only one in a long series that seems to have learned little from the history of educational change efforts over the past few decades in which the systems features of the school were disregarded in favor of an exclusively discipline-specific orientation.

The notion of a free flow of information to maintain the integrity and proper functioning of the system is consistent with the pedagogical methods generally known under the generic title of "cooperative learning" (Sharan, 1994). According to these methods, students work together in small groups where they communicate directly with one another, assist one another, and determine collective goals and means of reaching them. In some of these methods students not only help each other and cooperate in learning given subject matter, but they also engage in investigating topics that they have identified and agreed upon and decide how to implement their plan of research. Many of these instructional methods distinguish classes conducted along lines of the systems model from those taught by the frontal approach to teaching consistent with the bureaucratic model. In the latter, the bulk of the communication is unilateral, from the higher-level authority figure to those at lower levels of authority or to the workers (teacher to student), and on occasion bilateral (teacher to student and student to teacher), but rarely multilateral (students with one another in a group). In cooperative learning the class as a whole functions as a system. The groups can coordinate their activities with one another, and coordination and communication are not restricted to the individuals within the groups. Thus, systems theory provides guidance for the conduct of instruction at the classroom level, not only for the conduct of the staff at the organizational level (Sharan, 1994; Sharan and Shachar, 1995; Slavin, 1990).

The restructured school of tomorrow will organize its staff to facilitate ongoing communication between colleagues:

1. working together in teams of 3 to 6 members devoted to problem solving in a variety of domains, with planning the nature of the instructional process and content being the primary topics;

2. working together in teams to gather information about the school's functioning in critical areas to provide the staff with feedback as a basis for problem solving and decision making and to determine the relationship between means and goals in the conduct of the school's educational operations;

3. working together to formulate schoolwide policy in all of the areas of human behavior in the school and to maintain vigilance regarding the implementation of the policy.

All of these organizational structures and procedures ensure the school's high-level functioning as a social system.

The school restructuring movement has added a new dimension to the interpretation of the systems notion of communication in the field of education. There should be communication between *teachers* within and between departments dealing with different subject areas; it is equally important that such communication hold meaning for the *students*. The organizational change required to translate this notion into practical steps in schools is far greater in scope than that required to maintain communication among teachers. Implementation of this notion provides a concrete example of the deeper significance of systems concepts to school learning. The intention is to extend the application of the systems model into the arena of the curriculum, to radically reduce the custom of dividing the curriculum into self-contained cells determined by traditional disciplinary divisions, and to create transdisciplinary clusters that integrate several disciplines into units that are meaningful for young people's grasp of themselves and of their environment. For high school students the disciplinary divisions, so typical of the bureaucratic approach to organization, are not particularly meaningful, as these students are not yet on the road to becoming practitioners or investigators of the specific disciplines, as are university students. Traditional divisions between domains of knowledge only limit their ability to explain to students the world they live in and their own experiential connection to that world. This topic will be discussed in length in later chapters.

THE COMMUNITY MODEL

In his book on developing community in schools, Thomas Sergiovanni (1994) bases his work on the distinction introduced by the German sociologist Ferdinand Tonnies in 1887 between gesellschaft (society) and gemeinschaft (community). The former has the quality of an enterprise where relationships are based on contractual agreements or regulations; the latter shares the associations of family relationships grounded in emotions and values. Tonnies ([1887] 1957) wrote (quoted by Sergiovanni, 1994, 8–9):

The theory of gesellschaft deals with the artificial construction of an aggregate of human beings which superficially resembles the gemeinschaft insofar as the individuals live and dwell together peacefully. However, in the gemeinschaft they remain essentially united in spite of all separating factors, whereas in the gesellschaft they are essentially separated in spite of all the uniting factors. (1957, p. 64)

Building on a basic commitment to caring for and a connection with individuals, school organization modeled in light of the communitarian vision displays features that contrast with those typical of bureaucracies. On the other hand, the communitarian model shares several important elements with the systems view. The systems and communitarian views agree on the need for cooperation between teachers concerning all aspects of their work in school, including the setting of school policy and goals. Teachers are empowered, individually and collectively, to design and implement their work in accordance with the explicit policy of the school. Such cooperation can yield a heightened sense of shared responsibility by teachers for the conduct of the school as a whole. Communication is primarily lateral, between colleagues, rather than vertical, from the top down. Extensive studies of unprecedented scope verify the superior effects produced by communally oriented organized schools, compared to those that functioned according to the bureaucratic model. (Bryk and Driscoll, 1988; Bryk, Lee, and Smith, 1990; Lee, Bryk, and Smith, 1993; Lee and Smith, 1995; Newman and Oliver, 1967; Newman and Wehlage, 1995).

Some versions of the idea of a "community" school emphasize the inclusion of parents in the planning and carrying out of various activities in the school. Parents' participation in school activities is certainly most desirable and beneficial. However, their appearance in the school for a few hours now and then resembles "visiting" more than "belonging," in the sense discussed by Tonnies. The idea of the communitarian school presented here refers primarily to the relationships among the people who spend their working days in the school and define their presence as "belonging," namely, teachers, administrators, and students.

It is important to distinguish between the images of "school as social system" and "school as community," despite the overlap between the two. The main feature of the communitarian notion concerns a mutual approachability between people without regard for formal status or position, such that they will evidence in that setting a degree of caring for others, both teachers and students; it holds that this feature is accepted as a basic value underlying human relations in the school. Cooperation among teachers and students in the preparation of a school policy statement, for example, is consistent with both the communitarian and the systems models. However, effective communication as a necessary component in the function of a social system does not entail a statement about the quality of human relations in the school in general. The communitarian approach specifies that interpersonal communication of concern and caring for others' well-being is the basis of social interaction in the school. This basic value, if realized to a reasonable degree, will determine the atmosphere in the school, above and beyond the patterns of behavior determined by the school's organizational structure.

There are, of course, many ways to cultivate this value in schools, among them methods developed as part of a systems approach to school organization (Schmuck and Runkel, 1972, 1994). However, in order to develop such an atmosphere, teachers and students must participate in formulating a policy statement that spells out the implications of communitarianism for daily life in the school, and the statement must be accepted by them as the foundation of the school's organizational functioning and of their own behavior in school. Without it, the school might function well as a social system, but not as a community.

It follows that the image of the school as a community differs in intention from images of the school as a bureaucracy or as a system. The latter two describe the structure of the organization as a whole, whereas the former does not. Its scope is purposely restricted to the realm of human relations in the institution and is particularly suited for application to schooling, which is a moral as well as an instrumental undertaking of the community at large. We are not likely to seek communitarianism in courts, libraries, universities (although many claim that the university is, or could be, a community), hospitals, or industries. Communitarianism as an organizational model can be applied only to settings where members or participants share common values that stress their mutual acceptance and caring for one another, as characteristic of a community (Bryk and Driscoll, 1988; Kruse, Louis, and Bryk, 1994). The bureaucratic and systems perspectives stress the design of the structure and processes of production, not the quality of human relations.

The rise of the notion of the school as a community may have been motivated, in part at least, by the high levels of alienation, disconnectedness, intergroup animosity, and crime and violence that characterize contemporary society in the urban megapolis. Such divisive phenomena have created a distinct feeling that we have lost the closely knit social life that existed some fifty years ago in towns and in city neighborhoods. Most recently, the shopping mall has sapped much of the social connectedness that survived urban sprawl. That sense of connectedness with others, a basic confidence that other people in the environment are approachable and potentially concerned, is the essential feature of a sense of community. It is this sense that some educators now seek to reconstruct in schools, because it provides an indispensable support for young peoples' learning and personal growth and adjustment, as well as a sense of well-being on the part of the adults who work in schools. Feeling and knowing that one belongs to a social entity that cares, a school that is a "home away from home," is antecedent to young people's intellectual progress in school (Sarason, 1974, 1985; Sergiovanni, 1994; Sizer, 1993).

SCHOOL ORGANIZATION: THREE MODELS UNDER ONE ROOF

Certain features of bureaucratic schools and of schools organized along the systems or the communitarian models are indeed mutually exclusive—logically, psychologically, and organizationally. A subject-specialized, discipline-oriented school with clear division of teachers and classes by subject matter, along with a high percentage of classroom time devoted to verbal transmission of information by teachers (frontal teaching) and a school schedule that allows little or no time for collaborative staff work devoted to cooperative planning, problem solving, and decision making by teachers (mainly because instruction by solo practitioners does not require or invite cooperative staff work), is usually associated with a hierarchical structure of authority, however benign. This form of organization is simply not compatible with either a systems or a communitarian model of schooling and cannot coexist with the other two models in an organization.

On the other hand, a number of organizational features and goals are shared by the communitarian and systems approaches to school. It seems relatively certain that no degree of restructuring aimed at establishing the school-as-community idea will eliminate *all* of the distinctive aspects of bureaucracy or of social systems from the arena of school organization and administration.

The Unique Contribution of the Bureaucratic Model to School Organization

What unique features of bureaucracy are likely to remain part of the organization of restructured schools?

1. Some schools may decide to transfer authority and responsibility for the school's organizational conduct from a single principal to a committee of teachers. Some differentiation in levels of authority in the school, whether the carrier be one or several persons, will probably continue into the future. Even idealized visions of reconstructed secondary schools heretofore have not recommended that the principal's role be eliminated or stripped of its authority in many areas of school life, although that suggestion has been brought up by serious observers of schools (Sarason, 1997). None of the existing methods for delegating authority to teachers advises that teachers become involved in all aspects of decision making that traditionally have been the prerogative of the principal. Models of participative management generally distinguish between categories of tasks that should or should not be submitted to teacher committees or teams for consideration and decision making. Teachers patently do not relish the role of decision makers when the task does not fall within their realm of competence

or impinge on some aspect of their work. An example is dealing with the building superintendent about the care of the physical plant, a topic likely to be
viewed by teachers as falling exclusively within the principal's decision-making
authority. The principal's role has received attention from many investigators
of school administration (see the extensive literature cited by Hoy and Miskel,
1987, 336–350). Both a hierarchy of authority and the differentiation of roles
among administrators and teachers seem to remain permanent fixtures of school
organization.

2. Bureaucratic organization always includes the documentation of events
with written records, and schools typically maintain extensive records of students' academic work and behavior. (Unfortunately, as schools rarely if ever
document their modes of operation and their consequences—what was done in
the school that led to students' behavior and learning—few schools can produce
a history of their activities. Why one school has many high achievers in science
and another in music often becomes a mystery a few years later.) Documentation
is determined by the need to supply statistics to governing bodies that fund the
school's operation and the need to provide parents with some record of their
children's progress for purposes of their continued educational or vocational
career.

3. At this time it seems that schools will continue for many years into the
future to employ teachers whose professional training consists primarily of their
disciplinary specialization with a thin frosting of education and methods courses.
Schools necessarily will have to continue, if not increase, their in-service education efforts for teachers and administrators. Schools of higher education continue to maintain separate courses of study for teachers of different academic
subject matter. Few institutions offer systematic study for all teacher candidates
together on crucial subjects such as: How are schools organized, and what is
the teacher's role in school organization? How do teachers function as members
of a teaching staff? What are, or can be, teachers' roles in formulating school
policy, in terms of collegial relationships, student-teacher relationships, pedagogical matters, and so on? Unlike prospective physicians, teachers do not
achieve a common professional background before specializing in their particular subject matter. In education, the opposite is true: prospective teachers study
their disciplines first, and only afterward, often as an afterthought, do they get
a glimpse of topics related to teaching. Hence, teachers are not educated to
develop a sense of responsibility for and involvement in the school as an educational unit. Consequently, they usually remain focused almost exclusively on
the problems of their own classes and discipline. Schools seeking to restructure
themselves and to cultivate their students' pursuit of knowledge per se, not
necessarily in a specific discipline, will have to assume the responsibility for
extending teachers' professional horizons, to enable them to function in the new
professional environment created by the school of tomorrow.

Nor can schools realistically anticipate counteracting the fact that institutions
of higher education are compartmentalized by subject matter. Many schools of

education within universities maintain special programs for the preparation of teachers in each and every disciplinary domain, such as music, biology, or literature. Their students do not study together how to be teachers or what schools are like; rather, they study "their subject" and how to teach it. Consequently, universities and schools of education will continue to graduate teachers with subject specialization. University-based schools of education are unlikely to dismantle this state of affairs, nor are they equipped to educate prospective teachers as generalists who conceive of themselves first and foremost as teachers and only secondarily as the guardians and teachers of specific subject matter. However high schools may succeed in designing and implementing integrated curricula and overcoming the boundaries of subject-matter departments, many secondary school teachers will enter the profession expecting to focus their teaching efforts within disciplinary domains. Multidisciplinary teams in schools, as suggested several times in the following pages, may succeed in partially transcending this limitation, but they will have to take it into consideration.

4. Methods of "remote control" of schools employed by school authorities at different levels of government (districts, counties, states) continue to impose uniformity on schools without reference to the specific social and psychological needs of their clienteles, local classroom conditions, student interests, and so on. We cannot foretell to what extent it will be possible to convince school authorities to decentralize educational decision-making power and forgo their control over such features as:

1. quantity of curricular material to be "taught" during given periods of time,
2. use of standardized tests to assess academic achievement when such tests bear no relationship to what students have learned,
3. determining the number of hours, per week or month or semester, that given subjects are to be studied, regardless of student interests or involvement,
4. how many hours teachers are to spend in the classroom as a factor determining their salary.

This kind of external control over classroom teaching by central authorities is one of the powerful factors guarding the bureaucratic structure of schools. Genuine decentralization that grants pedagogical and fiscal autonomy to schools will make possible the extension of the systems and communitarian models into a broader spectrum of school functioning and reduce adherence to the bureaucratic model.

The Unique Contribution of Systems Theory to School Organization

Careful consideration of systems theory reveals that it too has critical contributions to make to the desired operation of schools that should not be disregarded. Although some systems features overlap with the communal approach, others are unique to systems theory. Two features in particular of systems theory that are not part of the communal approach are (1) the concept of feedback for self-regulation and (2) the goal-oriented nature of systems for transforming input (throughput) to yield a product of some kind.

One salient problem for schools is the absence of adequate feedback procedures to monitor throughput processes (organization and instruction). It is notoriously difficult for schools to establish clear links between means and ends and to have personnel engage in ongoing improvement of their work to reduce the effects of positive entropy, that is, a gradual (or rapid) deterioration of the system's operations, the use of inefficient or outdated methods of operation, and the like. Clearly, the development of methods for obtaining feedback on the nature of its operations would significantly enhance the school's ability to function effectively. Furthermore, the implementation and maintenance of these systems properties most often require a bureaucratic structure for purely administrative purposes such as the distribution of funds according to the school's policy, distribution of persons to given spatial areas, preparation of appropriate records for teachers, acquisition of supplies, and so on.

To yield a product is clearly a goal not of a community (gemeinschaft) but rather of an enterprise (gesellschaft). Nor do communities need feedback to regulate their "communal" aspects of functioning. Nevertheless, many other functions performed in the community require feedback. For example, communities must control certain aspects of the events occurring within their geographic space, events that result from the myriad of input-output processes that are in perpetual motion in any community (e.g., construction of buildings and roads). Also, negative entropy, often following in the wake of feedback, must be provided to counteract the breakdown of certain vital functions, such as public health, garbage collection, monitoring the purity of drinking water, and police presence. Such functions are performed through the operation of departments within the local government, and the departments are typically operated along bureaucratic or systems lines. The possibility for human relations characteristic of community life is sustained by the bureaucratic and systems features of the more formally organized domains of the community, while the communal features are almost in the nature of emergent qualities.

Schools, like other social service institutions, have a distinct goal requiring that they transform inputs into products, albeit "products" defined in terms of human development. Schools' more salient products are (1) professional satisfaction for teachers and administrators (derived from different sources) that they have accomplished their jobs with reasonable success, and (2) growth and development—intellectual, emotional, and social—for the students, however those goals may be defined. From the point of view of "product production," schools with both bureaucratic and systems features serve the community at large, as well as their own internal communities. The position taken here is that the adoption of systems features in many of the schools' realms of operation can create significantly better conditions for productive learning than the predominantly bureaucratic modes of operation that have prevailed heretofore.

The Unique Contribution of the Community Model to School Organization

Despite the manifold tasks performed by departments and organizations on behalf of the community for the welfare of the public, the "communal" aspects of a community's goals lie in creating a supportive social-emotional environment for its members by virtue of the community's *existence*. This existence provides the social conditions needed to sustain interactions among persons, not the specific products produced by a particular transformation (throughput) process activated by the various organizations on behalf of the community (Barker and Schoggen, 1973). The *existence* of community as its primary mission legitimates and supports the *existence* of the people who comprise the community without being grounded in some justification that transcends the person or is separate from the person (except for the justification that emanates from the "law of the land"). *The communitarian image of schools proclaims that teachers and students are to receive encouragement, support, and acknowledgment because they work in or attend the school, that is, they are citizens of the school. Their citizen status needs no justification by reference to achievement or any other external criterion, apart from fulfilling the school's fundamental expectations from its citizens that they exercise their citizenship in a manner commensurate with the requirements of collective existence as accepted in most human communities.*

Notwithstanding its distinctly positive and appealing qualities, the model of the school as a community can be applied only to *some* aspects of life in schools, leaving others to be described or represented by the bureaucratic model and by the systems model employed in tandem. As we have seen, this is precisely the case for the functioning of a real community, whose proper operation almost inevitably requires notions such as feedback and transformational throughput. The latter two notions are provided only by reference to social systems. The feedback process is necessary only because of the school's system properties as a transformational setting, that is, one whose goal direction is intended to yield products emerging from the system's throughput operations.

No complete catalogue of organizational features has been compiled that identifies which functions of schools are distinctly bureaucratic, which are more akin to a systems conception, and which are derived from the notion of community. Some features are obviously identified with one of the three models. Many more must be considered to complete the picture. What is encouraging to this author, as will become evident in the following chapters, is that the range of school functions that have assumed features of the systems and communitarian models has expanded markedly in recent years and apparently will continue to do so. Extending the systems and communal features of the school into more of the functions for which they are appropriate is one goal of this book. Obviously,

Figure 1.1
Values, Human Relations, and Mode of Organization in Three Organizational Models of the School

	Bureaucratic	*Systems*	*Communitarian*
Values	Efficiency, control and supervision, regularity	Cooperation	Care and concern for others' well being
Human Relations	Formal, clear division of roles to minimize conflicts	Open flow of information, collegiality, flexible roles	Every member of the school is approachable regardless of status
Mode of Organization	Defined hierarchy, one class-one teacher-one subject, curricular emphasis on academic disciplines, uniform schedule, documentation	Short-and long-term problem-solving and project teams among teachers and students, trans-disciplinary curriculum, flexible schedule	

© Hanna Shachar and Shlomo Sharan.

many human situations arising in schools will be resolved more successfully as they progress in the process of organizational clarification.

The chief characteristics of the bureaucratic, systems, and communitarian models of school organization, divided into the domains of values, human relations and mode of organization, are summarized in Figure 1.1.

Organizations of all kinds that display this multimodel composition share the ambiguity and conflicts that frequently arise from the sometimes contradictory expectations, norms, or regulations that govern their operation. Many educators are sensitive to the conflict inherent in acknowledging teachers' and students' dignity as members of the community, independent of their performance in their school-specific roles, especially in light of the *educational and hence inherently moral* purpose of the school itself. Just how this basic recognition of personhood in the school community—of teachers, of administrators, and of students—is integrated with the goal-directed feature of the school as a social system often poses complex and troubling dilemmas for school personnel. The recognition and resolution of these potential conflicts should appear in the school's educational policy statement (see Chapter 5). In order to provide some basis for judgment in these matters for administrators, teachers, and perhaps even students, the school's policy statement can determine moral priorities that can assist everyone in deciding which of the school's functions must be given higher priority in specific situations—its bureaucratic, systems, or communal values.

The foregoing discussion underlines the importance of retaining a multi-image approach to understanding school organization rather than dichotomizing these images into one or another type and then identifying each alternative as more or less desirable. In the case of schools, we suggest a perspective in which bureaucratic, systems, and communitarian elements all contribute to our goals for the restructuring of schools to meet the needs of the future. We do not ascribe to theorists and researchers a lack of awareness that schools with communitarian or systems features are generally bureaucratic in other features. Our purpose was to explain why the dichotomous manner in which organizational models are often presented is not realistic. Theoretical conceptions should be faithful to the reality they intend to represent.

CONCLUSION

In the graphic representation of the traditional school and the restructured school portrayed in Figure 1.2, the three models divide the organizational space among them, each model relatively dominant in different functions of the organization, but all overlapping in some functions. No "map" has been drawn thus far identifying all the functions of a school and indicating whether each function belongs to one or another of the three organizational models. Hence, three major domains of human relationships in schools were selected to appear in the figure under the title of "functions."

In the restructured school, the values and goals of the school as a community provide the foundation of human relations for everyone at all levels of the school. The standards of interpersonal relations suggested by the image of the school as a community should occupy first place in the school's policy statement and educational priorities, even though a significant portion of the relationships at the administrative level are instrumental and hence more akin to the systems than to the communitarian model. The school's operations as a social system include collaborative staff work for planning, problem solving, and decision making for all major aspects of school life, so that priority can be given to creating the conditions for productive learning (Sarason, 1997). Open communication between the administration and the staff is carefully cultivated to maintain a high level of functioning in the school as a system. Special emphasis should be placed on gathering data about the school's operations that provide ongoing feedback to the staff about the effectiveness of its activities.

The integrated curriculum (third row) is consistent with a systems perspective, although a few subjects still may be studied as separate units, not integrated with others. On the other hand, the bureaucratic model leads to the total separation of different disciplines still typically found in most schools. Evaluation of student achievement (not in the figure) derives from both the systems and the bureaucratic models of school organization. Evaluation for purposes of feedback and self-regulation is consistent with the systems perspective, while evaluation for record keeping, accountability to outside authorities, and the like is more in keeping with a bureaucratic orientation. The existence of some hierarchy

Figure 1.2
Hypothesized Proportions of Three Organizational Models in Traditional and Restructured Schools in Different Areas of School Functioning

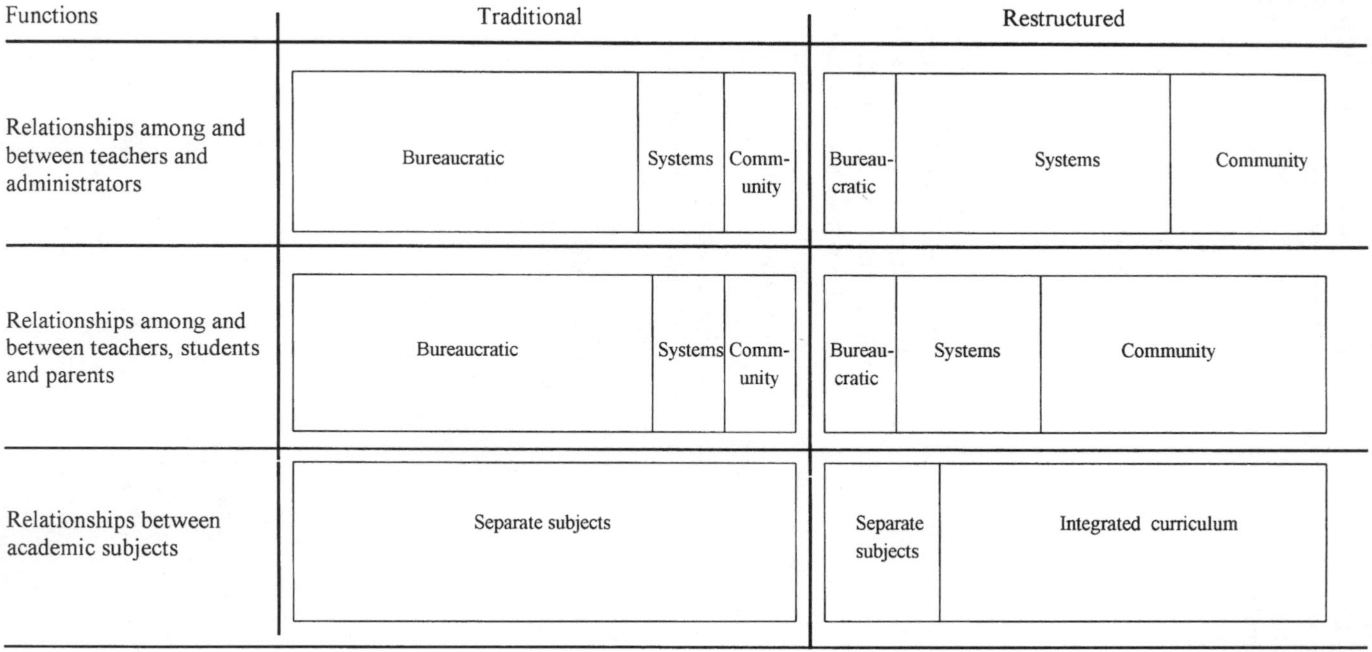

Functions	Traditional	Restructured
Relationships among and between teachers and administrators	Bureaucratic · Systems · Community	Bureaucratic · Systems · Community
Relationships among and between teachers, students and parents	Bureaucratic · Systems · Community	Bureaucratic · Systems · Community
Relationships between academic subjects	Separate subjects	Separate subjects · Integrated curriculum

© Hanna Shachar and Shlomo Sharan.

of authority in the school, such as the principal, team leaders, and subject matter coordinators, as well as the monitoring of various formal features of school life (such as attendance, building security, acquisitions, and record keeping of all kinds), also belong to the bureaucratic aspect of the school's organizational behavior.

Clearly, schools function in all three models simultaneously, affecting all levels of the school's work, including classroom teaching and learning. Grasping the operation of the school from this multimodel perspective can provide educators with organizational flexibility and degrees of freedom that the one-model school cannot achieve.

Chapter 2

Schools Today

INTRODUCTION

What kind of school would we like to see emerge in the near future? How would our school of the future differ from the schools we have today? When we decide on what we wish to incorporate into tomorrow's schools, how can we change the schools to make them similar to what we want to see for the future? It is one thing to describe what we want for the future, or even to build such a school from scratch. To do that, of course, we would have to select, or "retrain," only those personnel who agree with us and who have the skills to make this vision a reality. That would be a challenging and difficult task. But it is quite another thing to transform existing schools into our vision of what they should be. Authorities on school change agree that major school reform is a long and hard journey (Cohen and Spillane, 1992; Elmore et al., 1991; Glickman, 1993; Louis, Kruse et al., 1995; Murphy, 1991; Murphy and Hallinger, 1993; Sarason, 1983, 1990, 1995a, 1995b).

It appears that many people in the professional community have yet to appreciate how complex genuine school change really is. But do we have a choice? There is no denying the need to improve today's schools, and they will not simply become better and more sophisticated in the course of time. The "spirit of the times" (zeitgeist) will not enter the schools by osmosis. If that could happen, schools would be far better and very different from what they are today. Witness the multitude of changes in industrial and commercial institutions over the past two decades. Schools have not "absorbed" similar changes, although they were "in the air." There is no evidence to support the view expressed often by many educators that genuine improvement goes on all the time. In order for schools to get a lot better, what we have now must be changed, and

changing schools for the better is the cardinal challenge confronting education
today.

Before we talk about *how* to change the schools we have today, we present
a short description of how schools function now, followed (in Chapter 3) by an
outline of how we envision schools of the future. We know that a description
of schools *in general* has limited value because schools vary a great deal even
within a particular district, not to speak of an entire country. We do not presume
to describe what schools, and secondary schools in particular, "look like" and
what they do. No one, for example, has documented how teachers perform their
work in the classrooms in any given locality. To do so would be an enormous
and complicated task, and we are not likely to have such information in the
foreseeable future. However, many enlightening works in the professional literature tell us a great deal about how secondary schools operate (Barr and Dreeban, 1983; Barth, 1980; Berlak and Berlak, 1981; Grant, 1988; Jackson, 1968;
Lightfoot, 1983; Powell, Farrar, and Cohen, 1985; Rutter, Maughan, Mortimore,
Outson, and Smith, 1979; Shedd and Bachrach, 1991; Stodolsky, 1988; Wehlage, Rutter, Smith, Lesko, and Fernandez, 1989).

We are able to point out some of the basic features we have encountered in
"typical" schools. Remember that schools have many more features in addition
to the functions, arrangements, and methods discussed here, in structure as well
as in programming. Our presentation of the traditional school and classroom is
admittedly a critical one, not just a factual description of a "typical" school,
as it focuses on what we think must be changed. But, this critical approach does
not mean to be critical of teachers or school administrators. The world's schools
are staffed by millions of teachers and principals who face a challenging task
each day. Enormous effort is invested in performing this task according to high
standards of personal and professional ethics. Every school day, millions of
students enter their classrooms and are instructed in vast number of subjects.
They study a wide range of concepts and skills related to literary, technical,
artistic, social, and scientific enterprises of all kinds. Whatever critique is made
of schools, here or in other publications, cannot ignore the enormous contribution schools make to the development of the younger generations and of society
in general. It is impossible to conceive of modern society without schools and
the dedicated people who work in them. No one intends to point an accusing
finger at any one group, such as teachers or principals, as if the blame for the
problems of contemporary schooling could be laid at their doorstep. Nor could
the conditions of schooling be the consequence of any one group's fallibility.
Changing what teachers do in classrooms is only one of many critical elements
in the equation of change.

Many people are nevertheless aware that dissatisfaction with schools and criticism of their operations are more widespread and receive more public attention
than at other times in recent memory. Much of the criticism aimed at schools
comes from deeply concerned observers and scholars who are not trying to
debunk schools, as some authors did several decades ago (Doll, 1993; Elmore

et al., 1991; Fullan, 1993; Goodlad, 1984; Lee, Bryk, and Smith, 1993; Sarason, 1982, 1983, 1990, 1995b). The knowledge and experience about schooling gained over the past few decades lead rather unambiguously to the conclusion that schools and schooling are definitely in need of overhaul.

No vision of schools in the future, as portrayed here or by other authors, can be proven at this time to be the best of all possible visions. The "proof" of how such schools will affect people lies in the future, which rarely turns out as anyone predicted. We can only plant the seeds of the tree whose fruit will be harvested by our descendants. Naturally, we hope that the future's verdict will be favorable. In the meantime, based on what we know from contemporary thinkers and research, we present the features of school organization, teachers' and principals' professional roles, and the curriculum that we would like to see in schools of the future.

The conception offered here of the school of tomorrow is best understood by comparison with typical schools. Our concepts of the ways in which schools could function better are based primarily on a "systems" theory of organization and on the concept of the school as a community. We compare those approaches with the way schools operate today, whose organization is largely based on the theory of the school as a bureaucracy. Why the bureaucratic patterns of school organization and classroom teaching dominate the educational scene in so many schools and countries or how and why these patterns became part of education's professional legacy are questions that deserve separate, book-length treatment. Whatever is the historical background of this heritage (such as the influence of bureaucracy as a model of human organization that developed in wake of the Industrial Revolution), we will focus on the patterns of teachers' work and on classroom life, as found in many schools.

Schools in different districts and/or countries have had different histories. These varying courses of development could have important implications for planning how to change the way these schools operate. A change agent asked to help a school restructure its organization and teaching methods will have to inquire about the school's recent past and to learn about the background of the social and structural situation with which he or she must work. A change agent must take the past and the future (as he or she would like to mold it) into consideration at every step of the way.

The pragmatic approach to school change that we describe also defines the realistic scope of a change project that can hope to accomplish its goals. Consultants can help schools change how they design the curriculum and how they establish relationships among students, teachers, and principals. Change agents may also assist principals to establish and maintain relationships with their counterparts in other schools as well as with members of various settings and institutions in the community.

But isn't it well known that school policy and the behavior of principals and teachers are frequently affected by forces originating from beyond the "reasonable scope of change" that we just mentioned? Examples of such factors are national, state, or district testing programs, mandated curricular requirements, or various features of teachers' contracts that calculate salaries on the basis of the number of classroom teaching hours. Teacher education programs in local colleges and universities influence new teachers entering the profession. And what happens when supervisors impose in-service training courses that the teachers, or even the principal, never asked for and may not even want? That these topics were excluded from consideration here does not mean that such factors cannot threaten to wipe out with one swoop what change agents worked hard to achieve in a school. The decision to limit the scope of our discussion primarily to events located within the school and to relate it only secondarily to factors in the community outside the school stems from two main considerations:

1. School consultants, internal or external, often are not able to exert much influence on macrosocial factors such as political or professional decisions affecting schools taken by the legislature, the municipal board of education, or school districts. The wider the scope of affairs that the consultant tries to influence, the less direct investment he or she may be able to make in the school itself. Influencing macrosocial events usually requires forms of intervention different from those available to school consultants, such as interest groups, lobbyists, or invited committees of expert advisors, who operate on the basis of political dynamics. The kind of consultation to schools that is the focus of this book is primarily done through conceptual clarification, policy making, and professional retraining (Cohen and Spillane, 1992; Dalin and Rolf, 1993; Fullan and Stiegelbauer, 1991; Schein, 1988; Schmuck and Runkel, 1985). On the other hand, it is generally important for consultants to establish contact with major stakeholders in the change process who are outside the school, such as district superintendents or heads of municipal departments of education. These people must be brought into the circle of those whose advice and support are sought and who should be kept informed of the progress of the change project.

2. Available evidence suggests very strongly that school consultants who focus on a single school or on a set of schools in a given geographical area (such as a relatively small municipality or a neighborhood of a larger city) can eventually achieve the goal of restructuring the schools to function in the manner presented later in this chapter (Murphy and Hallinger, 1993; Rosenblum, Louis, and Rossmiller, 1994; Schmuck and Miles, 1971; Schmuck, Murray, Smith, Schwartz, and Runkel, 1975; Sharan and Hertz-Lazarowitz, 1982; Shachar, 1996). That agenda is a big bite to chew even for experienced and skilled school consultants.

SCHOOLS TODAY

Students and the Classroom

In the "traditional" classroom, students are seated in rows, and the teacher stands at the front of the room, from which point he or she delivers information, most often verbally, to the students. They are expected to listen to what the teacher says. The teacher also asks many questions. This view of the classroom, which could be seen from an imaginary "flying saucer" perched above a roofless school, with its pilot peering into the building, was ingeniously suggested by Seymour Sarason (1982). He wanted his readers to think about and identify at least some of the patterns of behavior that are typical of people in school while they are there. These patterns form the basic social structure of the school. Sarason called these patterns "behavioral regularities," which characterize the fundamental modes of operation found in an organizational setting.

Even today, with all the changes during the past few decades, a large percentage of the classes in secondary schools in the Western world (and probably with even greater tenacity in the Eastern world) look like the traditional classroom, though classes in many elementary schools no longer look or function in the traditional manner. Teaching still involves much lecture-type delivery of information to students, interspersed with many questions asked by the teacher, and answers given by the students—and filling out work sheets! That kind of teaching goes on even when the students don't sit in rows any longer but in small groups, clusters, or other patterns. Changing the seating arrangement does not contribute much to changing the method of teaching. It actually makes matters worse when teachers continue to lecture or ask the entire class many questions while half of the students are sitting with their backs turned toward the teacher.

In all classrooms in public education, the teacher is an authority for the students in more ways than one. In the traditional classroom this authority includes both intellectual and social matters. The content of students' learning activities, the pace at which subject matter is to be taught and learned, how students are supposed to relate to one another in the classroom, and the manner in which students are evaluated are determined or controlled by the teacher. Constant evaluation is one of the hallmarks of traditional teaching. Teachers must submit official reports both to chart their students' progress and to ascertain whether students are learning what teachers are teaching them. It is no simple challenge to find out if students learn and understand what teachers teach! Students rarely have any influence on these matters, despite the opportunity that may be offered to them now and then to choose a topic for special study.

In this kind of classroom, the textbook and the teacher are the primary sources of information; communication among students unsolicited by the teacher is frowned upon. It simply interrupts the teacher, who does most of the talking in the class. As students are not supposed to talk to one another, conversation among students during class time is relatively rare and often surreptitious. Students are not taught or encouraged to view their peers as potential resources for knowledge and understanding. To do so not only interrupts the teacher but, perhaps primarily, also violates the accepted norms of a competitive society. "Each one for him or herself" is the rule loudly trumpeted in traditional schools as fundamental to their code of acceptable student behavior. Each student is responsible for his or her learning only, no matter what other classmates might do or learn. This rule is one of many intended to maintain order, predictability, and social stability in the classroom, at least as these terms are defined in our heavily populated schools and classrooms.

These arrangements are not altogether surprising when we remember that there is only one adult in each classroom to teach and control a large number of students. The prevailing bureaucratic conception of school organization and classroom teaching is usually a one-way (teacher-to-student) form of information delivery, which becomes a two-way exchange when students ask for clarification or answer teachers' questions. That kind of social situation requires that teachers exercise a relatively high degree of control over the students. Teachers are held responsible for making sure that students pay attention and comply with the rules. Control of a large number of students in the classroom involves the exercise of the teacher's power. The use of the teacher's power is considered to be most effective when the students are organized to work alone and not with others (Goodlad, 1984; Sarason, 1982, 1983, 1990, 1995b; Shachar and Sharan, 1994). Most of the time in school, students are required to concentrate on learning by themselves and to make believe that they are not surrounded by their peers.

Perhaps the most unfortunate aspect of traditional whole-class instruction is its superficiality. The mass information-delivery method of teaching by lecture, the speed and frequency with which these lectures are given, rarely allows teachers to delve deeply into problems and to explore their implications in directions opened up by their students' questions and curiosity. It would be difficult to prove that the superficial quality of school learning is a direct result of the lecture-and-question method of teaching. But let us examine these facts about school learning:

1. It rarely involves students in an in-depth exploration of topics.

2. It rarely involves students personally, intellectually and emotionally, in their studies. Schools transmit a great deal of information to students, who are asked in turn to provide concise replies to teachers' questions in order to demonstrate their mastery of the information. Students are not asked to ''pursue knowledge'' by researching topics to gain a broad perspective on them or to solve problems regarding these topics in relation to their own lives or to the world. (Goodlad, 1984; McNeil, 1986; Newman and Wehlage, 1995; Sarason, 1983)

3. Some alternative teaching methods have been found to help students learn with a greater degree of interest and understanding than they show when studying in classrooms conducted with the lecture-and-question approach, as extensive research on cooperative learning has shown. (Cohen, 1994; Slavin, 1990; Shachar and Sharan, 1994; Y. Sharan and S. Sharan, 1992)

It appears that the traditional classroom in the bureaucratic school works under so many rules and constraints that there is little alternative to teaching in the manner described here. Research confirms that students' social or intellectual characteristics, such as coming from a relatively low socioeconomic level in society, do not keep them from learning high-level ideas or seeking solutions to complex problems through careful investigation. Systematic assessments of children's intellectual functioning after they participate in cooperative learning through group-centered inquiry does not support the claim that students from lower-class or middle-class backgrounds learn less or less well than if they had been taught with the traditional whole-class method (Johnson, Maruyama, Johnson, Nelson, and Skon, 1981; Newman and Wehlage, 1995; Shachar and Sharan, 1994; Sharan, 1980, 1990; Sharan, Kussell, Hertz-Lazarowitz, Bejarano, Raviv, and Sharan, 1984; Slavin, 1983, 1993).

Many teachers explain their continued practice of the traditional lecture method by pointing out that students need to be spoon-fed information or they will fail. Teachers see the lecture method as the best way to help the students. A more objective explanation is probably quite complicated. We speculate that the practice seems to be the result of organizational schoolwide rules and constraints of various kinds, as well as previous training, traditions, and habit, and not primarily a matter of making sure the students will learn (Barnes, 1976; Chubb and Moe, 1990; Jackson, 1968; Lee, Bryk, and Smith, 1993; McNeil, 1986; Thelen, 1981).

In the traditional school, the principal often functions in the same role in respect to the teachers in the school as the teacher does in respect to the students in the class. The principal is the authority for the teachers, much as teachers are for their students. Principals frequently relate to the staff as a collection of individuals, just as teachers conduct "whole-class instruction" as if the class is a collection of individual students unrelated to one another. Just as each student is asked to be responsible for his or her work without reference to classmates, each teacher is responsible for his or her classroom independent of other classes and teachers in the school. The latter feature has been characterized as the "loosely-coupled" aspect of school organization (Weick, 1976).

This organizational arrangement keeps each *classroom* operating as a separate unit, almost as if there were no other classrooms in the school. Rarely do teachers and students from nearby classes cooperate in planning or carrying out learning activities. This sharp separation of classes into individual teachers' territories is a direct consequence of the bureaucratic organization of the school, which calls for a clear division of labor among "workers" to avoid duplication of effort and to foster efficiency (Bidwell, 1965; Bidwell and Quiroz, 1991). This approach to understanding the organization of classrooms and schools allows us to see the parallel between the students in the classroom and the classroom in the school: Students sit "alone" as solo learners in a large group of peers. Everyone works on the same task but must make believe that "there is nobody there" except himself or herself. This isolation is repeated at the level of the classroom, as a unit within the school. Educators in elementary schools will probably object that this description is outdated, as their schools have adopted flexible arrangements of seating and collaboration among students. However, a national survey of high schools showed clearly that the vast majority of class-rooms are conducted in the traditional fashion (Cawelti, 1994).

The consequences of teacher isolation and their lack of collaboration with colleagues on matters of curriculum and instruction are many and far reaching. Teachers who are not involved in systematic work with their colleagues in small groups devoted to the examination and improvement of their work are unlikely to appreciate the benefits and difficulties of cooperative learning for their students (Sarason, 1976).

The School

Remarkably, the school as an institution is relatively isolated within the community it serves. It is an unusual school that maintains active relationships with the community beyond basic public relations. Schools do not consider the local community, or communities some distance away, as a potentially rich source of experiences and information for students. Some schools may view the community as a place where students can learn about many aspects of life, such as the professions, commerce and industry, and government but they are few in number (Sarason, 1983; Sarason, Carroll, Maton, Cohen, and Lorents, 1977; Sarason and Lorentz, 1979). In the eyes of teachers and parents alike, school learning means learning that takes place within the walls of the school.

Some schools do have work-study programs, in which students work several days and attend regular school on other days. Those programs do not affect schools in general. Work-study programs usually are restricted to students at the lowest levels of academic achievement who are tracked into work-oriented rather than academic-oriented forms of schooling. By and large, the vast resources of the community, where adult social, economic, political, artistic, intellectual, and service activities occur, are regarded by schools as outside their territorial bounds. Restriction of the concept of learning to something that takes place within school walls and to topics chosen by the school is one of the most effective means schools command to control public access to educational progress for children. Everyone must pass through school in order to get to the next stage of learning on the accepted ladder of educational progress. That provides teachers and schools with a great deal of power over students and over "official" knowledge (Sarason, 1983; Young, 1971). In a world where people learn all the time and from an increasing number of sources easily available to the public, without the power of control over formal learning schools could become an endangered species.

The conception of school learning as confined to the space within the school hampers the school's ability to relate learning in school to life outside school. Indeed, schools have guaranteed that school learning is actually preparation for more school learning and not preparation for life, as is widely proclaimed. What do schools mean when they talk about schooling as preparation for life? It seems clear that the meaning is that a diploma is needed to move forward on the road of educational and economic advancement. When using the expression "school as preparation for life," probably few people mean that one needs the knowledge learned in school in order to live a better life as a person and as a member of society. Schools are conducted as if getting into college is equivalent to life itself, and that is why schools claim to be "preparation for life." No wonder so many students have come to view school as a rite of passage, as something one has to live through, not as an instructive experience in its own right. As a result, they invest only minimal mental and emotional energy in their schooling, to fulfill the formal requirements for graduation.

Of course, schooling as preparation for more schooling is a legitimate and worthwhile goal, and schools always have claimed to prepare students for study at higher levels of education. Nevertheless, as educators we would be deluding ourselves if we thought that the masses of students, whom every national school system must educate, can be motivated to invest genuine effort in learning when they know that the goal of school learning is more learning and do not know how such learning is related to their lives or to life in the real world. If students do not gain a deep personal appreciation for the value of learning—for the pursuit of knowledge and for their intellectual development—society has not derived the expected benefits from its educational efforts.

The School and the Principal

Research on how high school principals spend their workday revealed that, on average, over 80 percent of each day principals met with one other person, such as a teacher, a parent, or an official from the local municipality or the school system. A small fraction of the day was spent with groups, as in a committee meeting. Meetings with large groups of teachers were as rare as once in two or three weeks (Gali, 1983; Rosenblum, Louis, and Rossmiller, 1994).

Only the principal is expected to have a view of the school as a whole organization. It is not yet popular for teachers to become responsible for school-wide problems and to cooperate with other teachers on a daily basis to solve these problems, albeit with the leadership of the principal. Many teachers say that they do not have the professional background or preparation to function in that capacity, nor are all teachers prepared to assume such responsibility as part of their role as teachers. Decisions affecting the school as a whole are made almost exclusively by the principal, with or without consultation with teachers.

Schools organized in this fashion, however many the new departments or subjects added to their programs over the years, retain their fundamental character as bureaucracies. The division of labor among teachers and the hierarchy of authority and control found in most schools are the basic features of bureaucratic organization (Bidwell and Quiroz, 1991; Lee, Bryk, and Smith, 1993; Shachar and Sharan, 1995). The conception of tomorrow's school, which guides our work, seeks to change this feature of schools today.

THE EDUCATIONAL SYSTEM

Our analysis of the isolation of teachers and principals in schools, compared to organizational arrangements by which they can interact with colleagues, can be carried one step further. We have already stressed the striking parallel between the role of the teacher in respect to the students in the class, and the role of the principal in respect to the teachers on the staff of the school. Taking this line of reasoning one step further, there seems to be a distinct parallel between the supervisor of a school district (as in the United States) or the executive director of the Ministry of Education (in countries with centralized school systems). He or she stands in relation to the schools in the school system much as the principal stands in relation to the teachers in a given school. There is little or no contact between different schools in the school system, each being a separate entity, not connected to other similar entities in the same system. In general, interschool collaboration or interaction is notoriously difficult to establish and maintain, except for competitive sports and a few other extracurricular activities, even though schools have the same goals and teach similar, or even identical, subjects at given grade levels. Many attempts to establish leagues of cooperative schools have been short lived. Since there is only one principal per school, the principalship is probably the loneliest job in education.

It seems, therefore, that a similarity of organization exists between all levels of schooling, from the classroom to the entire local educational system (Shachar and Sharan, 1995). The organization of one level, such as the classroom, is similar to, and perhaps determined by, the organization of its larger settings, the school and the school system. It is widely claimed that teachers have a great deal of autonomy in the classroom, but a great deal of what teachers do in the classroom reflects the organization and the norms of the school, not just the personality of the individual teacher. In turn, the school reflects the organizational and behavioral norms accepted by the larger school system. Schools that do not conform to these norms, such as experimental schools or those that have adopted distinctive innovations in organization and instruction, are constantly under pressure to adopt the practices used by the majority of teachers and schools in a given system. Unless the nonconformists are private schools not controlled by the district or Ministry, these innovations are unlikely to survive in the long term (Chubb and Moe, 1990).

It is clear that any attempt to change classroom organization and teaching methods faces a formidable challenge. Beyond doubt, the effort to change schools has not made remarkable progress precisely because the impediments are many and complex (Tyack and Tobin, 1994). The road of change leads through many points of opposition from people who have vested interests. Our knowledge of what to do and how to do it and our will to struggle with these problems are not always strong. Further, one more basic feature of life in schools, and in secondary schools in particular, must not be neglected, that is, what and how much students are required to study at any given time.

THE CURRICULUM

Except for a handful of experts, everyone takes for granted that a school is made up of many classrooms and that each classroom has its own teacher. Students are assigned to these classrooms in fairly large groups, usually somewhere between 15 and 35 in many Western countries. Israel has many classrooms with 40 or 42 students. Still larger numbers of students per class are common in many countries of the Far East. Apart from a handful of schools, however, the principle of "one class, one teacher" (Sarason, 1982) is close to universal as the basis for organizing the work of teachers and for placing students in classrooms.

Almost universally, this manner of organizing schools results in classes devoted to just one subject or discipline. Not only do high school teachers define their professional identity in terms of the subject they teach, they expect to teach that subject alone in a class where no other teacher will be teaching (Darling-Hammond, Bullmaster, and Cobb, 1995; Grossman and Stodolsky, 1994; Johnson, 1990; Petrie, 1992). That role is similar to that of the university professors who taught the teachers. The teacher's profession, primarily in secondary schools, is not defined as being educators but in terms of the subject they teach. From the students' point of view, each class, lasting 45 or even 90 minutes, deals with a subject probably unrelated to the one studied just before or after it. From one class to another, or from one teacher to another, students encounter a different realm of study every hour of the school day.

The number of such classes varies from place to place, and certainly from one country to the next. In many states in the United States, for example, students study five or six subjects at any given time, often attending each class at the same time every day, except for courses like gym, art, and music, which may appear one or more times a week. Typically, Finnish students take seven to ten subjects at a time. Israeli high school students study fourteen or more subjects at a time. Some classes are held once or twice a week, others three or four times a week. For these students, juggling the curriculum is an acrobatic feat, not to speak of the radical fragmentation of meaning and the lack of relationship among subjects or integration of the material typical of school learning today.

This way of organizing schools and school learning shows that schools are distinctly behind the times. Until recently, factories distributed the manufacture of each element of a given product among different departments or production lines. The various parts were then brought together at the assembly line for the production of the complete product. But, over the past few decades, many factories have adopted a *systems* model of internal organization. Forms of work previously assigned to different departments are now integrated and performed by a team of a single department. In the more sophisticated industries, products are planned and produced in their entirety by a single team that includes all the expertise needed. Such integration expands considerably the range of tasks that each group member may be called upon to perform. Also, team members co-operate frequently, making it possible for the team to fulfill the broader scope of its responsibility. Extending the breath of the task to be accomplished by a single team prevents to a significant degree the boredom or burnout that can gradually build up because of daily repetition of a task. Employees also find greater challenge, responsibility, and interest in their wok (Hackman and Oldham, 1980). Equally important, in the systems form of organization people are much more likely to give expression to a higher level of thinking, they are likely to improve the way they work, and superior products may even be produced (Morgan, 1986; Thelen, 1954; Zander, 1982). In short, many industries have advanced far beyond the assembly-line organization that was the standard mode of industrial operations for decades.

However, the school curriculum retains its bureaucratic design as a collection of separate parts that have little or nothing to do with one another (Darling-Hammond, Bullmaster, and Cobb, 1995; Doll, 1993; Grossman and Stodolsky, 1994; Petrie, 1992). Schools long ago became accustomed to the production-line or linear conception of curriculum. Teaching and learning were also thought to progress in a definite sequence that dictated what should be taught first and what later. This design of curriculum and instruction was also adopted from the bureaucratic-industrial model, as developed and disseminated by Ralph Tyler and his disciples in many countries (Doll, 1993). Also, curricula and textbooks are still aimed primarily at teaching rather than at the needs of learning and the learner. The discipline-centered curriculum goes hand in hand with the way schools, classes, and the work of teachers and students are organized. The subject-matter departments are the mirror image of the organization of the curriculum and of the classes in the school (Lee, Bryk, and Smith, 1993; Powell, Farrar, and Cohen, 1985; Siskin, 1991; Siskin and Little, 1995). By now, of course, it is hard to tell which is the cart and which is the horse. It could very well be that the existence of subject-matter departments dictates how curriculum and classes will be organized, but the question of what comes first or what causes what is only of academic interest. William Doll captures this state of affairs in the following concise statement:

Many curriculum critics, including Oliver and Gershman (1989), point out that current curriculum design is based on fragmentation, isolation, atomization—not on the flowing of experience. Curricular subjects, class schedules, grade levels, lesson plans, even teaching strategies are represented in particle form. (Doll, 1993, 69)

This structure of the school and curriculum has negative consequences for a host of educational goals. Among the goals schools seek to achieve that are not served well by the way schools are organized are:

1. teachers' professional growth through mutual support and feedback to one another regarding the way they teach;

2. the development of students' modes of thinking (Ladwig and King, 1992);

3. the cultivation of a "world view" so students can learn to appreciate the interrelatedness of various phenomena in society and nature;

4. the stimulation and implementation of an investigative orientation toward knowledge;

5. the deepening of students' perspectives on provocative, life-related "issues," which are almost never unidisciplinary;

6. studying the modes of operation of the community in which students live.

The present form in which teachers receive curricula does not take into consideration an interrelated or systems view of phenomena or events. Were that the case, many changes would have to be incorporated into curriculum planning. The planners would have to include in their work a wide range of interrelated subject matter reflecting the nature of real-life experience. They would have to grant students a wide range of choice in the selection of "issues" for study through inquiry and in different ways. Students would not be occupied in performing tasks that confirm what teachers or textbooks know already. If such features became typical of school curricula, that alone would hail the end of an era in curriculum planning. It would end the practice whereby the "transmission" concept of teaching and learning rules supreme and preplanned academic contents are delivered by subject-matter teachers who do not see themselves as educators. It would also mark the end of school learning dominated by disciplinary encapsulation (Barnes, 1976; Doll, 1993; Petrie, 1992). But the end of that era is not now in sight. Schools will have to recognize that school organization, methods of classroom teaching, and the design of the curriculum are interdependent. Significant change in the status of the separate academic disciplines in the school curriculum will have to occur if other changes in organization and instruction are to be implemented (Petrie, 1992; Sizer, 1993). "The issues of classroom and school governance are in theory and practice identical. . . . Governance and subject matter are, in a phenomenological sense, never experienced as separate variables" (Sarason, 1995b, 172). Whatever change is planned in the work schedule of teachers so that they can collaborate on the school's educational policy or school problems will almost assuredly not affect classroom teaching unless the change includes the redesign of the curriculum as well (Grossman and Stodolsky, 1994; Siskin, 1991).

Integrating the curriculum to reduce the number of separate subjects students must study at one time and to broaden the scope of their studies to make school learning closer to real-life problems is a complex affair. Subject-matter teachers have a great deal of "vested interest" in the way the curriculum seems to protect their special roles in the school. There is the danger that schools can become entangled in the conflicts over disciplinary, multidisciplinary, or transdisciplinary approaches to knowledge that plague colleges and universities (Petrie, 1992). Unfortunately, public education does inherit some of the consequences of these debates because they affect the education of teachers. But we must not lose sight of the fact that the goal of public education is not to define or protect the integrity of academic disciplines. The mandate of public education (and of the education of youth in general) is to contribute to the cultural and intellectual development of the students, to help them understand themselves and the world in the past, present, and future. Our mandate is to arouse students to want to learn and to appreciate the profound significance of learning and knowledge. Hence, the primary concern of public education is pedagogical, not epistemological. The universities should cease imposing on the education of the youth demands for the kind of fragmented and specialized knowledge that stems primarily from the epistemological definitions of disciplines currently accepted by the universities. (Even in universities, the definition of disciplines continues to change; many new departments have been established in recent years with titles of disciplines that did not exist only a few years ago.) Universities should be called upon by leaders of public education to relinquish or relax their pressure on secondary education. This pressure is expressed through the medium of the discipline-oriented curriculum. It is ironic that the negative implications of the overloaded, discipline-centered curriculum has been documented by and come under fire from university-based investigators. Obviously, these are not the people who decide what academic background will be required for entrance into the universities or how students seeking teaching credentials are to be prepared for their profession. As educational thinkers and researchers have very little voice in such matters, much of educational research seems to be mostly an academic exercise.

Another irony lies is the fact that in many professions, as they are practiced outside the university, there is widespread recognition of the need for building "organizations in which there is a good deal less specialization (read "disciplinarity") and a good deal more integration (read "interdisciplinarity") (Petrie, 1992). Integration of different disciplines can be undertaken by the schools through their organizational and pedagogical efforts. These should be aimed at providing a dramatic increase in the meaning and sense of school-based learning, as well as in the culture of the schools where teachers are concerned (Lee, Bryk, and Smith, 1993; Sarason, 1982, 1990). Making sense out of the curriculum as a whole, rather than viewing it as a collection of unrelated topics, is still left largely to the students. Not surprisingly, they fail to do what schools and teachers do not even attempt to do.

One way of cultivating interdisciplinary studies in secondary schools is through the creation of interdisciplinary teams of teachers. Through collaborative planning of potential topics of study and investigation by small groups of students, teams of teachers can create an interdisciplinary course of study (Darling-Hammond, Bullmaster, and Cobb, 1995; Petrie, 1992). Teacher education programs in the universities aimed at preparing teachers with an interdisciplinary background and orientation are still in the future.

In sum, for all their differences, today's secondary schools are often large conglomerates of subject-matter departments and specialists concerned each with his or her classes, which are not few in number (Siskin and Little, 1995). One teacher's classroom is almost out of bounds for other teachers in terms of co-operation in planning their classroom teaching and for giving and receiving feedback to one another. This division of labor is one area where the basic principle of the theory of organizations as bureaucracies is most clearly seen in the operation of schools (Rowan, 1990). Bureaucratic school organization makes it next to impossible for teachers to interact during classroom teaching. Peer cooperation for planning and implementing innovative teaching is vital for providing experiences for teachers that contribute to their professional growth. They also are a source of assistance and support for teachers in coping with the difficult demands of daily instruction (Joyce, Wolf, and Calhoun, 1993; Shachar and Sharan, 1995; Smylie, 1994).

Enormous benefits for learning and for students' socialization can be reaped from interaction between classrooms within a school and between the school and many settings and people in the community. These opportunities are not yet exploited by schools. It is promising that some localities are beginning to view the bureaucratic model of school organization as less and less effective and relevant (Clark, 1985). However, if the past is any indication of the pace of change in schooling, we can anticipate that that process will continue to unfold for several decades to come. It is clear that the dominant role of the bureaucratic model in the design of schooling is shrinking. Gradually, it will be relegated to those domains where its function is still vitally needed and where no alternative has emerged.

Chapter 3

The Restructured School

STUDENTS AND THE CLASSROOM

The educational environment of the restructured school has many features that differ from its traditional counterpart. The key to the difference is the word *interaction*. In the restructured classroom, students face each other as members of small groups and work together cooperatively. This form of social organization is aimed at promoting communication and interaction among students. The teacher no longer stands at the front of the classroom. Indeed, the "front" of the room as the teacher's own territory has been abolished.

The instructional process has been altered radically, no longer consisting of the delivery of verbal information by the teacher to the students. Unilateral and bilateral communication between teacher and students does occur when needed, but students spend a significant amount of time in a process of cooperative inquiry. Small teams determine specific topics of study and investigate these topics much as in research conducted by adults (S. Sharan, 1995; Y. Sharan, 1995; Y. Sharan and S. Sharan, 1992, 1993). A cooperative team inquiry approach to learning emphasizes multilateral communication among peers who work together in small groups. This setting and pattern of communication invites active student initiative and participation.

Of course, students need assistance from their teachers to develop and practice skills for collaborating in small groups. Teachers will have to move from group to group, lending assistance wherever needed, serving as guides and resource persons. Here and there students study alone when required or preferred, with a range of technological aids for seeking information. Computer technology certainly affects classroom learning in many ways. Through the Internet and other modes of communication with peers, institutions, other classrooms, libraries, and data banks outside the classroom and even outside the city or country, with the appropriate equipment students will find a vast network of resources at their disposal (O'Neil, 1995; see *Educational Leadership*, 1995, vol. 53, number 2). The cognitive and social benefits that can be derived from this general form of classroom learning have been documented by a substantial research effort over the past two decades (Cohen, 1994; Johnson and Johnson, 1987; Shachar and Sharan, 1994; Sharan, 1990, 1994; Y. Sharan and S. Sharan, 1992; Slavin, 1983, 1990, Slavin, Sharan, Kagan, Hertz-Lazarowitz, Webb, and Schmuck, 1985).

This kind of classroom opens channels of communication among participants and affords them a moderate degree of control over their activities. It is a form of social organization that embodies the principal features of a systems approach to organization rather than the traditional bureaucratic model. Communication within the system is largely horizontal and multilateral, as among peers in a discussion, rather than hierarchical, unilateral, or bilateral, such as when teachers ask questions and students reply. All the elements within the system, such as groups of students, can be in communication with one another regarding their learning. The teacher functions as a classroom facilitator and guide, rather than as the dominant authority in all matters intellectual and social. The physical structure of the classroom has been altered to make possible direct communication in small groups, while the learning tasks in which the groups engage stimulate cooperative investigation, discussion, and problem solving (Sarason, 1982; Y. Sharan and S. Sharan, 1992). Learning has become a cooperative enterprise devoted to the formulation and investigation of genuine problems.

The classroom as a social system does not seek to afford teachers security through close control of student behavior to eliminate unpredictable events, as does the traditional classroom. It *does* seek to provide students with an emotionally and intellectually stimulating environment. In that kind of environment, students are more likely to be highly task oriented, precisely because they are not being overcontrolled by the teacher. Gradually students will assume greater responsibility for their learning because they were *given* such responsibility! School learning becomes more of a student-directed, teacher-guided pursuit of collective academic goals, rather than a contest to see who remembers more and faster than others and hence deserves a higher grade.

In such an environment teachers can feel professionally rewarded and personally secure without holding sanctions over the students' heads to ensure their compliance with the rules. It can be a place with far less emphasis on power relations and more on the free exchange of feelings and ideas than the traditional classroom. The interactive, cooperative classroom fosters a relaxed atmosphere through active cooperation with peers on academic tasks. Attention to the group task is sustained by students' identification with their classmates working in groups.

Students' identification with one another in a collective pursuit of knowledge is probably one of the factors that account for the distinct increase in students' motivation to learn observed in classrooms conducted with cooperative learning (Sharan and Shaulov, 1990). Motivation to learn is built up by features of the teaching method, not only by the promise of rewards or even by the subject matter, although these factors are not to be ignored. A higher level of motivation to learn means more genuine interest in learning, more pleasure derived by the students from their work, greater satisfaction from the process of learning. The press for a better grade probably will not disappear, but it can become a less dominant consideration in the students' minds and allow them to develop a genuine interest in the subject and in the process of learning.

Another way in which teachers' control of students' activities and behavior is relaxed in the interactive classroom refers to students' academic pursuits and products. In today's heterogeneous classrooms—heterogeneous not only in ethnic background but especially in interests and abilities—students pursue their study and inquiry in a great diversity of ways. That norm must be accepted and turned to the benefit of school learning in these classrooms. It is counterproductive to rely on uniform approaches to teaching and learning, nor should we expect uniformity in the products that will emerge from the students' efforts (Wolf, Bixby, Glenn, and Gardner, 1991).

Moreover, when small groups of students investigate a topic, even if all the groups in a class study the same topic, the group products will surely differ considerably from one another. Each group will naturally synthesize its information differently and create its own account of its work and findings. When all group members are considered as bringing valuable resources to their group and are encouraged to contribute whatever talents, experience, perspectives, and knowledge they possess, every group will produce its own product, which will differ from those of other groups.

When products differ, their evaluation obviously cannot be uniform. Schools and teachers will have to develop sets of criteria for evaluation that focus on the process of how students perform their tasks and how they design the presentation of their work. Presentations can assume a wide variety of forms and styles, depending upon the topic investigated and the opportunities and resources available to the students for exploring that topic (Sharan, 1994; Y. Sharan and S. Sharan, 1992; Wolf, Bixby, Glenn, and Gardner, 1991). An important feature of such presentations, such as exhibitions of various kinds or simulations of social and organizational situations, is that they integrate what students have learned into a meaningful message to other people. They demonstrate *what* students have learned and *how* they communicate what they learned to the public, first and foremost to their classmates and teacher (Newman and Wehlage, 1995; Sizer, 1993). This kind of evaluation rises much above the widespread practice of testing in terms of challenging the interest and minds of students.

The high-level practice of an inquiry-oriented form of teaching and learning can make productive use of interaction between classes or between groups of students from different classes, when interaction can expand students' opportunities for learning. Certain rooms in the school can be devoted to specific topics of inquiry during specified periods of time, after which the material or equipment can be dismantled. This conception emphasizes a flexible use of space and time preferable to permanently assigning particular rooms to specific functions. The tight link between room and function assignments in traditional schools parallels the phenomenon of teachers' disciplinary specialization.

It seems that school classrooms and hallway space are used to best advantage when they are not assigned to strict time slots. Teams of teachers should have the discretion to plan the use of space and time in a far more flexible fashion than has been customary (Cambone, 1995; Shachar and Sharan, 1995). Simultaneously, the assignment of students and teachers to classroom spaces will also undergo "defreezing" from the fixed schedule for an entire academic year frequently followed today. Such fluidity in the planning of space and time in schools, along with a more flexible assignment of teachers and students to these spaces, has long been practiced in some progressive elementary schools. However, the difference in organizational conditions in elementary and secondary schools makes it difficult to transfer experience from one kind of school to the other (Wilson, Herriot, and Firestone, 1988).

THE SCHOOL

Principals often work almost entirely without colleagues of similar status in the school. Large secondary schools may have one or more vice principals, each responsible for a well-defined task such as the teaching schedule, student discipline, or school finances. Rarely, however, is a vice principal responsible for coordinating different aspects of the school's operation, including its pedagogical policies and methods. Many principals function as one member of an administrative team whose members share a broad view of the school as a whole, in terms of all its major domains of operation. Principals and vice principals, not only teachers, must assume interdisciplinary roles. "Manager of the teaching staff" is no longer adequate as a definition of the principal's role. The principal's task of organizing the school as a complex social system now involves the maximum possible number of teachers and students in its organizational and educational processes (Murphy and Louis, 1994; Sergiovanni, 1993; Thomson, 1993).

The principal of a school viewed as a social system serves in a leadership capacity rather than primarily in a managerial role (Murphy and Louis, 1994). He or she facilitates and coordinates the work of the teacher teams or assists teachers pursuing individual projects. The principal is also a resource person who helps teachers define and locate the components needed to implement their instructional plans, including equipment, time, interclass interaction or cooperative efforts, and access to institutions, sites, or people outside the school as resources for student learning. Clearly, the pivotal role of the principal places him or her in a decisive position regarding the process of change and new ways of organizing the school and teaching (Lee, Bryk, and Smith, 1993; Lightfoot, 1983; Sarason, 1982, 1994; Thomson, 1993).

Similarly, rather than having only one teacher responsible for a given classroom, where that teacher works alone preparing and implementing teaching, tomorrow's school accomplishes its pedagogical work through teams of teachers. Team members share responsibility for all pedagogical functions and call upon one another to cope with all aspects of their work. The central importance of teamwork in no way diminishes the continued importance of individual thinking and preparation (for staff work as well as for classroom teaching) by teachers (Hargreaves, 1993; Huberman, 1993). Nor is it intended to take away the principal's prerogative to veto decisions that conflict with school policy. The problem of allocating time to teachers for teamwork in the restructured school is discussed in Chapter 8.

Research on restructured schools explored whether the redesign of teachers' professional roles to involve them in schoolwide problem solving and decision making affected their teaching and, subsequently, their students' academic achievement. No results of that kind have been found. Some researchers hastily concluded that restructuring did not matter, as no student benefits from restructuring were shown (Smylie, 1994). Such conclusions are premature. A close reading of these studies shows that the redesign of teachers' work frequently adds new elements to their job and may have made the job more interesting. However, redesign efforts carried out thus far have rarely changed "the essential structure and character of (teachers') work in the classroom" (Smylie, 1994, 132). As the students did not experience any change in the way teaching and learning were conducted, there seems to have been no basis for anticipating that students' academic achievement would be affected. Teachers' increased work motivation, hypothesized as a possible result of school restructuring, was not evaluated in this research, even though it is one of the first areas that could be affected by school restructuring. Only after organizational restructuring has included the adoption and practice of alternative teaching methods that actively involve and motivate the students will the time have come to evaluate how restructuring affects student achievement.

We do not assume that school restructuring in and of itself, including the redesign of teachers' roles, will affect student achievement. Rather, alternative instructional methods such as cooperative learning require the redesign of teachers' organizational roles as a necessary but not sufficient condition for the sustained implementation of new methods of teaching. Organizational change alone does not automatically equip teachers with new instructional concepts and skills; hence, it alone does not lead to improved instruction (Shachar and Sharan, 1995; Smylie, 1994). It is important for teachers to participate in collaborative efforts with colleagues to solve problems and make decisions regarding their teaching. Teachers working individually, without the support of colleagues and the administration, cannot be expected to make significant changes in teaching. "Limited interaction forecloses opportunities for collegial influence, motivation, learning and, therefore, change'' (Smylie, 1994, 155). Genuine change in teaching methods through intensive in-service training and coaching of teachers must precede or accompany changes in teachers' schoolwide roles and their active participation in decision making about the school's pedagogical affairs and arrangements.

Teacher teams, under the leadership of the principal, also engage in clarifying and determining the school's pedagogical and social policy. Members of the staff are not constrained to conduct their classes in a particular fashion. But they should know that there is schoolwide support and sanction for cooperative small-group projects, alternative forms of evaluation, individualized instruction and learning, the use of a wide range of sources for problem-centered learning, and the like, instead of the lecture method (Joyce, Weil, and Showers, 1992; Sharan, 1994). At times, these methods entail having students move among different rooms in the school or to sites outside the school, and not stay riveted to their seats all the time. Such changes in student behavior as a function of changes in teaching method require wide support from other teachers in the school as well as from the administration (Shachar and Sharan, 1994).

The organization of the teaching staff into teams facilitates communication among teachers, the giving and receiving of feedback about teachers' performance in different settings, and the pooling of human resources for mutual support and enrichment. For example, teachers can decide how information available through computer programs can be integrated into students' investigation projects in many curricular areas, rather than added on to the curriculum as a separate topic. Or, teachers can study their students' motivation to learn and consider what the school is doing to meet needs in this realm, rather than placing responsibility for the problem on the shoulders of a particular teacher. There is no lack of policy questions that await teachers' study, analysis, and planning. Again, these activities must be purposively planned by the teams. Of course, the sheer existence of teams of teachers for problem solving does not guarantee that the teams will perform such functions. Teachers can meet for hours to discuss what's wrong with their students' families, and none of the school's own organizational challenges will be mentioned. Nor will teachers be likely to discuss the teaching methods they use in their own classrooms. Someone, be it a teacher, a department coordinator, the principal, or a consultant from outside the school, must suggest an agenda of critical issues. Otherwise, teacher teams can become a convenient technique for avoiding the real challenges facing the school.

The team approach replaces the bureaucratic procedure of appointing individuals to be responsible for solving specific problems that affect the school as a whole. Individual teachers appointed to various ''fire-fighting'' roles might succeed in solving a problem for several students at a given point in time. At best, the solution will fit that student, but it will not be integrated into the operation of the school or become accepted practice for other teachers. Many problems that arise in a school are indeed of a personal nature, and an individual approach is sufficient and effective. Nevertheless, the "add-on" method of problem solving now typical of schools usually leaves many problems of policy and principle unsolved, to recur again and again. That situation is reminiscent of the fires that regularly consume large wooden buildings in various countries, where tradition forbids the use of other kinds of materials. Inevitably the structures will have to be rebuilt many times.

The integrated systems approach becomes particularly appropriate when teacher specialization and departmental divisions are not cast in cement and the school encourages teachers to fill the broad role of teacher educator instead of instructor in a discipline (Morgan, 1986). Gradually many of the teachers, and not just the principal, can begin to view the entire school as their organizational horizon.

Several authors have emphasized the potential pitfalls and inevitable conflicts inherent in collaborative staff work among teachers, as well as the need teachers have for personal solitude and individualism in the relentlessly intrusive school environment (Fullan, 1993; Hargreaves, 1993, Hargreaves and Dawe, 1990). Secondary schools are complex organizations that often have multiple, even conflicting goals that stem from the educational and disciplinary orientations of the teachers and the broad range of pedagogical demands made upon teachers by their students' educational needs (Firestone, 1982; Herriot and Firestone, 1984; Wilson, Herriot, and Firestone, 1988). Achieving a cooperative and consistent set of norms as a basic feature of the school culture is a great challenge to the school's leadership.

Furthermore, no set of organizational structures or procedures guarantees superior effectiveness or even improved working conditions for teachers. No method of human organization operates independently of the manner in which it is implemented. The purposes of collegial cooperation can be subverted by individuals and/or groups. What was originally intended to yield benefits for those involved can produce unforeseen negative consequences when these individuals or groups perceive the new procedures as threatening their stability, security, or power (Lieberman, 1970). Most citizens understand that the practice of democratic procedures by the government does not always ensure that the public good will be served by a particular legislative measure.

One report of teacher participation in school site councils in a U.S. school district tells how the teachers were unable to conceive of any change in the accepted roles for teachers. As a result, the existing hierarchical power structure remained unchanged despite the teachers' prerogative to create a more egalitarian form of governing their schools (Malen and Ogawa, 1988; Rowan, 1990). Democracy did not produce new forms of self-government when all the people involved had a long history of working in a bureaucratic school with a hierarchical power structure. Suddenly granting the teachers the power to change their situation had no effect on how they understood their job or on their professional behavior. Patterns of school governance yield only very slowly to innovation, as much because of what the participants have to unlearn as because of the need to learn new patterns, concepts, attitudes, procedures, and skills (Sarason, 1982, 1990).

Since all forms of human social organization carry the seeds of potential conflict, society must constantly reestablish improved forms of organization. No matter how effective the organization, there will always be disagreement. It is far more advisable to create the best organization possible and to cope with the inevitable disagreements than to remain tied to forms of school organization and classroom teaching that have proved that they cannot achieve the basic goals of education today. Cooperative staff work in schools must include methods for resolving disagreements among teachers and administrators in constructive ways. The continued concentration of decision-making power and control in the hands of the principal, particularly widespread in secondary schools, is not the preferred way to avoid the conflicts that will arise when teachers are empowered to influence how their school is run (Murphy and Louis, 1994; Sergiovanni, 1994).

Knowing full well that disagreement among school staff cannot be prevented, it still appears advisable to involve school personnel in the formulation of the school's pedagogical philosophy, policy, and goals, as well as in participation in continuous planning of how and by whom that policy will be implemented. Teams of teachers should focus on the identification of problems regarding the academic and social life of the students and teachers. Continuous identification of problems by groups of teachers who analyze these problems and prepare programs or procedures to deal with them is one of the distinguishing characteristics of schools that function on the basis of systems theory, in contrast with bureaucracies. Gathering information about the way the school operates and using this information to solve problems is how teams of teachers use feedback procedures for improving their school. Well-functioning social systems develop methods for receiving systematic feedback that can redirect the efforts of the organization. The use of feedback based on reliable information and used for planning the school's activities is a prerequisite for turning a school into a learning organization (Argyris, 1992; Argyris and Schon, 1978; Janis and Mann, 1977; Senge, 1990) (see Chapter 5).

Another approach to the prevention of conflicts among teachers is to divide large secondary schools into subunits or "houses" (Sizer, 1993). Large schools often have several vice principals. Each vice principal could assume the role of chairperson (at least for a defined period of time, since it is best to rotate leadership roles) for a multidisciplinary teacher team that will assume responsibility for the entire program of instruction to be conducted in that house. Included in its responsibilities will be curriculum design and development, scheduling, teaching methods, student evaluation, and students' academic and social welfare. The vice principals can serve as liaison with the principal and together form the administrative team for the entire school. There should be no expectation that this team's purpose is to create uniformity in curriculum or instruction for all of the subunits in the school. Problems of scheduling, curriculum, and interdisciplinary study projects and teaming are probably solved with much greater ease at the house level than at the level of the school as a whole. The house structure permits a much wider range of diversity and opportunity for creative teaching projects than might be undertaken when planned at the schoolwide level. But even in such circumstances, there are many topics of potential disagreement between the teachers, especially teachers of different subjects. The house chairperson and the school principal will have to exercise considerable leadership if they wish to have an interdisciplinary or transdisciplinary curriculum accepted by the teachers as a school norm (Lee, Bryk, and Smith, 1993; Siskin, 1991; Siskin and Little, 1995; Sizer, 1993).

The creation of semiautonomous teams of teachers who incorporate in their collective knowledge and skills the disciplinary domains the school seeks to include in the curriculum can constitute an effective organizational unit within the school. The faculty designated for this unit then assumes responsibility for a broad range of pedagogical and organizational topics that significantly expand the role of the teachers and calls upon each and every one to cultivate the professional self-image of the teacher educator (Lieberman, 1988; Louis; Kruse, et al, 1995). This is one approach to realizing in practice many of the positive features of the school as a social system. It also provides another avenue for circumventing or precluding several of the negative aspects of the school as a bureaucracy. The question of curricular interdisciplinarity and cross-subject interaction among teachers entails many complexities that need to be resolved gradually (Little, 1995; Siskin and Little, 1995).

It is necessary to say, however, that, even the ''house'' structure calling for semiautonomous units with their own staffs within the larger high school does not spell the end of bureaucracy, nor is it intended to do so. A hierarchy of authority is still a necessary component of school governance in many schools, though not in all. Within a context of participative management, involving house coordinators, subject-matter leaders, and teachers in the decision-making process through open channels of communication with the school's leadership, the role of the principal as the school leader with ultimate responsibility for the conduct of the school can have a consolidating effect on the teaching staff. The need for autonomy and close-to-the-action planning and decision making is not a call for anarchy, disorganization, and lack of responsibility.

The ''house'' structure has also been adopted by many schools to avoid the undesirable consequences of very large schools and their negative affects on teachers and students alike. Ever since the pioneering research by Barker and Gump (1964) that documented some of the negative consequences of large school size, a substantial research literature has substantiated their findings in a wide variety of domains and with ever-growing sophistication and specification. In short, moderate-sized high schools (400 to 800 students) exert the most desirable effects and allow for the development of more productive organizational, pedagogical, and social processes than large schools of more than 900 students (Fowler and Walberg, 1991; Lee and Smith, 1995, 1996). Moderate-sized schools foster a sense of community that large schools find difficult to cultivate. As many large schools cannot reasonably be abandoned, the house structure seems to be an obvious option for achieving the goals of the smaller schools while retaining the large physical structures.

THE CURRICULUM

There are many ways to organize the curriculum of secondary school students. In presenting some ideas that appear to have promise, our aim is to draw attention to the critical aspects of students' program of study in secondary schools and how some educators have already proposed to change existing models.

Of decisive importance is the principle that a genuine revision of students' programs of study is dependent upon changes schools must make in all other aspects of their organizational and instructional policy. The teaching schedule of all teachers in a school and the teaching methods employed will determine whether a truly significant change can be made in the content of the curriculum. These elements intersect at the crossroads of curriculum change. No one element can be successfully changed independently of the others. The interrelatedness of teaching method, curriculum, and instructional innovations is one of the central implications of understanding schools as systems rather than as bureaucracies.

Specifically, fundamental change in the study program of secondary school students entails a revision of the principle of ''one class, one teacher, one subject'' that perpetuates the professional isolation of teachers. Interdisciplinary teams of teachers, working together on curriculum development, can achieve these four goals:

1. reduction in the number of subject domains studied at the same time;
2. integration of different subject domains to create suggestions for broad problem-centered projects for student investigation;
3. adopting, mastering, and implementing interactive, cooperative approaches to learning whereby small groups of students decide upon, plan, and carry out investigations of problems stemming from the general topics suggested by teachers; and
4. adoption of a set of criteria for evaluating the students' performance of their investigation. Evaluation should not be limited to a set of test questions that might tap some aspects of the information gathered. Evaluation must demonstrate to the students that the entire process they carried out during the investigation was part and parcel of their learning experience and deserves recognition.

Finally, if schools (often through the principal's acting as a member of a principals' forum, as discussed later in this chapter) can arrange for students to investigate topics outside the school, groups can plan to make use of a range of communal settings (industrial, commercial, judicial) as resources for their research work. Such inquiry projects can truly revolutionize tomorrow's schools and their students' learning experiences.

One implication for curriculum could be that students might study only a few subjects at any given time, for relatively short periods whose length is not necessarily determined in advance, such as modules lasting six, eight, or twelve weeks. During the period, students devote maximum concentration to a few topics that can bridge several disciplines (Doll, 1993a; Grossman and Stodolsky, 1994; Petrie, 1992; Sizer, 1993). The teachers who have specialized in the component disciplines may collaborate in suggesting problems that students can investigate and potential resources to be examined. Among these resources will be organizational settings (industries, offices, laboratories, clinics, museums, musical groups), skilled and professional people in the community, and libraries, relevant computer programs, and the like. The length of time devoted to investigation projects on any particular day can be determined by the team of responsible teachers in relation to the requirements of the topic under study, not by uniform time slots imposed on all classes simultaneously. It may be considered advisable to devote several days entirely to a particular project and only then to go on to study other subjects. Several teachers can collaborate as a team in guiding the students in their work. Teachers will also meet at regular intervals to discuss the groups' progress and decide upon steps to be taken in the future.

Once more we encounter the challenge of rethinking the manner in which time is distributed and utilized in the organization of the school and its curricula (Cambone, 1995; Sizer, 1993) (see Chapter 8). Of particular concern here is that school personnel must recognize the interrelationship of all major features of the school's operation when dealing with the design of the curriculum. These features include:

1. the nature of the topic under study: Is it a broad, integrated, interdisciplinary topic or problem?
2. the desired duration of an instructional unit: What length of lesson is appropriate on a given day, and for how many days or weeks (or months, if necessary) should the investigation continue?
3. the teaching method employed: Does the process of learning require laboratory work, visits to sites or experts in the community, extensive library research, construction of a model, or frequent discussions by group members to clarify their work with peers?

The traditional format of curricula usually focuses on the subject matter to be taught, independent of schoolwide organizational features and unrelated to a wide perspective on how teachers and students spend their time in school. Nor is the typical curriculum a guide for teachers in their use of innovative teaching methods such as investigations carried out by cooperative groups. Such curricula may not be helpful as a guide for restructuring the school's instructional effort, although they can serve to suggest general domains of study that teacher teams may wish to include in their curricular planning.

THE EDUCATIONAL SYSTEM

Schools can help each other without pitting one school against the other in some form of competition, whether in sports or in an academic contest, although both are popular forms of interschool contact. The administrative team within a school, consisting primarily of the principal, the vice principals, "house" or subunit coordinators, and other special personnel (perhaps guidance counselors), is only one way that a principal may function as a member of a team. If indeed the view point is valid that the classroom reflects teachers' relationships at the school level and that principals' relationships with teachers reflect their relationships with district officials, cooperation among teachers and disciplines at the school level may need its counterpart in cooperation among school principals within a given neighborhood, town, or city. Why should a principal working as a solo practitioner appreciate the need for and dynamics of collegial cooperation? The significance of teacher cooperation could probably be much enhanced in the eyes of the principal when he or she cooperates with principals from other schools on matters confronting all of them.

Cooperation among principals in such a forum can be singularly productive if several schools, even two or three, are engaged in adopting and implementing school reform involving the curriculum, teaching methods, and teachers' work roles. The principals' forum could explore the implications of these changes and clarify what principals must do to make them a reality. This forum could help the principals focus the schools' energies on accomplishing the goals of school restructuring and keep the school on course. Frequently, the attention of principals and teachers is diverted to other topics before they have had a chance to acquire skill and competence in the use of methods they were in the process of learning. In many schools where the authors served as consultants, it was common to see a diffusion of teachers' energies by having them attend a series of in-service courses on a wide variety of topics unrelated to the challenges of the restructuring program in which they were engaged. Course offerings available from private or school-system sources often caused principals and teachers considerable conflict and confusion and diverted their efforts (Louis, 1994). At times, switching horses in midstream occurred because of pressure from district office officials or from people at the level of the national Ministry. These people, who had their own agendas, were not aware of the difficulties entailed in long-term restructuring of the school or of the time and energy it required from everyone involved. In some projects, school-system officials often were more interested in reporting high attendance at courses they were funding than in concentrating on the long-term goals that particular schools had set for themselves. At times, these officials required staff to attend in-service courses during the same day or week that these teachers or principals were committed to attend workshops related to the restructuring project for which the officials did not have direct responsibility.

The principals' forum also has potential political importance for presenting to the public the rationale of the school reform project. Parent groups have been known to voice objection to reform within schools, especially when its significance is not made clear to them and their participation is not invited. Principals are responsible to the public and must involve parents and other interested community members in the conception and goals of the change effort from its inception (Lee, Bryk, and Smith, 1993; Sarason, 1993, 1995a). That task is accomplished far more easily, and with greater effectiveness and conviction, when it is performed by a group of principals working together.

Doubtless, principals can also ban together to ward off complaints or demands for change from parents or other members of the community, even when these may be quite legitimate. Teamwork can become a double-edged sword that can work against, as much as on behalf of, progress. If that happens, parents will have to turn to some other court of appeal. In general, however, principals are most likely to seek ways to accommodate their parent population.

Of course, principals of different schools can disagree about the policy and process of change much as any group of teachers from the same school. Their smooth cooperation is no less an idealized vision than is the picture of constructive teacher collaboration in schools. Once again, the potential for disagreement or conflict between participants in the principals' forum or for exploiting the group as a force for retaining the status quo of power relations is not a convincing argument against the potential benefits to be reaped by the principals and by the public from a collective undertaking of the kind described here (Smylie, 1994). Principals can appreciate the value of working together for a common goal without expecting to reach consensus about matters of policy or procedure. Nor need diverse decisions affecting particular schools undermine the overall purpose of cooperating with other principals on school policy and how to present it to the public.

The principals' forum can perform many functions in addition to providing mutual support for implementing school reform and for involving the community in this process. A principals' group can make a decisive contribution to student learning by arranging for students to investigate various topics related to community life in community settings or to participate in programs in community settings. Principals as a group link community institutions with the schools, a task that teachers are unable to undertake. Once that is accomplished, teams of teachers could work out the details of students' study or service projects in the community. Once again, the point of these projects is to enhance learning through planned investigation and direct experience, not to provide the pleasant sight-seeing trips that schools often arrange for students.

Moreover, if a principals' forum were to negotiate such study projects with community representatives (including the mayor, city council, chamber of commerce, or the departments of health, police, and firefighting), the programs would become municipal policy rather than the pioneering effort of individual schools.

The ideas expressed in this chapter about teacher collaboration for participation in schoolwide problem solving and decision making, especially in regard to educational policy, are certainly an inherent part of the conception of the school as a community. Such a conception is supported by sophisticated and extensive research on school restructuring, as well as by leading proponents of communitarian school organization and administration (Bryk and Driscoll, 1988; Lee, Bryk, and Smith, 1993; Little, 1995; Newman and Wehlage, 1995; Sergiovanni, 1994; Thomson, 1993). The notion of the principals' forum for initiating and maintaining an ongoing relationship between schools and the community, for the purpose of fostering student learning in real-life settings, goes beyond current calls for communitarianism within schools. Rather, it envisions the school as one of the important settings in the community at large, which should have access to other settings in that community on the basis of mutual benefit, just as various communal institutions expect to serve or benefit from the families who send their children to school (Sarason, 1983, 1995a; Sarason, Carroll, Maton, Cohen, and Lorentz, 1977; Sarason and Lorentz, 1979).

Furthermore, in this chapter we sought to relate each level of schooling to its wider social-organizational environment and to point out some ways of constructively utilizing their interrelatedness. Our purpose was to indicate how people learning or working at each level of schooling can cooperate with others working in the same or other organizational and communal settings to support and foster the goal of meaningful learning for the students. Every level of school life has its social context in which the relevant people can interact with one another to their mutual benefit.

SUMMARY

The school of the future portrayed here is the kind of school actually emerging in various localities today. Many of the elements mentioned here as the goals of the change process we seek to initiate already exist, though not necessarily in one school. Tomorrow's school, whose outline is presented here, can be implemented with the knowledge and skills available today. What we foresee is what we know can be done. In fact, this vision of the future reflects a nascent reality whose fulfillment is yet to emerge.

In a sense, the entire conception of school organization, curriculum, and instruction proposed here is an operationalization of a systems view of the relationship between the individual or the single event and the context or system in which the individual functions:

it is not the individual as an isolated entity which is important, but the person within the communal, experiential and environmental frame. In fact, the concept of isolated or rugged individualism, sacred to so much of modern . . . thought, is a fiction. . . . What is important, epistemologically and pedagogically, is a comparison of the patterns an individual develops operating in a number of different situations—This is an ecological, holistic, systemic, interrelated view. (Doll, 1993a, 92)

Among the chief characteristics embodied in the operation of the secondary school of the future, we will be able to observe the following:

Student Learning and Curriculum

1. School learning involves a considerable amount of investigation of problems by the students, often in cooperation with their peers while working in small groups. The problems are formulated by students and teachers together.

2. In order that students can carry out exciting investigations, they have access to a rich pool of resources, including printed materials, computerized data banks or communication networks, and major settings located in the community (industry, commerce, human services, government, the arts, communications, religious institutions, skilled experts, professionals, scientists, the legal system and law enforcement).

3. Investigations sometimes encompass a range of disciplines, thereby approximating real-life problems confronting people and society.

4. Students' programs of studies include three or four broad intellectual domains during any given portion of the school year, such as periods of six to eight weeks. One additional domain should involve physical activity.

5. Student evaluation emphasizes the manner in which students make use of the knowledge they acquired during a given project, namely, how they present it to others and what the entire project expresses and reflects about the students' comprehension and formulation of their presentation, whatever form it assumes.

School Organization and Teachers' Behavior

6. Teachers participate in multidisciplinary teams (which could also be organized into separate subunits or "houses" within the school, if that is desired). These teams have the authority and responsibility for planning and implementing the curriculum for the students in that "house" on a continuous basis, that is, instruction should be based on a cycle of planning, implementation and feedback. The teams' plans are consistent with the school's general policy without imposing uniformity on all groups of teachers and students in the school;

7. Members of the school's staff collaborate in formulating the school's pedagogical and curricular policy. The policy statement emphasizes preferred methods of instruction (see points 1–3) as well as the principle of interdisciplinary topics for group investigation;

8. Conflicts between staff members, or between staff members and the school administration, are resolved at the subunit level, if possible. Each team sets up accepted procedures for resolving professional conflicts.

9. Teams of teachers engage in an ongoing process of data collection about school events. These teams study and summarize the information for presentation to appropriate groups of teachers and/or parents in preparation for system-

atic problem-solving efforts. Teacher teams are empowered to prepare programs or plans for solving problems affecting the school.

The Principal, School Leadership, and the Community

10. Principals provide educational and organizational leadership to the teaching staff, so that teachers can function optimally in their roles. In particular, the school's work schedule allocates blocks of time to teacher teams for cooperative planning and problem solving on a continuous basis.

11. Principals form an administrative team consisting of team leaders from all of the subunits (houses, interdisciplinary teams, etc.), as well as other special school personnel. These teams deal with the implementation of school policy while affording teachers the flexibility to design instruction in response to their classroom experiences.

12. Principals represent the school to the public, including parents and the community at large. Community groups are encouraged to participate in the formulation and implementation of school policy, without encroaching on the professional competence of the teachers in the design of instruction.

13. Principals participate in a principals' forum comprised of their counterparts and representatives from other schools in the community who share basic goals and who are willing to exchange expertise and human resources.

The conduct of schooling at all levels as a network of interacting systems contains the features that make it a community devoted to learning. Education in that kind of learning community is life as *lived* by people in many places, not only as preparation for life. Learning in that kind of environment is not a rite of passage. Rather, it partakes in the essence of the journey.

Models, Prescriptions, and Maps for Changing Schools: A Caveat

In the following chapters of this book, a select series of "models of change," procedures, "maps" of the road to school change, and methods are recommended and described. Indeed, it is the purpose of this volume to provide educators with goals of and roads to school change, as well as methods for accomplishing genuine improvement in school structure and operation. More than once in this book we quote the saying, attributed to ancient Chinese culture, that "if you do not know where you are going, any road will take you there." It is critical for educators to determine their goals as best as possible and then to work out how to proceed to reach those goals.

Just how far does the truth of this saying extend? Accepted understanding of how social systems operate has long recognized that rarely, if ever, is there only one satisfactory solution to a complex problem. That implies, as well, that there is rarely, if ever, only one way to reach a satisfactory solution to a complex problem. Consequently, the models of change appearing in this book (see Chapter 4) are not intended to constitute a genuine "map" in the sense that all the features of the road or the phenomena that will be encountered on the way to a destination are known and recorded—as if all that remains for the traveler to do is to proceed along the designated highway and, in time, reach the target. Nothing could be further from reality than to claim advance knowledge of what will happen during a school change project, no matter what "model of change" is being followed. A school restructuring project involves scores, if not hundreds, of adults, plus hundreds of students, over a period of years. The interactions among people, even those between the change agents and the teaching staff alone, are so numerous and varied and their consequences are so multiple that no map of the road to change could possibly provide a forecast of "what the weather will be like" when the project is halfway down the road. Nor can any substantiated claim be made that a specific set of procedures, such as those described in this and in other books, is known to be the correct intensity with which to apply methods of change or the sole sequence in which to order events, compared to other possible plans. The sheer multiplicity of the events precludes advance mapping with any degree of certainty.

We are suggesting here that sets of well-known elements (methods, procedures, social structures and processes) of human behavior in the school setting have the potential for supporting the school personnel's decision to improve the manner in which it functions. Exactly how these elements will be applied, combined, and coordinated, with what frequency, intensity, or expertise they will be implemented, and with what level of comprehension on the part of the "clients" are largely unknown and unpredictable. Yet, if any of these elements (such as teacher problem-solving teams, mutual assistance teams, or an inquiry form of learning) are omitted from the process of change, there is a strong likelihood that the desired change will not be realized. In short, the "map" of the road to change provided in these pages consists of necessary but not sufficient conditions for realizing the goal of genuine change in schools.

Under no circumstances are we saying that any road will lead to change. There is a kernel of validity to the Chinese adage about being able to choose any road if you don't know where you are going, without its implying that there is only one road that will take you to your destination after you have identified it! We are saying that there is more than one way of working with the various elements required for accomplishing school change; most of them must be included in the process of change (Miles and Khattri, 1995).

The question of whether there can be a "map" to guide the process of school change requires additional comment, because we set out to develop such a map in this book. Is that goal realistic? If such a map cannot be relied upon as a predictor of what will be experienced during the process of change, then it lacks the basic feature of any ordinary road map, which is that people can rely on it to get to specific places. People can check the accuracy of the markings on the map at the specified scale and replicate the map again and again. If that is not true about a "map" of school change, how can we advise clients about what road to take?

The decisive condition for replicating any map is that checks on the accuracy of the map must be made at the specified scale at which the map was originally drawn. Measurements taken at any other scale will find the original map to be inaccurate. The mathematician Benoit Mandelbrot explored this situation in the notion of the fractal as applied to some problems in geography. The problem of the length of a national border depends to a certain, but significant, extent on the "length of your ruler" (Gleick, 1987, 96). The more details captured by the instrument of measurement, the longer the border becomes. If you were to take every pebble on a sandy beach into account, you would get a much longer estimate of a coastline than when you measured that same coastline from a satellite. Mandelbrot observed that this process of enlargement of the coastline probably continues "down to atomic scales, where the process does finally come to an end. Perhaps" (Gleick, 1987, 96). That is to say, the change in the "length" of a national border may not be expandable to an infinite (so it seems) degree, however one measures it, but the amount of possible extension is far from negligible. It is certainly enough to become a bona fide causus belli if a neighboring nation laid claim to the difference in the length of the border between one kind of measurement and another! The analogy to the discrepancy between a model of change presented between the covers of a normal-size book and the real events that await a change agent in a high school of 150 teachers and over 1,000 students should be obvious.

There is one more important dimension to the analogy between Mandelbrot's fractals and the problem of the relationship between models of school change and the nature of the experience entailed by the actual process of change. This dimension is what Mandelbrot called the quality of self-similarity (Gleick, 1987, 103). Self-similarity is the recurring patterns of a given relatively large system, such as the school, in the smaller-scale system, such as the classroom, the curriculum, or the individual teacher or student. In systems theory the notion is the same: Smaller systems are embedded in larger ones in an infinite regress, and the smaller systems embody the features of the larger ones, ad infinitum. Classrooms in a school incorporate the basic features of the manner in which the school as a whole is organized and operates (Shachar and Sharan, 1995). A map or model of school change would have to deal, at least in principle, with every important level or subsystem of the school, from the school as a macrosystem down to the text a student may be asked to study, as a microsystem, and everything in between. Not only is that too ambitious an undertaking, but such detail would make any model, however excellent in conception, useless. After all, a model *simulates* reality at a drastically reduced level of complexity. Burdened with a myriad of details, it loses its functional value. Consequently, professional consultants, who are practitioner-scholars, must be trained; they can derive benefit from ''models'' because they have the background knowledge, coupled with field experience, needed to translate models into the complex realities of the school. Only in this sense is the work presented in this book to be taken as a ''model of change'' for schools.

Chapter 4

Mapping the Road to Organizational and Instructional Change in Schools: A Model

INTRODUCTION

Educational systems in many countries have spent large sums of money over the past several decades on a wide range of in-service teacher training courses and projects of various kinds (Corcoran, 1995). Undoubtedly, many teachers have acquired a great fund of knowledge and skills through these courses. This vast investment in in-service training was based on the assumption, at times more implicit than explicit, that it would lead, directly and indirectly, to distinct improvement in schools' pedagogical functioning and outcomes (see Figure 4.1).

An assessment of the cost-effectiveness and the pedagogical impact of these courses and projects is not readily available. Nevertheless, there appears to be no reasonable ratio between the investment of time, effort, and money in in-service teacher training and its outcome in better school functioning, the use of more sophisticated teaching methods, and pupil benefits (Dalin and Rolf, 1993; Fullan and Stiegelbauer, 1991; Hopkins, Ainscow, and West, 1994; Sarason, 1990, 1995b). This criticism does not invalidate the potential significance and impact of in-service teacher training (see Chapter 6). Indeed, schools undertaking a process of restructuring rarely will be able to realize their goal without considerable investment in in-service education for teachers and administrators.

In our view, the disappointing findings about in-service education indicate, inter alia, that it has often been conducted without adequate attention to conditions that make such experiences effective. Most important among these conditions are their schoolwide, organizational implications, such as new concepts about and approaches to the school's class schedule, the redefinition of teachers' roles and teachers' work in schools, and fundamental changes in the process of instruction and evaluation. The nature of potentially effective in-service teacher

Figure 4.1
Assumed Direct Relationship between In-service Training and School Improvement

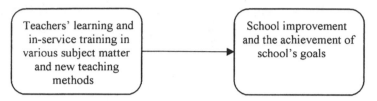

education in workshops and the design and conduct of these workshops are discussed later (see Chapter 6). Here we focus on the missing link between in-service teacher training and the improvement of schools. This link can be found in the time and effort needed to unlearn the prevailing professional behavior of all school personnel and to learn new patterns of behavior (Louis, 1994) (see Figure 4.2).

A working model of instructional and organizational change in schools can provide more insight into the reasons that many programs of in-service training remain ineffective and into how the process of school change can proceed with a much higher degree of effectiveness. The model appearing in this chapter unpacks the "missing link" in the chain of school improvement and details what must be added at a practical level, above and beyond efforts at in-service teacher training, in order to accomplish long-lasting improvement of secondary schools. Recent publications in Europe and the United States provide many insights into school change (Dalin and Rolf, 1993; Elmore et al., 1990; Fullan, 1993; Fullan and Miles, 1992; Hamalainen, Oldroyd, and Haapenen, 1995; Hopkins, Ainscow, and West, 1994; Joyce, Wolf and Calhoun, 1993; Murphy, 1991; Pink and Hyde, 1992; Sarason, 1990, 1995b). However, there is, as yet, no map of the practical steps that must be taken in order to create and maintain new traditions in schools and classrooms (Louis and Miles, 1990). Existing knowledge remains largely theoretical, leaving the road of implementation uncharted in many of its critical aspects. Otherwise excellent blueprints for successful school change have strangely failed to include classroom teaching practices as a major focus of their attention. Organizational specialists on occasion have forgotten that instruction is the school's primary (albeit not exclusive) mission, and school organization is one of the critical means to that end. The model appearing in this chapter and the procedures set out in later chapters to implement the crucial functions of the teaching staff provide some assistance to educators in making school restructuring a reality.

The need for significant change and improvement of instructional methods in secondary schools is no longer a matter of debate in many Western countries. Yet, genuine change and innovation are, at best, slow in making an appearance in the normative functioning of secondary education.

Figure 4.2
Teachers' Organizational Behavior as Mediating School Improvement after In-service Training

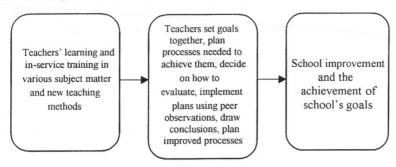

A varied repertoire of classroom instructional methods, under the general title of cooperative learning, has been developed and studied systematically over the past two decades. These methods are founded on principles emphasizing direct interaction and communication among students, as well as personal and group-centered responsibility for learning, rather than stressing the role of the teacher as the focus of teaching and learning (Cohen, 1994; Johnson and Johnson, 1987; Sharan, 1994; Slavin, 1990). Despite the impressive impact on students exerted by these instructional methods as assessed in many educational experiments and despite the recognition that these methods can revitalize instruction in high schools, they have not yet become an integral part of high school teachers' instructional repertoire (Shachar and Sharan, 1994; Sharan, 1990; Y. Sharan and S. Sharan, 1992; Slavin, 1983, 1990; Slavin, Sharan, Kagan, Hertz-Lazarowitz, Webb, and Schmuck, 1985).

Many elementary schools have successfully adopted basic innovations in organization and instruction over the past two decades. By comparison, high schools in general remain relatively uniform and traditional in structure and teaching methods. Quite obvious among the sources of this uniformity is the complexity of the organizational structure of high schools, as well as the absence of appropriate preparation offered by pre-service and in-service training programs for high school personnel (Sarason, 1993; Siskin and Little, 1995).

A MODEL OF SCHOOL CHANGE

The model of school change presented here was developed as part of a six-year effort to change the instructional methods and organizational behavior of teachers in fourteen secondary schools in several towns in Israel. The development of the model was prompted, first and foremost, by the repeated failure to notice any change in actual classroom instructional practices after teachers' participation in in-service training courses.

A second impetus for the development of the model was the decision made by the Israeli government to promote social integration actively in the nation's schools (Amir and Sharan, 1985). Governments in other countries, such as the United States, reached similar decisions. The decision aimed at preventing junior high schools (grades 7–9) from using students' grades as a basis for selecting which students they would take from among the graduates of elementary schools (at completion of grade 6) and to have students from all academic, socioeconomic, and ethnic groups represented in each school. The change in classroom population that occurred in the transition from relatively homogeneous neighborhood elementary schools to the junior high schools with a larger catchment area created heterogeneous classrooms in the secondary school in many countries. It soon became patently clear to educators that the traditional form of instruction directed at all students in the class simultaneously was no longer appropriate or effective for these heterogeneous classrooms.

Junior high schools in Israel also realized that the kinds of in-service training courses hitherto offered to teachers were inadequate to meet their needs. A broader perspective on the effect of the school as an organization on the instructional practices of the teachers was needed to cope with the demands of the new social and academic reality in the junior high schools. The recent professional literature has drawn attention to the critical role of the school as an organization in initiating and sustaining processes of instructional change (Hopkins, Ainscow, and West, 1994; Sarason, 1995a, 1996c; Shachar and Sharan, 1995). Genuine instructional change must take into consideration the restructuring of the school as an organization as well as the instructional needs of the heterogeneous classroom (Amir and Sharan, 1985; Elmore et al., 1991; Fullan, 1993; Murphy, 1991; Sarason, 1982, 1990; Shachar and Sharan, 1995; Senge, 1990).

The plan for school improvement presented here envisions working with schools for a period of four to six years in a series of stages. The entire plan is guided by concepts derived from two basic assumptions:

1. The school is a learning organization, consistent with a social systems approach to organization. (Argyris, 1992; Argyris and Schon, 1978; Banathy, 1992; Senge, 1990; Sharan and Hertz-Lazarowitz, 1978)

2. The organizational behavior of the teachers is one of the prime targets of the intervention program, alongside the teachers' instructional behavior in the classroom. (Sarason, 1982; Schmuck and Runkel, 1985; Shachar and Sharan, 1995)

The Organization of the School

Improvement in the school's functioning is not merely a result of improvement in the individual teacher's ability to teach better (Senge, 1990). The social/organizational unit for improving the functioning of the school is the group. If groups (of teachers) in the school do not learn and change together, change in their teaching behavior in the classroom will not be more than a passing episode. Change must be adopted as part of the school's pedagogical policy in order to reach adequate implementation and survive in the long run. Individual teachers cannot practice methods of instruction and evaluation over an extended period of time that clash with those practiced by their colleagues or fail to be accepted and promoted by the school's administration (Sarason, 1990, 1996c; Smylie, 1994).

The validity of this basic principle for change in secondary schools has long been ignored; secondary school teachers generally participate as individuals in in-service training projects devoted primarily to a given subject matter. Subject expertise was, and is, considered by secondary school teachers as one of their primary sources of legitimacy and professional power (Little, 1995; Siskin and Little, 1995). It was erroneously anticipated that teachers would derive immediate benefit from participating in in-service workshops on instructional behavior in their classrooms.

Of course, in many schools teachers have learned a great deal as individuals, but without this new knowledge exerting any discernible force for improvement on the overall functioning of the school. What is required is a distinct change in the way we conceive of the teacher's role and function in the school and the distribution of space and time in the work schedule of teachers, allowing them to use the knowledge they acquire to benefit the school as an organization. Our conception of the school's organization must include the development of new roles for teachers and the redefinition of existing roles, including that of the school principal (Darling-Hammond, Bullmaster, and Cobb, 1995; Murphy and Louis, 1994; Smylie, 1994).

The revised conception of the school as an organization must include a number of elements heretofore widely regarded as dictated by authorities outside the school, such as boards or ministries of education. Of particular relevance is the school's approach to the planning and use of time, such as the duration of instructional units during the day, the length of the school week or year, or the number of subjects taught per unit of time (often conceived as being 45 minutes to an hour) or per day. Many people become acutely aware of these temporal boundaries when they try to change them (Cambone, 1995). That statement was actually written by Kurt Lewin, in slightly different language, many decades ago. The process of school restructuring cannot ignore the temporal regularities that govern people's behavior in school, which must become the object of renewed examination and creative planning (Sarason, 1982; see Chapter 8).

Changing Teachers' Organizational and Instructional Behavior

A change in instructional behavior on the part of teachers involves learning entire patterns of new behavior. This change can take place over a series of stages beginning with the teachers' exposure to new concepts, the acquisition of new skills, the unlearning of old concepts and ways of thinking, and the internalization of the new behavioral patterns that comprise the method of teaching being learned now (Sarason, 1982).

It has become fashionable to explain schools' resistance to change as stemming from teachers' lack of motivation to learn new methods, from their conservative orientation, from the absence of adequate compensation to teachers for undertaking change, and from their objection to innovations. However, a more productive approach to understanding the impediments to change in schools is found in the fact that, more often than not, teachers are asked to change their instructional practices while simultaneously adhering to the norms and modes of behavior prevailing in their school. Indeed, even while participating in in-service training courses geared to exchanging methods currently practiced for newer ones, the teachers continue to be evaluated in terms of their ability to produce expected outcomes while conforming to the old patterns of behavior. For example, while learning alternative methods of evaluation, teachers are required to submit student grades in the traditional form on predetermined dates. School systems thereby transmit a double message to teachers, the essence of which is a profound contradiction between proclaimed goals and existing norms. What the school says it wants teachers to learn and what it demands of them in their work at best appear to have nothing in common. Or, what is worse, the different approaches to teaching may be sharply at odds. No wonder piquant remarks are circulating about the ironies of change in schools, such as "changing teaching practices in schools is like replacing a wheel on a speeding train" or "it's like fixing a broken motor on an airplane in flight." Sadder still is the simile of school reform as the stubborn attempt to ride a dead horse (Sarason, 1994, 1995b).

Conditions Necessary for Initiating the Change Project

The model appearing in this chapter concentrates on the practical steps to be taken in developing a successful school restructuring project. Before the inception of the change project, several preconditions must be fulfilled and some preliminary steps taken.

Several months before the end of an academic year and before the schedule for the new academic year has been planned, a meeting is held with the school's administration to discuss the organizational requirements of the project. These include setting aside time for teachers' in-service training workshops (40 hours), for special school personnel such as department heads or coordinators (80 hours), and for school principals and vice principals (50 hours). Only when an initial agreement provides for these training activities to take place with the relevant personnel and for the necessary time to be allotted can the implementation of the four-stage program begin. In this agreement, teachers' in-service training activities must be given a new status in the overall planning of time distribution in the schools (Cambone, 1995). In the new conception, teachers' needs as learners must be acknowledged as of equal importance to the needs of the students as learners. The prevailing view perceives teachers' in-service training experiences as events transpiring on the periphery, which may or may not affect the school in the course of time by some process of gradual assimilation. Meanwhile, the main features of the school's operation remain unchanged and largely indifferent to the contents and message developed in the teachers' in-service courses.

The plan of work presented in the model proceeds through four stages, each one to be implemented simultaneously on four different levels of the school or with four different groups of personnel (see Figure 4.3).

STAGE 1: LEARNING WHAT TO DO

The Principal

The first step to be taken with the principal is to enlist his or her collaboration as the person who will facilitate changes in the school. To this end, the principal must acquire an appreciation for what constitutes genuine change, compared to what was traditionally considered to constitute change. Genuine change means a distinct alteration in the patterns of relationships among people in the school, in terms of the roles typically occupied by both teachers and students (Sarason, 1993; Little, 1995).

a. The principal grasps the essential features of the new teaching methods that the teachers are studying in their in-service training course, as well as the nature of the changes that the teachers must undergo in order to learn and implement the new methods.

b. The principal learns how to lead the teaching staff in systematic problem solving and decision making (Deal and Petterson, 1990; Thomson, 1993). The subject of the school's organizational regularities, particularly those determined by considerations of time and its distribution, must be one of the main topics addressed by the teaching staff and principal when they undertake to identify and solve schoolwide problems.

c. The principal reaches an appreciation of the parallelism between the manner in which teachers experience their work in classrooms and the manner in which they function as members of the teaching staff and that these two levels of the teacher's life in the school are profoundly interrelated (Shachar and Sharan, 1995).

These three sets of concepts and skills constitute the essence of positive school leadership. Principals of secondary schools have become largely occupied with administrative aspects of school operation, leaving them little or no time or motivation to give in-depth attention to the pedagogical needs of the school (McCarthy, 1985). The drift to an administrative from an educational role for the principal may have been inevitable in light of the considerable organizational complexity of the large urban high school.

Nevertheless, many principals express genuine concern about the teaching and learning processes in their schools and the need to change them, perhaps even radically. However, few principals seem to appreciate the nature of the connection between their role as principals and the process of instructional change that must occur in the school if their vision of effective teaching is to be realized.

Figure 4.3
A Four-Stage Working Model for Instructional Change in Secondary Schools

	Stage 1: Learning what to do	Stage 2: Learning how to do it	Stage 3: Expanding the change process	Stage 4: Institutionalizing the change
Principal	Defining the principal's role as facilitator for changing teaching methods in school	Setting up a schedule for collaborative planning by teachers	Expanding the use of new instructional methods; Facilitating development of alternative evaluation	Establishing the new instructional methods as a norm in school life
Subject-Matter Coordinators	Defining the role of coordinators; Acquiring necessary skills to lead collaborative planning by teachers	Leading team planning; Sharing observations of classrooms and drawing conclusions	Developing teamwork and planning alternative evaluation	Ongoing assessment of goals and means of the new instructional methods
Teachers	Introducing the new instructional methods; Initial implementation	Collaborative planning of lessons; Implementation with peer observations	Ongoing team planning and implementation; Develop alternative evaluation	Regular use of new methods of teaching and evaluating
Students		Initial exposure to new learning methods	Developing skills for cooperative and self-regulated learning	Mastering different learning techniques and social skills

Quite often principals seem to believe that an external change agent must be imported into the school who, given the proper resources, will carry out the appropriate changes and set the school on a new path. The program described here seeks to return principals, to some degree, to the role of the school's educational leader and to provide him or her with the motivation and sense of competence needed to expand the role (Murphy and Louis, 1994).

Subject-Matter Coordinators

However skilled or charismatic the principal may be, schoolwide change cannot be accomplished by him or her alone. Of critical importance for the implementation of change is the support of many internal change agents allied with the principal's vision and capable of serving as leaders of various teacher sub-groups within the school. Subject-matter coordinators or department heads can fulfill this role if given the proper preparation. Hence, in this working model for change, the in-service training program for these personnel is sufficiently extensive to include the acquisition of all the skills required for them to become active internal change agents. Subject coordinators also learn the new teaching methods along with the regular classroom teachers, but in addition their course encompasses the following:

1. problem-solving models with teacher teams,
2. concluding agreements with teachers about their roles and responsibilities in the school,
3. identifying teachers' resistance to change and helping teachers cope with these feelings and attitudes,
4. learning communication skills, including giving constructive feedback as part of a process of peer observations in classrooms aimed at helping teachers implement the new teaching methods,
5. learning how to lead teachers in the preparation of a work program for the academic year (or a given six-week period) regarding their team's activities, such as team meetings, and
6. learning to negotiate a work schedule with the principal that ensures mutual understanding of the coordinators' roles and activities.

Teachers

The teachers' course is a series of experiential workshops aimed at acquiring the concepts and skills of three to four different teaching methods, as well as criteria for evaluating the processes and products of student learning with co-operative learning methods (Joyce, Weil, and Showers, 1992; Sharan, 1994; see Chapter 6). During this course the rationale and the philosophy of the different methods are investigated and discussed by the teachers. The workshops also explore in depth the many manifestations and implications of the heterogeneous classroom and the difficulties teachers will encounter in their work with such classrooms.

Stage 1 frequently requires more than one year to be completed. The main reasons are that schools experience turnover in personnel, new teachers arrive at the school who did not participate in the first year of the project, and often teachers who were originally reluctant to join the project may wish to participate. Consequently, a new set of workshops must be undertaken.

STAGE 2: LEARNING HOW TO DO IT

At stage 2, each school should receive on-site consultation once a week. The consultants should be the same people who conducted the in-service training courses for the teachers and the principal. The main goal of these consultations is to assist the teachers and principal to plan and carry out the methods and procedures acquired during the in-service course. Collaborative planning of each step in the implementation of the new teaching methods in the classroom should be given a far more central role than was ordinarily recognized in the past. It was often assumed that the acquisition of a new method by teachers led directly to its classroom implementation. The on-site consultation provides support to the staff for having confidence in its initial efforts.

The Principal

The first order of business is for the principal and consultant to establish a schedule of meetings for the subject-matter coordinators and their respective teams of teachers. These groups have responsibility for planning a year's work in their particular subject areas in light of the pedagogical methods they have acquired recently. Thus, the principal, with the help of the consultant, has to reassess the entire teaching schedule for the staff in order to solve any problems in providing time for teams to meet (see Chapter 8).

A second task for the principal and consultant is to plan how to inform the staff about the school's new educational policy and goals and about the principal's expectations as to how teachers can assist in their articulation and implementation. The principal may request that teachers tell him or her how many lessons they will conduct with the alternative methods of teaching. Subject-matter coordinators could be asked to submit a plan for new approaches to student evaluation as part of the effort to change classroom instruction.

Subject-Matter Coordinators

The subject coordinators or department heads comprise an identifiable group within the school, less as part of a formal hierarchy than as an example of the expanded role of teachers in the restructured school (Darling-Hammond Bullmaster, and Cobb, 1995; Smylie, 1994). Members of this group maintain four sets of relationships with other personnel or groups, as follow.

1. They have a schedule of meetings with the principal in order to negotiate a mutually acceptable work schedule for the coordinators, to exchange ideas and information, and to provide ongoing updates to the principal on their activities. Such meetings take place twice or three times during an academic year. More frequent meetings could prove burdensome for the coordinators, who already have a heavy load of meetings scheduled throughout the year.

2. They maintain contact with one another by regular meetings in order to coordinate the activities of their respective teams of teachers. Two or three meetings should be held during the year, unless otherwise required.

3. Each coordinator meets regularly with his or her team of teachers who

teach the same or related subjects. These meetings take place once a week or once every other week. The coordinator engages in team building, having teachers assume responsibility for different roles and cultivating a sense of the team's collective responsibility for its work in the near future. Meetings of coordinators and teachers are also attended by the trainers who conducted the in-service courses. The trainers assist the coordinators to plan the meetings with the teachers, giving them feedback about the conduct of the meeting as well as about its content. The trainers attend these meetings, which are one of the most critical elements in the implementation of the entire model. It is during this segment of the program that teachers' behavior undergoes change, as they become members of teams of peers who are engaged in altering the professional norms of the school.

4. Coordinators can establish multidisciplinary teams, if desirable, who are responsible for teaching an integrated curriculum, such as conducting a study project using computers where the subject matter cuts across two or more subject areas (Siskin and Little, 1995).

Teachers

Teachers participate in small groups that can be composed of same-subject teachers or teachers of different subjects, as they wish. The purpose of these groups is to engage in cooperative planning of lessons designed according to the principles of the alternative instructional methods they learned in the in-service training courses. The plan includes both criteria for peer observations during the implementation of the lesson and criteria for evaluating students' performance during the lesson. (For details of how to implement mutual assistance teams, see Chapter 6.) Teacher teams also plan how to obtain feedback from the students regarding their perception of their new patterns of learning in the classroom.

At this stage of the program, it is unrealistic to anticipate that these teacher mutual-assistance teams for cooperative planning and implementation will be able to go through more than two cycles of planning and mutual observation during the course of an academic year (see Chapter 6). Teacher teams may meet more frequently to assist one another in planning ongoing instruction (Sharan and Hertz-Lazarowitz, 1982).

Students

Groups of students are exposed to teachers' initial attempts to practice the new methods in classrooms. These steps focus on helping students to cooperate with one another and to plan their work together as autonomous groups within the class.

STAGE 3: EXPANDING THE CHANGE PROCESS IN THE SCHOOL

A consultant from the project staff will continue to assist school personnel once a week during the third stage. The instructional and organizational processes of change have not yet reached a stage of institutionalization. Hence, school personnel—the principal, subject-matter coordinators, and teachers—will continue to need the injection of energy and motivation from their consultant in order to maintain the momentum of change.

The Principal

The principal must attend to two main tasks during this stage:

First, the principal must extend the scope of the change process in the school to encompass more teachers than in the previous year and involve them in teacher problem-solving teams and must motivate teachers to increase the frequency with which they implement the alternative instructional methods in their classrooms. The principal can facilitate this process by formulating operationally defined goals in collaboration with the teachers who will implement them.

Second, the principal must assist teachers to work out alternative forms of student evaluation consistent with the principles of the alternative teaching methods. Many of these methods place as much emphasis on the process of learning as on the acquisition of specific information. Alternative instructional methods require assessment of the learning process itself, which is not amenable to evaluation by traditional means of testing. What is sought is an estimate of the use students can make of what they have learned, not only an estimate of the contents of what they studied (Wolf, Bixby, Glenn, and Gardner, 1991).

Subject-Matter Coordinators

The coordinators' tasks derive from their collaboration with the principal. They consist primarily of planning how to implement the school's policy regarding the continuation of the change process with the teachers in their team.

1. Meetings of teachers and coordinators should be devoted to increasing the number of class sessions taught with the alternative methods, and to the development of specific procedures for implementing alternative assessment of student learning.

2. The coordinators' tasks during this stage also include the continued expansion and improvement of peer observations in the classroom through mutual assistance teams.

3. Coordinators are assisted by the consultant from the project team to reach a high level of professional mastery of the alternative teaching methods, as well as acquiring skill in devising means for alternative evaluation.

By so doing, the school consultant will be able to transfer responsibility for assisting the teachers during the next year to the coordinators. In this manner it will be possible to discontinue the school's dependence on external consultation and to ensure the institutionalization of the instructional and organizational changes (Dalin and Rolf, 1993; Huberman and Miles, 1984; Joyce, Wolf, and Calhoun, 1993).

Teachers

Teacher teams engage in the cooperative planning of a greater number of class sessions using alternative teaching methods. The teams concentrate on planning and implementing class sessions in which teammates conduct systematic observations. A portion of the teams' meetings must be devoted to discussing problems arising during the lessons and proposing solutions to these problems (Little, 1982). The teachers' observations can then be based on a short list of guidelines that team members formulate prior to the lesson that draw the observers' attention to various events during the implementation of the alternative method. Teams also develop specific procedures for using alternative methods of student evaluation.

During this stage, teachers have the opportunity to invite the school consultant from the project team to visit their classes, conduct observations, and participate now and then in the team meeting. At that meeting, the consultant can help teachers plan solutions to problems that arise in the classroom. By this time, the school consultant, who was also the teachers' original trainer at the beginning of the project, has been accepted as an integral part of the staff and is not seen as an outsider who comes to give advice and depart.

Students

Students develop a set of skills for interpersonal interaction and for collaborative and independent learning as members of a small group. These are skills that the students generally were not called upon to cultivate in traditional classrooms, such as the ability to cooperate and communicate with their peers in a constructive manner, to accept responsibility for the pace and scope of their learning, and to develop the ability to assess and document the process of learning that they carried out in order to provide feedback to themselves and to their colleagues in the group.

STAGE 4: INSTITUTIONALIZING THE CHANGE

The principal's behavior at this stage will determine whether the school will cross the "point of no return," that is, will succeed in institutionalizing the changes acquired thus far and enable observers to identify essential changes in the school's behavior. Even after the school has progressed along the stages described in this model of school change, several forces threaten the school's progress and may cause it to retreat to previous patterns of functioning. Such forces arise from both external and internal sources. Examples of external forces are:

1. school supervisors or district personnel whose ideas and views differ from those of the principal;
2. standardized tests administered by national or district-level organizations that constrain teachers to devote all of their energies to preparing students for the tests;
3. pressure from higher levels of the school system's administration to submit detailed documentation of the school's programs and activities (Chubb and Moe, 1990);
4. parent pressure groups with different agendas; and
5. the need to guarantee adequate pupil registration at this school rather than other competing institutions.

Examples of internal forces are:

1. teachers who enjoy relatively high status in the school who opt not to join the change effort;
2. subject-matter coordinators not equally endowed with charismatic leadership qualities to conduct effective teamwork with teachers;
3. teachers burned out by change projects previously conducted in the school that failed to yield results despite the teachers' investment of time and effort (Corcoran, 1995); and
4. a large percentage of faculty turnover in the school.

At this stage the school has acquired all of the methods, skills, and procedures needed to sustain the changes it has adopted. However, in light of the danger posed by the forces just enumerated, it is recommended that the school consultant from the project staff should continue to appear at the school, albeit infrequently, to assist school personnel if needed.

The Principal

The principal is now prepared to present to the staff a clear set of short- and long-term goals. These goals should be designed and articulated in cooperation with the coordinators and teachers and should embody what has been learned thus far. The statement of goals should be accompanied by suggestions for means to achieve those goals, such as the amount of classroom time to be devoted to alternative teaching methods (Cambone, 1995), as well as measures to evaluate processes and products.

Once such a statement has been formulated, the principal and staff present it to a number of groups relevant to, but outside of the school. These groups can include parents, school system functionaries such as supervisors, and the municipal department of education. The principal and teachers will be asked to respond to questions and even to the challenges of various kinds that frequently arise during such presentations. The school consultant can assist the principal and teachers to plan these meetings carefully to succeed in achieving their purpose. Their primary purpose is to enlist the support of these groups on behalf of the change process in the school and to give all stakeholders an opportunity to participate in the process (Sarason, 1995a). Since school personnel rarely receive professional preparation for the task of engaging in public relations efforts of this kind, the prospect of holding such events can provoke anxiety (Sarason, 1993). Again, the assistance of the school consultant can be critical to allay the concerns of the school staff in this matter.

After the teaching staff has been involved in a wide range of activities regarding school policy and has experienced the stages of development described in this model, the principal can request the team leaders to submit work plans for a year that incorporate the new policies and norms. Introduced in this fashion, these policies have a high probability of becoming the new traditions of the school as an organizational entity.

Subject-Matter Coordinators

In collaboration with team members, the coordinators prepare plans for the year's work, which they will submit to the principal. The plans need not include a great number of details, but they must include the following points:

1. the nature of each team's collaboration during the course of the year, including a minimum of three sessions during the year of peer observations and feedback regarding the implementation of the new teaching methods;
2. the teaching methods employed by teachers in their classrooms and with what frequency and scope they will be employed;
3. methods of student evaluation;
4. the nature of the teams' interaction with parents, particularly in respect to the use of the new methods of teaching and evaluation; and
5. the exact relationship between the agreed-upon short-term goals and the specific activities in which the teacher teams will engage during the course of the year.

Teachers

The expectation at this stage is that teachers will employ alternative instructional methods in their classrooms up to 60 percent of instructional time. Membership in teams should provide teachers with a relatively clear picture of how their colleagues are functioning. Each team should have developed collective responsibility for its members' instructional practices. The teams should be engaging in an ongoing manner in cooperative planning of the specific content and process of instruction for all the students taught by the teams' members, not just for the classes taught by each teacher individually. Cooperative planning of instruction, coupled with mutual peer observation and feedback, should dispel the sense of isolation widely found in traditionally organized schools (Joyce, Wolf, and Calhoun, 1993; Little, 1982; Rosenholtz, 1989). This process encompasses teachers' decisions about curriculum and instructional methods.

Students

The contents of this last element in the model constitute the primary goal of the entire process—that most of the students should master a variety of techniques for learning, inside and outside the classroom. They should also acquire skills for cooperative planning and implementation of study projects with their peers. Students should have become familiar with a variety of methods for collecting information and evaluating their work and products. The success of this process can be assessed by the extent to which the students display genuine interest in what they study and are internally motivated to learn, so that learning is not a phenomenon largely dependent upon the teachers' or the schools' system of sanctions.

CONCLUSION

This chapter describes assistance and consultative efforts that a school can require for its professional improvement and development. Of decisive importance is the availability of a high-level professional team of consultants who can assist school personnel at all levels for an extended period of time of no less than several years. Our experience with the preparation of professional school consultants devoted to school change (who are not responsible for other, often-conflicting roles such as school psychologists, academic researchers, or private entrepreneurs of various kinds) is that candidates for this role must have at least the requisite qualifications for participating in a consultant-training program: (a) They should be experienced teachers with a reputation for excellence. (b) They should have filled various roles in their schools so that the tasks of leadership are not foreign to them. (c) They must have experience in functioning as members of a team that engaged in problem solving and receiving feedback. Of course, these people should have a high-level academic background (Schein, 1988).

Another topic that received considerable attention in this model is the problem of staff time for meetings, a topic that haunts school improvement efforts like a ghost (Cambone, 1995). Schools, unlike many other kinds of organizations, appear to have a singular lack of flexibility in their use of time. They are subject to the imposition of work schedules by external, often politically determined forces. These schedules are frequently adopted from antiquated conceptions of the school and bear no essential relationship to the contemporary tasks of teaching and learning (Sizer, 1993). The political echelons of the school system who seek to have schools improve their level of functioning must come to understand that schools require a substantial extension of teachers' work time, in any of a wide variety of forms, in order to allow schools to reach for goals consistent with the requirements of our times. Paradoxically, although many aspects of schooling have been altered with the aim of improving teaching, the temporal dimension of teachers' work has remained largely unchanged, as if new structures, tasks, and methods can be performed and maintained within old time constraints (National Education Commission on Time and Learning, 1944; see Chapter 8 in this book).

Schools in general, and high schools in particular, are very complex organizations, which often serve large populations of students (over 1,000) with diverse needs, have numerous departments, offer a wide variety of courses in many subject areas, and maintain large staffs of teachers (150 or more). Changing organizations of such complexity cannot possibly proceed in any mechanistic way according to the prescriptions of a given model, including the one presented here. The change model offered here emphasizes two critical elements:

1. In-service training for school personnel is insufficient to produce significant change and many additional steps are necessary, as set forth in the model; and

2. All levels of school personnel must participate, more or less at the same time, in the process of change.

Implementation of this model will, in the course of time, endow teachers with decidedly greater empowerment and extended control over their professional work in schools. It also provides the specific contents of teachers' expanded roles. Such empowerment is frequently mentioned as a sine qua non of school improvement and restructuring (Rowan, 1990; Lee, Bryk, and Smith, 1993). The stages of the model identify the transformations in staff professional skills and functioning needed to help schools decide where they are going and what road to take.

Chapter 5

Integrating the School's Systems

The portrait of tomorrow's schools drawn in this book depicts the school as an organization comprised of four main subsystems:

1. the staff system (distribution of teachers to tasks and their patterns of interaction),
2. the instructional system (classroom teaching and learning),
3. the curricular system (domains of knowledge), and
4. the students.

All of these subsystems exist and function in schools today. What distinguishes the schools we envision for tomorrow is a change not in these basic components, but in how they are organized and related to one another and in how they are integrated into the larger system of the school as an educational organization (Wilson and Daviss, 1994). The way in which the school's subsystems are co-ordinated and interrelated determines their impact on teachers and students alike and gives the school its special character.

Tomorrow's schools will constitute a significant advance in sophistication and effectiveness over the schools of today. They will overhaul the present bureaucratic style of school organization, retain the bureaucratic model for specific aspects of the school for which it is most appropriate, and extend the social systems and communitarian perspective into most of the areas of the school's functioning that entail social interactions. For the past century to our own day, the fundamental structure of schools has preset curricula mandated to specific cohorts of students (classes) who are taught by individual teachers in separate rooms (Sarason, 1982). This kind of separation of groups and subjects is consistent with the concept of the division of labor and specialization of function that is fundamental to bureaucratic organization in general. Tomorrow's schools, following the ideas of a systems theory of organization and of the school as a community, will emphasize the interrelatedness of parts within the system, the integration of the system as a unit or "whole," and the connection between the system and its environment, the community. They will inject a high degree of communication and integration among the three component subsystems of the school, as well as between the system and its environment (Banathy, 1992). Such integration will significantly reduce the extent to which teachers, along with the subjects they teach, will be set apart in different rooms for relatively short class periods (45–50 minutes) as they have been heretofore, and still are, in many schools. The time when space (classrooms) and time (class periods) are separated into small units through which large cohorts of students are processed every day in an unalterable sequence appears to be coming to an end, slowly but surely.

In the social systems and communitarian conceptions, the school's organization will have considerable flexibility and mobility among its component elements (teachers, students, departments, disciplines, grade levels). Students and teachers will participate and collaborate in making critical decisions regarding teaching and learning. Furthermore, instruction will not consist primarily of transmitting quantities of information from teachers to students, mainly through teachers' verbal presentations followed by teachers' questions. Instead, students will actively pursue knowledge through processes of problem solving, discussion, investigation, simulation, and so forth as individuals or in teams. Students will have access to a wide range of information resources. These sources will include, first and foremost, their teachers, whom they can approach freely for assistance and who see their role as one of providing support, encouragement, assistance, and direction for students. Students will also have access to professional people who are not necessarily their teachers, to various experiences in real-life settings where the relevant knowledge is used, to computerized information of many kinds, and to printed sources of all kinds usually found in libraries. School learning will involve different kinds of experiences associated with the direct investigation of the topics under study. In this fashion, schools will be transformed from production-oriented institutions (English, 1993), whose product is students' marks generated according to a preset plan, to institutes for learning through a wide variety of means that characterize the active pursuit of knowledge. In such schools, the instructional and organizational processes will be designed to implement the school's explicit educational mission, while taking into consideration and responding to students' interests, needs, and successes. Teachers will be aware of these conditions through continuous feedback that they arrange and utilize.

This conception of the school is possible with a relatively high level of coordination or coupling between the major subsystems that make up the school's educational and organizational core. It also requires that tomorrow's schools be guided by a rejuvenated vision of the educational process, not merely by greater managerial competence. The vision of tomorrow's school proposed here encompasses a far broader horizon of the educational enterprise than previously found in most schools. It seeks to release students and teachers from many of the constraints imposed on their thinking and behavior by the bureaucratic-mechanistic paradigm of organization that still prevails in many educational systems. As noted, these constraints consist primarily, though not exclusively, of the following features:

- disciplinary insulation,
- solo practitioner scheduling,
- curricular uniformity for large cohorts,
- uniform delivery of instruction, including content and pace, to entire classes of students,
- uniform evaluation procedures for classrooms of students usually in the form of testing,
- restriction of formal learning to classrooms,
- achievement as a product of the individual's talents unrelated to those of others, and so forth.

Schools today continue to assign large numbers of students to classes by age or achievement level. Classes are required to study a relatively long list of subjects presented sequentially each day. Quite striking is the fact that these subjects, more often than not, have no relationship to one another. By contrast, in tomorrow's schools there will be a community of instructors and learners engaged in the pursuit of knowledge, often focusing on solving critical problems. There will be a systematic and yet free flow of information among teachers working in teams, and between these teams and the other subsystems of the school. Disciplinary compartmentalization will yield to an interest-centered, integrative perspective on the pursuit of knowledge. Interaction among teachers and integration of varied subject matter are aimed at increasing the meaning of what students learn and raising the level of their engagement in the process of learning. Broad intellectual goals, such as relating knowledge to real-life problems and making creative use of this knowledge or the nature of the relationship between different social or natural phenomena, will largely replace the widely accepted goal of today's schools of increasing students' mastery of specific subjects (Little, 1995; Joyce, Hersh, and McKibbin, 1983; Newman, Wehlage, and Lamborn, 1992: Sergiovanni, 1994; Sizer, 1993). The communitarian aspects of the school will emphasize a sense of approachability among colleagues at all levels, that they can count on receiving the support they need to feel accepted in the school's social environment.

Curricular uniformity for large cohorts of students is deeply entrenched in the organizational tradition of secondary schools. This uniformity refers to what is taught at any given time to large classes of students, all of whom are expected to learn the same thing. It also refers to what is taught during a long period of time such as an academic semester or year. Curricular uniformity is a tradition in public schooling that is not easily changed despite its obvious shortcomings, only one of which is that students are required to study given contents "whether they like it or not." By that we are not referring primarily to the fact that students may be required to study given knowledge domains. Rather, the reference here is to the phenomenon that, whether a subject is an elective or a requirement, teachers feel constrained to "cover" given quantities of curricular material during specified periods of time for all students. Those who can't keep up are considered to be low achievers, slow learners, failures, incompetent, lazy, or what have you. The academic material studied is not adjusted to students' successes in learning, their interests or curiosity, even within the knowledge domains determined by the teacher. Nor can students pursue problems that may arise during the course of study that lead in directions not accommodated by the curriculum.

Teachers are often pressured by administrators and especially by standardized testing to "run with the material," which means to cover as much ground as possible. These images, borrowed from football and other sports, make it seem that teachers carry packages of information with which they must "run" to some mythical goal across the "field" in the face of an opposing team. Images from competitive games are in wide use and often influence people's thinking. Even teachers' work is often viewed as successful only by comparison with some imaginary opponent (the clock, the official curriculum, other teachers) whom they outrun. The image of teachers' "feverish" need to "cover the ground," that is, to set forth the "whole field of knowledge" before the students so they shouldn't "miss" anything important, was cited and roundly criticized by John Dewey at the beginning of the twentieth century (Dewey and Dewey, 1915, 12). We should also recall that, in this matter, Dewey was citing fundamental ideas of teaching presented clearly by Rousseau in the eighteenth century. Indeed, many of the concerns addressed in this book, about the nature of school learning, the structure of the curriculum, school community relations, and the like, were articulated by the Deweys over 80 years ago when writing about the Schools of Tomorrow (1915). From the point of view of pedagogical "theories in use," the ideas that actually guide practice, it is rather sobering to realize that we have not advanced very far in the past two hundred years. In our day, toward the end of the century that Dewey opened with his vision for the future, Theodore Sizer placed the motto "less is more" at the head of his efforts to reform high school education and to emphasize quality of learning over quantity of teaching (Sizer, 1993).

The operation of the high school as a "rapid curriculum delivery system" can be represented as a one-way progression repeated over and over again, as follows:

Curriculum → Instruction → Evaluation

This sequence is one of the fundamental regularities of much of schooling—and of secondary schools in particular (Sarason, 1982).

A distinctly different approach emerges from the conception of the school as a social system where information about the process of implementation (teaching and learning, in the case of the school) is constantly gathered for purposes of feedback to the implementers. The feedback may or may not result in changes in the manner of instruction, depending upon its message. Whatever the case, change is possible at any time in light of the feedback about teachers' and students' actual behavior, rather than having teachers base their lessons on the predetermined requirements of the curriculum. When the systems conception of instruction becomes part of school policy, teachers display a very different orientation toward the work of instruction. What was once conceived to be a repetitive linear progression now becomes a series of cycles or spirals, as follows:

> Curricula as guidelines → instruction accompanied by process evaluation → feedback → planning → new curricular/instructional methods plans → instruction, etc.

However, the implementation-feedback-planning-renewed implementation cycle is not sufficient for making a profound change in instructional method or vision. In order for feedback to serve as a basis for overcoming the current uniformity in teaching, teachers must recognize the variability in learning interests and progress among different subgroups of students and make a point of introducing significant differentiation into the processes of teaching and learning.

The adoption of this comprehensive vision of school organization promises to replace today's schools with an effective and edifying alternative. The guidelines for this alternative are prescriptive in terms of the schools' general organizational and operational structure. But we seek to abolish what we perceive to be the essence of the bureaucratic school, namely, the prescription of specific curricular contents taught in given periods of time and in a particular sequence by individual teachers acting as subject-specific experts. The alternative proposed here provides the framework for organized creativity, not for permissive anarchy or for bureaucratic rigidity (von Bertalanffy 1956, 1968).

In order to function in the manner described here and achieve the goal of high-level student engagement and success in learning, schools must undergo a thorough process of restructuring. The main purpose of this book is to assist educators to clarify their conception of the restructured school. We also present a set of organizational methods and procedures vital for implementing the process of restructuring and for maintaining its cardinal features for a long period of time.

SETTING SCHOOL POLICY

Among the earliest steps to be taken in the process of restructuring a school is the formulation of the school's policy statement, which will guide the school's work. The formulation of a policy statement is often recommended before a consultant or principal embarks upon a process of restructuring. The entire staff or at least a "critical mass" of the teachers should be engaged in formulating the school's fundamental educational policy. The policy statement, beginning with a statement of the overall vision or mission, should mention the fundamental goals and principles governing the operation of the school. These include organization, pedagogy, curriculum, interpersonal relations at all levels, and school-community relations.

There are different approaches to the formulation of a school's policy statement (Caldwell and Spinks, 1988; Hopkins, Ainscow, and West, 1994). Some authorities favor an elaborate statement that serves almost as a blueprint for the school's operation. Others suggest a relatively short statement whose main purpose is to provide a set of general guidelines. On the one hand, the policy statement must be sufficiently concrete and descriptive to make it possible for administrators and teachers to derive from it specific organizational and pedagogical conclusions. On the other hand, only in the last section of the statement called "action plans" does the policy statement set forth the specific content of the procedures to be carried out. For example, the policy statement can assert that the teaching staff will participate in project teams whose goal is to gather information and provide feedback to the staff on all critical aspects of the school's operation. However, which project teams should be set up or how they are to function will be specified only in the final section of the policy statement. In the approach presented here, a school policy statement should include beliefs, mission, policies, objectives, strategies, and action plans (Cook, 1988; Kaufman and Herman, 1991).

Beliefs. Following the above outline, the policy statement would begin with the basic beliefs that teachers and administrators have about teaching, learning, school organization, curriculum, and school-community relations. To ascertain what these beliefs are, it will be necessary to gather relevant data. Beliefs can be organized under several important categories of life in schools, such as beliefs about student learning, the behavior of administrators, teacher participation in school governance, the nature of staff and curriculum organization, and school-community relations.

A school staff might believe that learning is fostered most efficiently by competition among students and that schools should reward those who prove their superior achievement by excelling in relation to other students. Private boarding schools frequently pride themselves on their competitive and elitist ethos. That will be an entirely different kind of school than one where the staff believes that the citizens in a society should learn to cooperate, that cooperation in fact makes possible the conduct of most aspects of modern social existence, and that the school is a micro-society that should foster cooperation and mutual assistance among teachers and students.

Mission. The mission statement derived from the basic beliefs should serve to concentrate the school's energies on an agreed-upon purpose. If this can be done—and it is admittedly easier said than done—the school can go a long way toward avoiding fragmentation of human and material resources. The mission statement can foster a sense of belonging and identification with the school on the part of staff and students. As such, it must avoid being a vague, wishy-washy statement that means everything to everybody. It is usually restricted to one sentence.

The mission statement shown here reflects an egalitarian approach rather than one based on beliefs about the virtues of competition:

The Nordau School seeks to achieve a high level of student engagement in the process of learning by providing opportunities for teachers and students to have a sense of belonging, ownership, and participation in decision making regarding the school's operation at all levels, by conducting instruction largely through inquiry methods that foster student cooperation, and by having students experience, and come to appreciate, the direct relation between school learning and life in the community.

Policies. Formulation of the policy statement will probably require many meetings and discussions. If the teachers have faith in the principal that the policy statement expresses genuine operational intentions and is not a pronouncement intended for purposes of public relations, it can rally staff members around its implementation. The statement will breed a great deal of cynicism if it is a transparent propaganda ploy. Since the policy statement almost certainly concerns how decision-making power will be distributed in the school, the use of such statements for purposes other than that for which they are intended is not a rare phenomenon (Sarason, 1996a).

A list of specific policy statements on a range of topics essential to school life appears at the end of Chapter 3, following a discussion of the rationale behind those statements. In general, policy statements assert clearly what the school intends to do to fulfill its major functions. According to some authorities, negative policy statements should also be formulated, stating clearly what the school will *not* do.

Examples of policy statements are:

• The fundamental premise of this school, which takes precedence over all other policies, is that each teacher and student is a citizen in the school community and should enjoy all the privileges of full citizenship, which include basic acceptance of their human dignity, acceptance of their need for support from their environment, and their right to approach one another for contact, human exchange, or assistance, without regard to their relative standing in the school in terms of any specific criterion.

• The school will not implement ability tracking in any aspect of its academic program.

• All students can succeed in learning. This school is devoted to making it possible for all students to learn and derive a sense of satisfaction and pleasure from their learning experiences. To succeed, students need acceptance, encouragement, and support.

• Decision making about curriculum, instructional methods, school-community relations, and all other aspects of the school's educational program will be made by the principal in conjunction with the teachers. Details of how and when teachers will participate in making decisions about issues affecting the school appear in the section of this statement devoted to the school's strategies.

- The fundamental premise of this school is that excellence in teaching will ultimately yield high-level learning. Excellence in teaching can be achieved when the school provides teachers with the time needed for cooperation in the planning and implementation of instruction. Hence, the school will strive for quality, not merely for quantity, at every level of its operation.

- The principle of quality over quantity will be applied to curriculum planning and to students' study programs. Each student will be permitted to study a maximum of three knowledge domains at any given time. These domains can be changed at the end of each module (eight or ten weeks), if so desired.

- Teachers will participate in teaching teams, but no teacher will engage in classroom instruction for more than four hours on any given day. The remainder of the workday will be devoted to individual activities or teamwork of various kinds.

- The curriculum will be adjusted by obtaining feedback about ongoing teaching and learning; it is not a blueprint that must be followed as written.

- A portion of students' learning experiences will take place in community settings of varied kinds, including local government, commerce and industry, and health facilities.

Objectives. What must the school achieve in order to carry out its mission? The objectives are the goals set out in the statement of the school's mission. The mission statement is, as noted, limited to one sentence. That can help the school concentrate its efforts on a very small number of objectives included in the mission statement. However, few as these objectives may be, they usually demand all the energy, expertise, and devotion that the staff can muster.

Some authors on this subject assert that objectives should be formulated in strictly behavioral terms, setting out just exactly what students will learn and what proportion of students must learn the stated contents to qualify the school as having reached its objective. Those authors argue that "process objectives," such as the kind of experiences students should have or the broader values or intellectual abilities they should acquire, are too general and elusive to be measurable. Hence, they do not qualify as true objectives.

Our view is that the demand to formulate concrete behavioral objectives ignores the essential characteristics of education and seeks to force educational experiences into a materialist and mechanistic mold. In education, process and product are a continuum, not sharply distinguishable, as Dewey argued early in this century (Dewey, 1922, 1939). Schooling strives to cultivate students' habits of mind and behavior as manifested in a variety of modes of expression and activity, including reasoning, speaking, writing, social interaction, and aesthetics. If not, whatever else the school accomplishes in terms of visible results that may enhance its public image (such as that 100 percent of the twelfth grade has graduated), it has not fulfilled the essence of its mission, only its external trappings (Dewey, 1933; Sizer, 1993; Wolf, Bixby, Glenn, and Gardener, 1991). While these may not be negligible and will always play a role in public education, outcome-based teaching can, and often does, breed superficiality paraded in the form of the number of questions answered correctly on a test, the number of graduates, and so forth (McNeil, 1986). Many qualities can be quantified and measured, in education, psychology, and other approaches to the study of human behavior. The view that quality and quantity are opposites or that they are entirely separate is patently an oversimplification. They should both be viewed as a matter of priority, not as mutually exclusive. Yet, for decades education has witnessed how many quantities (number of correct answers, number of papers written, number of pages published, and so forth) quite frequently are devoid of quality. Too many graduates of our schools, including university graduate schools, have a paper-thin education. Educational objectives should focus first on quality, and only second on quantity.

No one should construe this explanation to mean that we are free to ignore quantity altogether by claiming to achieve quality education for a relatively small number of students. When significant percentages of a nation's high school graduates cannot enter college because they are unable to pass baccalaureate examinations, as occurs in a number of European and Middle Eastern countries, quantity speaks eloquently about the quality of the education offered to the public.

The sample mission statement presented earlier directs attention to the critical importance of student engagement in learning (a concept that overlaps with, but is not reducible to, motivation to learn). Engagement can be conceived of and evaluated as an important effect of the total learning environment on students' behavior. Rarely, however, is student engagement mentioned among the outcomes that schools insist on measuring, perhaps because it is difficult to evaluate by written tests of any kind (Newman Wehlage and Lamborn, 1992). Engagement in learning is a process objective that might be equal in significance to any other category of effects that the school might wish to assess. Like many other process objectives, engagement in learning can be conceived of in multiple ways, as an outcome (dependent) variable or as a mediating variable that affects many aspects of learning, some part of which can be called "achievement." The distinction between outcome and process objectives appears to be artificial and potentially misleading.

That is not to say that the school's objectives should be stated in patently idealistic terms that defy clear definition. Such global statements, although widely accepted truisms, become trivial precisely because they often mean nothing in particular. Perhaps the most often repeated statement of this kind is the assertion that the school strives ''to have students realize their full potential.'' Obviously, such statements are meant to enhance public relations, not to express the educational goals of a school.

Objectives should be closely tied to the school's statement of its mission. The sample mission statement shown earlier is focused, among other things, on student engagement in learning, based on student's interests and their appreciation of the life-related meaning of their studies. That focus distinguishes the objectives of this school from those of the traditional academic high school, which stress the mastery of large quantities of disciplinary information. Such information is selected and presented by teachers on the basis of a mandated curriculum and what they understand to be the knowledge required for proficiency in the fundamentals of each discipline.

Strategies. What resources does the school intend to commit to the achievement of its objectives? *How* will the school proceed to accomplish these objectives? Objectives need not state the specific procedures to be taken, which are to appear in the next, and final, section of the policy statement, which is devoted to action plans. However, the basic strategies should be spelled out unmistakably, in broad terms, to clarify whether the staff is proceeding according to agreed-upon strategies or whether the school is or is not implementing its policy.

The following strategies are critical but do not exhaust the list of strategies needed:

- Teamwork will be the basic strategy of human organization in this school, at the level of the administration, teaching staff, and classroom.
- The teaching staff will carry out its primary responsibility of instruction through the medium of multidisciplinary teaching teams.
- Teams of teachers, coordinated by and in collaboration with the principal, will be responsible for identifying and solving major educational or human relations problems arising in the school or between the school and the community.
- The school will seek and provide adequate in-service training for teachers who wish to acquire greater skill in the organizational or instructional methods of teamwork.
- The objective of high-level student engagement in learning will be pursued, inter alia, through limiting the number of different knowledge domains students will study at any given time (perhaps three, or a maximum of four).
- Teaching teams will be allocated sufficient time (four hours or more) as part of their weekly work schedules to engage in ongoing planning of curriculum and instruction in light of feedback received about previous instructional events.

These strategy statements appear to be straightforward. Nevertheless, many terms widely employed in education do not have a single, unambiguous referent, and they often mean different things to different people. Team teaching is certainly a popular term, but closer examination of how it was implemented by different schools and teachers led, in one study, to the identification of nine different kinds of practices that were all called team teaching. Ironically, only one of these nine types involved having two or more teachers work together in the same class at the same time, which is what many educators understand by the term ''team teaching'' (Hall and Hord, 1984, 127–128). For the purpose of creating an operational map for implementation, specific action plans must be made. Strategies must be translated into tactics.

Action Plans. A complete action plan is too detailed and too dependent upon each school's circumstances to present here. Cook (1988, 129) provided an excellent summary of the elements that should make up an effective action plan. These are:

1. a specific reference to the strategy the plan is intended to implement,
2. a statement as to the particular objective it seeks to achieve,
3. a detailed description of the steps required to accomplish the plan,
4. an indication of who will do what, and
5. a timeline for the plan (such as the length of the instructional module).

The policy statement can be prepared under the leadership of the principal if he or she is able to direct the necessary long-term discussions by the teaching staff. External consultants can also serve in this capacity as part of their task in the school restructuring project. However, if it later is found that the principal engaged an external consultant without intending to implement the plan, the consequences can be particularly destructive.

STAFF ORGANIZATION: A NETWORK OF INTERACTING TEAMS

The basic strategy indicated in the strategy section of the policy statement is the use of teamwork on the staff and student level. The organization of the teaching staff into project teams usually takes teachers' preferences into account, including the preference not to be a member of any team. The teams provide the substructure on which the multidisciplinary curriculum and inquiry-oriented learning can be implemented. Teams are also part of the organizational structure that maintains channels of communication among elements within the school and with settings outside the school (compare Hopkins, Ainscow, and West, 1994, 167–177). Project teams work on a range of topics that the school must cope with if it is to maintain a systems form of organizational and instructional superstructure. Without the ongoing work of these teams, a school can quickly revert to the typical bureaucratic model of organization and operation. The relative absence today of teacher participation in schoolwide decision making and the need for a high level of cooperative decision making as prerequisite for school restructuring in the future have been observed repeatedly. A forceful statement on this subject was made by Bruce Joyce and colleagues:

The combination of autonomy in the classroom, relative lack of formal structures for decision making, low levels of surveillance and supervision, and the use of the informal social pressure to maintain classroom privacy and resist collective decision making result in paradoxical findings regarding teachers' feeling of efficacy. Surveys report that many teachers believe they have great autonomy within the classroom, but are powerless with respect to overall district and schoolwide decision making. Both findings are correct. In most schools and districts teachers are relatively powerful within the classroom but experience low levels of involvement at other levels of the organization. The isolation of the classroom increases teachers' power within it while reducing their power outside it. . . . For our purposes this duality presents a serious problem because school improvement requires collective activity. Any attempt to create a better environment for education will have to decrease isolation, increase cooperative planning and sharply lengthen the amount of time in meetings. (Joyce, Hersh, and McKibbin, 1983, 69)

In terms of the conception of tomorrow's school presented here, the following project teams are recommended:

Interdisciplinary Curriculum Teams. One principle in the school policy statement will refer to the interdisciplinary character of the curriculum. The action plans will actually identify several broad domains of knowledge that students will study, instead of the traditional curriculum divided into the standard academic disciplines. Each knowledge domain will have a team of teachers responsible for defining transdisciplinary problems that students can investigate and be asked to solve. The teams will also prepare access to necessary resources for students, including sites or people outside the school where students can carry out a portion of their investigation or who can consult with, or be interviewed by, the students regarding their project. The curriculum teams will collect information about the impact on teachers and students of teaching the various knowledge domains, in order to provide them with feedback and allow for further clarification of the curriculum. All of the teachers in a school will participate in at least one and perhaps two of these teams.

The establishment and operation of these teams incorporate the school's policy on the distribution of teachers to subject matter and the organization of the student body, in terms of blocks of time to be spent with given teams of teachers (see Chapter 8, "Restructuring Time in Schools"). Clearly, these teams form the organizational and pedagogical backbone of the school.

Teaching Methods in Use. This team's primary purpose is to survey the implementation of teaching methods in classrooms by the school staff and to provide them with feedback. It should be made clear that the team's work is intended to assist the staff to improve instruction, not to supervise or monitor teachers' behavior. This delicate topic requires much discussion, explanation, and cooperation among teachers to avoid any buildup of bad feelings. Yet, it is important for a school staff periodically to receive systematic information about how teachers function in the classroom. That kind of information is relatively unknown in today's schools; its absence strengthens teachers' sense of isolation and of teaching "behind the classroom door."

The team that surveys the use of teaching methods in the school does not operate all year. Its operation is determined by local circumstances. Often it functions for one or two months during an academic year.

Mutual Assistance Teams. One of the most helpful and important teams for teachers is the one devoted exclusively to short-term instructional planning and mutual observation. Three teachers, or four at most, plan class sessions together in terms of both process and content. They also prepare a short list of three or four criteria that direct their observations in the class to determine to what extent the plan is being implemented. One of the teachers leads the class while two others observe both the teacher and the class according to the criteria determined in advance. Immediately after the lesson, the team meets to give feedback to the teacher who led the class and to plan the next lesson to be led by another member of the team. This cycle of planning, teaching, feedback, and replanning can be repeated two or three times during the course of the year.

It might be convenient for the curriculum teams to function in the capacity of mutual assistance teams as well. That depends on the teachers' preferences and on other factors. What must be stressed is that the mutual assistance team focuses primarily on teaching method and only secondarily on curricular substance. It may not always be possible for the same team, such as the curriculum team, to switch functions and perform a distinctly different role, that is, mutual assistance devoted to the process rather than content of instruction. The work of the mutual assistance team is elaborated on in detail in Chapter 6.

The three types of teams discussed thus far focus directly on classroom instruction. The following types of teams focus on schoolwide topics.

Class/Teaching Schedule Team. Teachers can submit requests to this team or committee to change the length of a given class session or sessions, the day on which the class meets, the frequency of class meetings during a specified period of time, or the location where the class will conduct its work. The team sets up criteria for submitting and accepting these requests.

Survey-Feedback Teams. Not all topics related to the school's policy require the work of standing committees or teams. It is always possible to set up a team ad hoc to investigate topics and to provide the staff with feedback. The teams are disbanded when they complete their task, although at times ad hoc teams can function for relatively long periods of time, even several years if necessary, but that is usually not effective. An example of one such team well known to different schools today is the team whose job is to identify slow learners at risk of failing in a subject and provide them with special assistance. On the level of a schoolwide problem, a team can be set up to determine the nature of the tests given in the school, the frequency of testing, the use of alternative evaluation methods, and the like (compare Hopkins, Ainscow, and West, 1994, 142–152).

When the team presents its findings to the staff and the staff decides to proceed with a problem-solving sequence, the team that carried out the survey on this topic can be disbanded. Another team can assume the responsibility to evolve and implement a solution to the problem. The work of these survey-feedback teams is discussed in greater length by Schmuck and Runkel (1994).

School-Community Relations. This team's first priority is to plan for involving the parents in the school's work, above and beyond the planning of social activities for the students. But the school's relationship with the community should not end with maintaining close relations with parents, as important as that may be. Schools can establish productive relations with many different settings in the community where students can be helped to carry out study and service projects of many kinds. The local municipal government or township should have an ongoing relationship with its schools to assist them in developing ties with the various institutions and settings (private and public) in the area. Local government must assist in creating the legal and procedural framework needed to make student study outside the school a matter of routine. Otherwise, it will remain a special event dependent upon unusual dispensations from school-district authorities, the police, and other official bodies.

In short, this team's domain of activity, along with the principal's, is to establish channels of communication with the larger social system in which the school is embedded. Communication with different settings in the community is imperative if teaching and learning are not to be conducted as if they were isolated from the world and restricted to the classroom. Unfortunately, today's schools are far too isolated from society in terms of implementing their educational programs (Banathy, 1992, 137–138; Dewey and Dewey, 1915; English, 1993; Sarason, 1983).

DIFFERENTIATION AND INTEGRATION: PUTTING THE PARTS OF THE SYSTEM TOGETHER

If the network of teacher teams, led and coordinated by the principal, can fulfill their functions reasonably well (after further training and experience), the school will be able to maintain the necessary cycles of planning, instruction, feedback, problem solving, and replanning that make the school a learning organization (Argyris, 1992; Senge, 1990). The school will have succeeded in establishing and operating multilateral channels of communication that will maintain its systems operation. It will give administrators, teachers, and students a sense of belonging, effectiveness, and influence on their school's work.

It is recommended that the staff examine the teams' work several times during the year and ascertain whether they are indeed functioning and how. Many committees established by various organizations exist on paper alone and never produce anything. Some never meet! The systems approach to organization emphasizes a high level of participation by teachers and students in the processes of decision making. These processes affect all of the major dimensions of the school's operation.

In Table 5.1, all of the dimensions have been grouped under three major categories: administrators', teachers', and students' behavior (determining *what* is to be done by each group); work design and tasks (determining *how* work is to be accomplished by each group); and space-time allocations (determining *where and how long* work is to be done) (Shachar and Sharan, 1995). By contrast, the same dimensions of school operation involve only a very low level of participation when schools function according to the bureaucratic model of organization.

The scales shown in the table can be used to assess the extent to which the school involves the relevant persons or groups in decision making, both at the classroom and at the schoolwide, organizational level (Shachar and Sharan, 1995). These scales are applicable to the work of the teacher teams as well as to the instructional work of teachers with students.

Table 5.1
Three Scales for Assessing the Degree of a Bureaucratic (Low Participation) and an Open System (High Participation) Approach to School Organization

	Bureaucratic Model					Open System Model			
	(low level participation)					(high level participation)			
Teachers' administrators' or students' behavior	1 2	3	4	5	6	7	8	9	10
Work design and tasks	1 2	3	4	5	6	7	8	9	10
Space/time allocation	1 2	3	4	5	6	7	8	9	10

We predict that there will be a relatively high level of consistency between the assessment of events at the classroom level and those at the organizational level. All major subsystems of the school are interrelated, and classroom organization and operation often reflect closely how the teaching staff is organized and operates. The team structure is intended to maximize the participation of all relevant groups in decision-making processes regarding the implementation of the school's educational policy. More specific details about the behavioral patterns to which the scales refer appear in other publications (Shachar and Sharan, 1995; Sharan and Shachar, 1994).

THE PRINCIPAL'S "OPERATIONS FORUM"

Some of these teams must communicate with one another and, at times, co-ordinate their activities. (The mutual assistance teams, however, need not meet with other teams or report to the entire staff. Their work is self-contained). The frequency of their interaction depends on how much they require consultation with and help from other bodies within the school. However, given the tendency for teams to work alone and to avoid being "interferred with" by persons outside the team, the principal must establish an "operations forum" that meets regularly so that the staff is updated on the work of all the teams. This forum could be attended by the principal and team representatives, by a portion of the entire staff, or by all teachers and administrators if that is feasible and productive. Not all meetings of the operations forum need be attended by the same people, but there must be a stable core of participants at all of the meetings during a given academic year (compare Hopkins, Ainscow, and West, 1994, 171–177).

The discussion at this forum will focus on the intersection of the school's three subsystems—staff organization, instruction, and curriculum—and on progress made and problems encountered. To participate productively in these discussions, teachers must develop an overview of the school as a system. That means they must understand the interrelation among the system's parts. It is the principal's task to have teachers acquire this overview and to ensure that they have the information necessary for them to participate fully in the operations forum. That is required in order for the school to shift some responsibility for directing its operation from the principal to the entire staff. That state of affairs—part of the vision of tomorrow's schools—will emancipate the principal from the role of sole educational administrator and make it possible for her or him "to lead from the center," that is, to assume the role of educational and organizational leader.

The various teams represent the school's need to differentiate its functions to cope with a wide variety of topics simultaneously. The meeting of all the teams, or their representatives, in the operations forum is a way to maintain communication among the subgroups operating in the school. The team meeting should consist exclusively of reports made by members or representatives of the various teams and their reactions to each other's reports. The team meeting is where the social system feature of the school is most visible. It serves as the coordinating hub of the organization that integrates the operation of the different departments, teams, or functions of the school as a whole (Lawrence and Lorsch, 1986). The manner in which these teams perform their functions can be quite varied and cannot be anticipated in any one set of guidelines.

SUMMARY

Figure 5.1 represents in diagram form the main structural features of the innovative school and their interrelationship. The four subsystems of the school form a concentric ring around the core of school policy. The work of the subsystems is directed by this policy, as well as providing feedback to the continuing process of making policy. Interaction between policy and implemention couples the inner core of ideas to the level of practice. Each subsystem also interacts with, and is directly or indirectly coupled to, the other three subsystems. The extent to which this intrasystemic coupling is more or less tight or loose depends on how the work of the staff is organized and implemented. In the school organization suggested here, all the conditions exist for a relatively tight coupling of the school's four subsystems, as far as the world of schools is concerned, even if the understanding of "tight" coupling differs in this context from that of industrial or commercial organizations.

Figure 5.1
Integrating the School's Systems

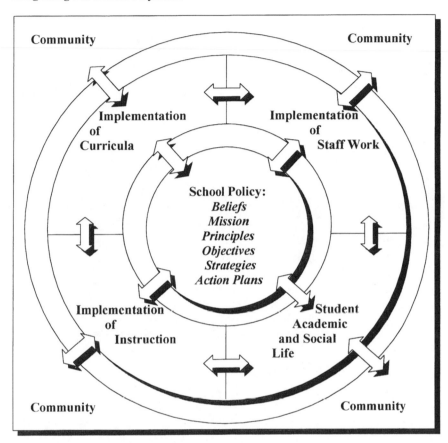

© Shlomo Sharan and Hanna Shachar.

Similarly, implementation of the school's policy through activity of the four subsystems is constantly interacting with the larger community (however the definition of community may vary for different purposes). The macrocommunity provides the environment for the microcommunity or school, as a whole, and interacts with the structures and levels of the school.

Chapter 6

Experiential Workshops for In-service Education: Developing New Norms and Skills for School Personnel

The myth that schools will change by deciding to adopt new methods of organization and instruction was relegated unequivocally to the realm of wishful thinking following the studies on educational change by the Rand Corporation and in light of the penetrating comments by astute observers of schools and school reform (Berman, 1981; Berman and McLaughlin, 1977, 1978; Joyce, Hersh, and McKibbin, 1983; Sarason, 1982, 1983, 1990). Adoption of plans for school reform, it was learned, is only a first step, and not infrequently an exercise in public relations, generally with minimal realization of the time, work, and resources needed to accomplish the task. Of course, adoption of plans to restructure schools is often meant to be an expression of good intentions. Once the decision has been made that certain schools need to be improved, and plans are carefully drawn up, the next step is implementation. But implementation, to educators' great dismay, is a road strewn with obstacles of many kinds. Indeed, implementing genuine change in the school's organizational and instructional patterns is the main challenge to significant improvement in schools (Elmore et al., 1991; Louis, Kruse et al., 1995; Miles, 1964; Murphy, 1991; Murphy and Hallinger, 1993; Sarason, 1990; Watson, 1967).

First and foremost, no plan for improving schools can be implemented without personnel who have the vision, concepts, and skills needed to put the plan into practice. Where will these personnel be found? The majority of schools continue to function, pedagogically and organizationally, according to models that the restructured school wishes to overcome and leave behind. Consequently, educators have few sites where they can obtain the experience and ideas that comprise the essence of the restructured school. In fact, they have been socialized into patterns of ideas, procedures, and modes of operation that must be unlearned, or distinctly altered, before they will be able to function in the restructured school with any degree of comfort and competence (Sarason, 1993). On that point there is widespread agreement: "Perhaps no institution in our society has been less altered in fundamental ways than the school" (Lounsbury and Clark, 1990, 35). For that reason, the solution to school improvement efforts does not lie in the direction of opening new schools. The absence of long-standing traditions regarding methods of organization and instruction in new schools that beckons to school reformers is not sufficient to ensure the implementation of new ways of schooling without the knowledge and skills of expert personnel.

Nor can school systems look to the universities for appropriately trained personnel. Many institutions of higher learning maintain courses of study that prepare educators for schools as they are today, not for schools as they should be or how they will be in the future. It seems that many years will pass before universities will change their programs of study for educators, above and beyond offering courses about the use of computers in schools (Clifford and Guthrie, 1988; Goodlad, 1990; Goodlad, Soder, and Sirotnik, 1990; Sarason, 1993). In those instances where universities do provide students of education with a new vision and the competence to function accordingly, the graduates' dispersal among many school systems, coupled with their status as newcomers to the profession, means they can exert little influence on schools.

As matters stand today, the road to school restructuring leads through in-service training for school personnel, despite the negative conclusions reached by reviews of in-service projects (Fullan and Stiegelbauer, 1991, 316; Hopkins, Ainscow, and West, 1994, 60–62; Sarason, 1990, 1995b). Effective in-service education for achieving school change preferably is conducted on a school-by-school basis, so that members of a given school have an opportunity to develop a common vocabulary and set of ideas about their work.

An entire staff need not participate simultaneously in the same workshop. That is patently not possible in schools with more than 30 teachers. Nor does it imply that school restructuring can be accomplished solely by means of in-service courses for teachers or administrators. Many different processes of change must be set in motion, particularly in high schools, which are typically large and complex organizations. These processes of change must encompass all of the schools' subsystems (Chapter 4). School consultants need a variety of methods and approaches for initiating and maintaining these changes (Arends and Arends, 1977; Dalin and Rolff, 1993; Hopkins, Ainscow, and West, 1994; Joyce, Hersh, and McKibbin, 1983; Huberman and Miles, 1984; Neale, Bailey, and Ross, 1981; Schmuck and Runkel, 1985, 1994; Watson, 1967).

One can distinguish at least three different arenas in which change processes must be pursued by anyone seeking to improve schools: the technological, political, and cultural arenas of change. Different authors have recognized the importance of the same three arenas of change, although they attributed somewhat different meanings to them (Berman, 1981; Hopkins, Ainscow, and West, 1994: House, 1981; Joyce, Wolf, and Calhoun, 1993; Sarason, 1995a). Our view of what these domains refer to is expressed in the subheadings of the following list. Note that the exclusion of any of these people or topics from the process of change can boomerang later, disrupting what has been accomplished. The agreement and moral support, at least, of the people outside the school must not be neglected. They must also be invited to participate in change activities, although in our experience few people are free or sufficiently interested to do so. The direct involvement and participation of all of the people, or nearly all, within the school is critical.

1. The political arena
    a. the school district or local department of education
    b. school supervisors of various kinds
    c. teachers' unions
    d. school-community relations (parents and local government)

2. The cultural-organizational arena
    a. schedule of classes/teachers, the use of time
    b. teacher teams for curricular development, problem solving, and decision making as a recognized part of teachers' work
    c. school structure (departments)
    d. relationships among the different departments
    e. students' organizations, school-wide functions, etc.

3. The technological-instructional arena
    a. student's assessed needs and interests
    b. curricular requirements and offerings
    c. interdisciplinary studies
    d. methods of teaching and learning
    e. resources for students, including libraries, computers, laboratories, etc.
    f. sites for study in the community

We will not undertake to present the methods available, or required, to change current practices in these areas to conform more closely to the goals of the restructured school. That task deserves an entire book to itself. Rather, in this chapter, we wish to focus on in-service education for school personnel through the medium of the experiential learning workshop. In that setting, the processes of teamwork among teachers and of classroom instruction can be simulated, analyzed, and practiced. Hence, in our view, it is one of the more powerful tools available to school consultants, principals, and others who actively pursue school restructuring.

In this chapter we treat two topics:

1. *Workshops as a Learning Environment*: in-service education and/or re-education of school personnel through the experiential workshop to develop the concepts and skills needed to implement the processes of school restructuring.

2. *From the Workshop to the School*: what must be done to accompany teachers from the workshop into the school in order to provide them with the support

and assistance necessary for transferring what they learn in the workshop with colleagues to their work in the classroom.

WORKSHOPS AS A LEARNING ENVIRONMENT

Experiential Workshops and School Change

Teachers who join a school improvement project that makes demands on their time will want to know how long it will take and whether it is worthwhile. What is the potential effectiveness of school restructuring in general and of the particular methods employed to implement it in particular? Why is the experiential workshop any more effective than the myriad of courses and lectures that they have attended heretofore?

Duration of the Change Project

Many school systems continue to treat in-service teacher education as occupying a set number of days when teachers have paid time off according to their union contracts or work agreements. The substance of the educational events that take place during these days is frequently different for each day or two. Rarely is a single organizational or pedagogical innovation pursued consistently for an entire year or more. This unfortunate state of affairs has been noted by several distinguished researchers and authors (Fullan and Stiegelbauer, 1991; Joyce and Showers, 1988; Slavin, 1989).

School consultants regularly encounter another phenomenon that testifies to the widespread lack of realistic planning for in-service teacher training. A school almost invariably has teachers attending a smorgasbord of in-service training courses at any given time, some of which are likely to present conflicting or even contradictory approaches to instruction. When teachers vote for adopting a change project, they may already be participating in two or more different in-service courses. They take it for granted that the new project will be added on to what is already an overburdened schedule of teachers' activities. Since high school teachers are often oriented primarily to teaching their special subject and less oriented toward students' pedagogical needs in general, regardless of the subject involved, teachers are attracted to in-service courses that stress subject matter and not the reorganization of the entire curriculum, the staff, and the methods of teaching. After all, subject-matter in-service courses may help teachers with what they have to do tomorrow in their classrooms, while the change project workshops promise a bag of gold at the other side of the rainbow. Principals, too, often view the number of courses in which teachers participate as a sign of the school's progress, even though the various courses attended by the teachers have no discernible focus. Not many high school personnel will ask if there is any consistency between geography, literature, and biology courses offered to teachers as part of their in-service training. Authorities on school change warn that having competing programs in the same school is the royal road to failure, if not for all of the programs, certainly for a program as demanding as schoolwide restructuring. Leadership must be exercised to keep the school on course, free from competing projects that drain the time and energies of the staff (Miles, 1986, quoted in Hopkins, Ainscow, and West, 1994, 38).

No wonder that teachers may be skeptical about the potential effect on the school of another set of workshops. No wonder, too, that they will need detailed explanations and much firsthand experience to understand why a change project should require four to five years to accomplish its goals. There is much variability in the length of time that different schools need to acquire competence in a new method of classroom teaching, such as cooperative learning. Nevertheless, it is close to certain that a high school restructuring project will need a minimum of three or four years of consultation and workshops, devoted to the functioning of teacher teams for data gathering and problem solving and to the acquisition of alternative forms of instruction and evaluation (Murphy, 1991; Sharan, 1994).

The staff must be reminded that the number of times groups of teachers from the same school are free to participate in three-hour workshops is quite limited and frequently cannot be arranged more than once in two weeks at best. Ten workshop sessions per academic year, for the same group of teachers, is often the maximum time investment a school can manage and still meet its ongoing responsibilities. Ironically, schools cannot be restructured if they do not function, and yet restructuring a functioning school, as many consultants have observed, is like changing a flat tire on a moving bus (Louis, Kruse et al., 1995)

Not only is time for consultant contact with the teaching staff very limited, the new methods of operation learned by administrators and teachers need time to be tried and ironed out to gradually become institutionalized or, in other words, integrated into the daily functioning of the school (Miles, 1983; Miles, Ekholm, and Vandenberghe, 1987). Schools as organizations have completely different temporal cycles than do individuals. That is a perspective that teachers, accustomed to focusing on their classrooms and not on the school, generally lack and that they will appreciate more as the project unfolds.

Potential Effectiveness of the Change Project

The question of effectiveness can refer to two different issues: (1) Are restructured schools effective in terms of student learning and teacher satisfaction? (2) Can the workshops and other methods employed to bring about basic changes in the school achieve their goals? The first question is discussed in Chapter 3. It must be remembered that evaluating the effects of large change projects such as school restructuring takes many years. As of this date, the history of restructuring is not very long and available data are limited in scope. Nevertheless, the published information is more than encouraging (Newman and Wehlage, 1995).

Particularly dramatic, convincing, and at times inspiring is the case study of the Metro Academy by Mary Ann Raywid (Raywid, 1995) and the comments on this report by Louis, Kruse et al. (1995). Case studies such as this one portray schooling at a high level of excellence, as it is for the teachers and students of the Metro Academy and as it can be for the teachers and students in many schools (see also Fine, 1994). Unusual schools probably enjoy unusual conditions of one sort or another. But it cannot be gainsaid that a far better way of life in schools is possible, and the reality created in some schools deserves to be emulated. Several brief quotations from Raywid's description can convey the flavor of what the Metro Academy is doing:

Perhaps the most arresting qualities of restructured student experience at Metro Academy accrue from (a) the literally ceaseless efforts to make school a thought-provoking place; (b) the determined arranging and rearranging of the daily schedule to serve programmatic purposes, rather than vice versa; and (c) the unremitting efforts to provide necessary needed support for students. . . . Insistence on thought-provoking pedagogy is rooted in the Inquiry Method that is the school's theme and unifying thread. . . . the students . . . ask questions and examine the variety of ways they can be answered. . . . a second way in which the lives of Metro students and teachers differ quite extensively from the lives lived in most other schools is associated with the way in which the school schedule is viewed. At Metro, the schedule is not the all powerful structure to which everything must conform. Instead, it is designed, and constantly redesigned, to serve the programmatic purposes staff have selected. . . . A third characteristic of restructured student experience at Metro accrues from the staff's determination to provide whatever is necessary in the way of student support . . . increasingly familiar advisory groups . . . proactive trouble-shooting . . . three kinds of labs . . . to assure students get needed support. (Raywid, 1995, 48–55)

We must not lose sight of the challenge: If we don't try a new approach to schooling, one that is at least based on sound theory, a small but impressive body of empirical findings, and professional reasoning, how will we ever improve it? The answer to our great dissatisfaction with what schools are today cannot be found in repeating what we have already done countless times.

Regarding the question of methods for changing schools it should be recalled that experiential workshops have been used for many years as part of systematic efforts to change schools. They were not invented as part of the relatively recent school restructuring movement. Unfortunately, research publications frequently omit a description of how the restructured schools that were evaluated got to be restructured in the first place. What made them become what they are? How did they get there? An otherwise informative and detailed study (reported in a 60-page booklet) of the effects of restructured schools says only a few words about the fact that the schools made use of external change agents who helped introduce the kind of teacher collaboration and styles of student learning presented in this book (Newman and Wehlage, 1995). In no way is this statement intended as a criticism of the authors of that or any other particular research report. We wish merely to stress how regrettable it is that the practice and publication of educational research has seen fit to exclude so much of the practice of educational change as a seemingly unnecessary part of the story of research itself, even when change is what created the settings being studied.

An outstanding exception to this rule is the extensive work published by Richard Schmuck and colleagues (Schmuck and Miles, 1971; Schmuck and Runkel, 1970; Schmuck, Murray, Smith, Schwartz, and Runkel, 1975; see also Fullan, Miles, and Taylor, 1980). The report on the Multi-Unit School project by Schmuck et al. (1975) is about school restructuring at the beginning of the 1970s, long before that term came into vogue. The approach to staff reeducation employed in that project is in large part, though not exclusively, that of the experiential workshop described here. In some cases, the workshops described by Schmuck et al. (1975) were conducted during the summer, when entire days were devoted to training, instead of dividing the process into shorter sessions of three hours. In addition to the extensive data reported in their book, which cannot be summarized here, the change agent–investigators concluded at the end of their multiyear project that "the methods of consultation that we used in this action research show excellent promise of helping schools about to undertake serious structural alteration. The morale in a school that has achieved a high level of collaboration, inventiveness and use of personal resources is impressive and thrilling to see" (Schmuck et al., 1975, 372). In sum, the prospects for successfully engineering genuine change in schools are real and potentially effective. Again, implementation is the key to whether the effort will succeed in a particular setting. Given supportive organizational and environmental conditions, in-service experiential workshops for personnel working in one or two schools can cultivate new concepts and skills leading to marked changes in their organizational and instructional behavior (Sharan and Hertz-Lazarowitz, 1982; Sharan and Sharan, 1991). The precise nature of the experiential workshop, its theoretical and practical features, is discussed in the following section.

The Workshop as a Temporary System

Assuming that the goal of restructuring a school has been adopted by the staff of a high school, the staff will know that many new ideas and skills must be learned before the plan can be put into action. How will a staff of 70 teachers, for example, learn to work in teams to identify and solve schoolwide problems? How will they learn new methods to teach students to carry out inquiry-oriented study projects during class sessions that last from 90 or 120 minutes to as much as 240 minutes, instead of the usual 45 minutes? (see Chapter 8). Most teachers are accustomed to teaching primarily by various forms of lecture, followed by a question-and-answer interchange between the teacher and students or by having students fill out work sheets. Different instructional methods will have to be acquired.

Moreover, few teachers were ever asked to think about or discuss problems of schoolwide educational and organizational policy. Clearly, changing the school involves changing the professional behavior of many individuals who work in the school. School change depends on individual change, although the involvement and willingness of the individuals to undertake change is a function of, and is supported by, their membership in the organization and their concern for its future and for their own future as part of that organization. Having said that, we wish to stress that the focus of the restructuring processes presented in this book is on changing the school as a social system, not on changing individuals (Arends and Arends, 1977; Senge, 1990; Sarason, 1981).

One place to begin the process of the teachers' reeducation is by setting up one or two parallel series of workshops, each with 20 to a maximum of 30 teachers. It may be possible to conduct only one such series at a time, primarily because there may be only 20 to 30 teachers who are sufficiently involved and enthusiastic about the change to want to join the workshops at the very beginning of the process of change. Others may adopt a "wait and see" posture whether they voted in favor of the change or not. At the early stages of the project, the fact that unconvinced teachers wait on the sidelines may be a blessing in disguise. The consultant can concentrate, for a while at least, on the people within the larger system who are most prepared to learn. This initial group of volunteers also provides the consultant with a significant point of entry into the larger permanent system, which in any case cannot be encompassed in its entirety in any one reeducative effort (Hopkins, Ainscow, and West, 1994; Runkel, Schmuck, Arends, and Francisco, 1978). High schools are most often too large and complex to allow a change project to involve the entire organization simultaneously. "Innovators . . . are more likely to be able to control miniature, time-limited systems than those inherently permanent in nature [like a school]. Systems like . . . in-service institutes and workshops . . . are already in wide use" for this purpose (Miles, 1964, 486). Nevertheless, teachers or other personnel not included in the first series of workshops should be encouraged to join a second series. Their lack of participation can prove very disruptive to the progress of the entire project and radiate considerable dissatisfaction and conflict among the staff.

The important features of the training workshop as a temporary system were systematically and thoroughly explored and explained by Matthew Miles in a classic work on school change (Miles, 1964). The notion of the "temporary" system expresses the fact, inter alia, that the workshop setting is set up to have a relatively short life span. It may consist of five, eight, ten, or fifteen meetings, each one for two and a half to three hours in length. All participants know that it is a temporary arrangement directed at a specific goal. That goal usually cannot be accomplished by the entire membership of the organization working together at the same time, especially when the goal is to change the participants' patterns of professional behavior. Nor can it be achieved even with a relatively small number of people, such as 25, in one or two meetings of the workshop. If basic changes in instructional and organizational methods are the goal, then an entire series of workshops, later accompanied and followed by systematic coaching activities, are usually necessary. Unfortunately, too few people really comprehend how much time, effort, and resources are required to implement genuine change in schools, if the effort is to survive beyond the time when the external consultants leave the scene (Elmore et al., 1991; Fullan and Stiegelbauer, 1991; Hertz-Lazarowitz and Calderon, 1994; Joyce, Hersh, and McKibbin, 1984; Murphy, 1991; Sarason, 1990, 1993; Sharan and Hertz-Lazarowitz, 1982). The temporary nature of the workshop also carries the implication of limited time to accomplish its goals. This awareness can exert a certain pressure or induce a tension among participants that galvanizes their attention and energy. Some workshops do in fact generate very intense work and produce amazingly creative, even sophisticated results. Other meetings seem to be more of a social gathering, with participants enjoying the opportunity to converse with colleagues with whom they may otherwise not have much opportunity to meet. In such instances, the task at hand is given only partial attention.

Whatever atmosphere reigns in a particular workshop session, whether it be more task oriented or socially oriented, in the course of the series of workshops participants not only learn new skills but are free to practice them without risking failure in the "real" world. In that sense, the workshop is both an educative experience as well as a practice session anticipating later implementation of these skills in the permanent system, as Miles astutely observed (Miles, 1964). Removal of the threat of failure enhances the capacity of the workshop to induce behavioral change.

We have emphasized the individual nature of the learning experience and potential change that take place in the participants as individuals. Of no less importance of the social/organizational dimension of the workshop. Colleagues experience together the learning of concepts and skills. Gradually, with some sense of familiarity and emerging competence in the use of the relevant skills, the group grants legitimacy to these patterns of behavior, whereas prior to the workshops such procedures would have been viewed with suspicion or rejected outright. The emergence of new norms for staff behavior from the teachers' collective experience in the workshops is one of the most significant contributions of the temporary system to the process of schoolwide change. When *teams* make decisions to adopt new patterns of professional behavior, when teachers apprehend that what they learned comprises a *shared frame of reference* about effective ways of performing their work, only then can individual learning affect the course of action taken by the school as a whole (Argyris, 1992; Miles, 1964; Senge, 1990; Schmuck and Runkel, 1985). The gradual construction during the meetings of the temporary system, of a network of interpersonal linkages focused on models of operation that the group accepts as desirable and relevant to their needs, is the basis for the influence that the temporary system can exert on the functions of the permanent system or organization as a whole. Establishing and maintaining effective teams in the school for working on problems of curriculum, for monitoring and improving instruction, for identifying and solving many schoolwide problems, are the building blocks of the learning organization (Argyris, 1992; Senge, 1990).

Figure 6.1
The Experiential Learning Model

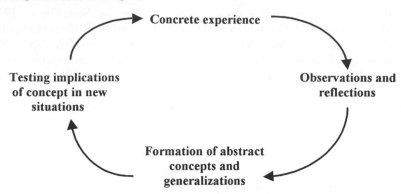

Experiential Learning in the Temporary System

The learning process during the time allotted to the temporary system aims at producing the cognitive, social-psychological, and organizational outcomes described previously. David Kolb's conception of experiential learning is related in essential ways to the notion of the temporary system and is ideally compatible to its methods and goals (Kolb, 1984; Kolb and Fry, 1975; Kolb and Lewis, 1986). Acknowledging the work of Kurt Lewin as one of the central sources of experiential learning, Kolb explains his model as follows (Kolb and Fry, 1975, 33–34):

The underlying insight of experiential learning is deceptively simple, namely that learning, change and growth are best facilitated by an integrated process that begins with (1) here-and-now experience followed by (2) collection of data and observations about that experience. The data are then (3) analysed and the conclusions of this analysis are fedback to the actors in the experience for their use in the (4) modification of their behavior and choice of new experiences.

Learning is thus conceived as a four-stage cycle, as shown in Figure 6.1.

Kolb and Fry (1975) explain that the group dynamics perspective on learning emphasized a socioemotional perspective, whereas the experiential learning model stresses that "learning and change result from the integration of concrete experiences with cognitive processes" (page 34). This latter point is particularly relevant to the work of school consultants whose work includes significant educative as well as reeducative elements. When assisting teachers and administrators to restructure their school, it is necessary to cultivate competence in the use of many instructional and organizational patterns of professional behavior that were previously unknown to the personnel involved. Methods for group problem solving were published in detail decades ago (Schmuck and Runkel,

1985) and even implemented experimentally in selected schools. In our experience, such methods are practiced in a very limited number of schools to this day. The very existence of such methods often constitutes a revelation for school personnel, including school supervisors, who favor school restructuring. Cooperative learning methods may be common knowledge among many teachers in elementary schools, but high school personnel often know only the term without ever having had any exposure to, not to speak of experience with, these methods of teaching (Sharan, 1994).

It follows that the experiential workshop should offer educators an opportunity first to examine the theory and practical steps that form a particular method for teamwork or for classroom instruction and then to carry out the method, in part at least, in the workshop setting. Skills, including the management and teaching of entire classrooms of students, cannot be learned from verbal information alone. The combination of verbal learning of theoretical material coupled with practical experience followed by reflection, feedback, and replanning as a simulation in the nonthreatening environment of the workshop is vital for the acquisition of new instructional skills.

Teachers in the workshop setting who are learning new methods of teaching sometimes function as both learners and teachers at the same time. They are on occasion, though not always, simultaneously both subject and object. Some teachers find that situation a bit confusing. A number of meetings are required until they are able to separate their roles as teachers and as students in the workshop in order to bring the understanding and skills they acquire to bear on their classroom teaching. For this and other reasons, a series of workshops (from eight to fifteen, as was noted) is imperative. The acquisition of skills for participating in teacher data-gathering and problem-solving teams, where the simulation in the workshop does not require a ''dual role'' of teachers who are also in the role of students in the classroom, is less complex.

Design of the Workshop

The design of the training workshop is based on Kolb's model, presented in Figure 6.1 (Joyce, 1992, Weil, and Showers, 1992; Joyce, Wolf, and Calhoun, 1993; Y. Sharan and S. Sharan, 1987, 1992; Hertz-Lazarowitz and Calderon, 1994). A carefully designed task provides the initial experience on which teachers and administrators can base their reflections and observations, formulate some generalizations regarding the theory and practice of the new method, and then engage in planning a lesson or series of classroom sessions in which they would implement what they learned. If available, the use of videotapes that show students conducting classroom activities of the kind being presented in the workshop are singularly helpful. Several authors have reported extensive use of videotapes in the conduct of instructional change programs (Joyce, Wolf, and Calhoun, 1993; Sharan, Hertz-Lazarowitz, and Sharan, 1981; Sharan and Hertz-

Lazarowitz, 1982). The activities viewed on the videotape are discussed, followed by group exercises/activities that embody the same procedures.

In the case of classroom instructional methods such as the various approaches of cooperative learning, teachers are able to experience the procedures during the workshop session. If the subject of the workshop is teamwork, teachers will prepare the materials they will need (such as a questionnaire or a set of questions for an interview) to carry out a survey-feedback procedure, during the interim between two workshop sessions. Results from the teams' work will be presented at the following workshop, to be held one or two weeks later. If some of the teams feel comfortable with the procedure after collecting the data or after practicing part of the teaching method in the workshop, they can implement that portion of the method in the school. This experience inevitably arouses many questions and serves as the basis for further reflection, generalization, and planning of future activities.

A feature of the workshop setting that lends it not only credibility but effectiveness as a learning environment is its authenticity. Participants actually perform the method being studied and do not just "talk about" it, as happens so often in typical school learning. That aspect of the experiential workshop should become part of the discussion during the "reflection" portion of the session. It is part of the new approach to instruction that the teachers can learn from participating in these workshops, namely, how to conduct classroom learning that involves *experience* as a basis for learning and does not rely exclusively on verbal transmission of information.

A potentially effective element of the experiential workshop is using the new method to be acquired by the participants as the object of investigation by teams, rather than having the teachers apply the procedures they are learning to some suggested topic (Y. Sharan and S. Sharan, 1992). One workshop session (2.5 hours) on Group Investigations would consist of the following (this need not be the first workshop in the series):

1. Objective: Learn basic elements of the theory and procedures of the Group Investigation method of cooperative learning.

2. Experience:
   (a) Participants go through procedures of cooperative planning, with pairs, quartets, and octets. At each stage, participants suggest topics they feel they must learn if they are to understand the Group Investigation method. Suggestions proposed and recorded at previous stages of this procedure are categorized by groups of eight members each. The category headings are presented as topics for investigation by interest groups.
   (b) Interest groups are formed, with four or five members per group. Groups decide what exactly they will investigate, how they will proceed to carry out the investigation, and how to divide the work among members. Workshop leaders provide resources for groups (published materials, videotapes).

3. Reflection:

   (c) Groups discuss the questions: Why were the procedures of cooperative planning performed in that particular manner? What was different about participating in pairs, quartets, and octets? What did these groups contribute? What are their problems?

   (d) What is the main message to be derived from this experience about Stage I of the Group Investigation method?

   (e) A representative from each group reports the essence of the group's discussion to the entire workshop.

4. Planning:

   (f) What kind of activities should comprise the next workshop?

This workshop appears too early in the series to ask the participants to implement in the classroom what was learned in this workshop session. Usually several workshops are held to give members an overview of the entire method and some practice in using different aspects of the methods before it is suggested that they apply the procedures in their classrooms. In the course of two or three sessions, the participants will have carried out a sufficiently large part of the Group Investigation method to begin applying part of what they learned and thereby to generate situations where they can test the conclusions and generalizations formulated in the workshop setting.

The Temporary System as a Microcosm of the School

According to one definition, an organization is a "group of groups" (Weick, 1969). The temporary system workshop functions precisely in that manner, with its component groups operating singly or interactively, as circumstances require. When a series of workshops encompasses 30 out of 70 teachers in the school, it more than represents the teaching staff as a whole. One way or the other, the temporary workshop system becomes a miniature replica of the school's staff and mode of organization. In that sense, the temporary system workshop is the most appropriate instrument for achieving the restructuring of the school where systems concepts (open communication between the various components, feedback as the basis for planning, involvement of all participants in maintaining the progress of the system to counteract positive entropy, horizontal rather than hierarchical organization) rather than concepts of the school as a bureaucracy (hierarchy, clear division of labor, and tasks according to specialization) constitute the essence of the school's vision and strategies.

The workshop is a recreation through simulation of the manner in which the restructured school should organize the work of its staff and the conduct of learning in classrooms. Thus, the temporary systems workshop operates in a fashion similar to the staff as a whole and to the classroom as a unit within the school. All of these levels of the school—the staff, the classroom, and the in-service training workshop—share the same essential features as an organization ("group of groups") that functions as a social system (Shachar and Sharan,

1995). When the principal is involved as a participant in the workshops, the transfer of organizational and instructional skills from the workshop to the school will be relatively smooth.

FROM THE WORKSHOP TO THE SCHOOL

Mutual Assistance Teams in the School

The mutual assistance team is an effective way of linking the workshop experience with classroom practice. The primary goals of the mutual assistance team are:

* to provide a support group for teachers in terms of their daily instructional work,
* to provide a group of colleagues who collaborate on planning and implementing specific class sessions, and
* to provide each member of the team with feedback on the implementation of the team's instructional plan as well as feedback on the performance of the class as a function of their plans and of the teacher's behavior.

In the typical high school setting, the mutual assistance team can be instituted only to the extent that the school (the principal and the staff) decide to disregard the accepted norm of "one teacher, one classroom" in order to establish communication among colleagues directed at helping them help each other improve their teaching and their students' learning. Receiving feedback from colleagues with whom one plans a lesson, in terms of what will be taught/studied and how the class session will be conducted, forms the basis for the restructuring of teaching. It makes possible the ongoing planning of instruction as a function of students' behavior, of their interests and successes. This approach replaces teaching as the delivery of "remote control curriculum" planned in isolation from the students and teachers who use (teach/study) it..

A basic requirement for using the mutual assistance team is that two teachers must be free from teaching to observe the third teacher who is a member of the team and that eventually each member will be observed teaching by the other two members.

Procedure

The specific steps in carrying out the work of the mutual assistance team described here are as follows (Dornbusch and Scott, 1975; Sharan and Hertz-Lazarowitz, 1978, 1982; Sharan, Gal and Stock, 1984):

1. Composing the team. This kind of team has only two or, better still, three members. Four members can make the entire procedure burdensome by the need to coordinate their teaching schedules. Members can be teachers of the same subject (as is often the case in elementary schools) or of different subjects. In the latter instance, the team will be identical with the multidisciplinary curriculum team (see Chapter 3), thereby avoiding unecessary duplication of effort. If the school's schedule includes blocked periods of 90 minutes or more (up to 240 minutes), it is particularly convenient for the mutual assistance team to serve as a teaching team as well, usually multidisciplinary, so that all of the team's members can be present for the entire class session.

It is important that team members be teachers who want to work together and who do not have serious difficulties in their personal relations with one another. A team usually works together for an entire academic year or more, if they so wish. However, it is recommended that teams exchange members after a year or two.

2. Planning the lesson. The team's first order of business is to decide on their goal for the class session or sessions they wish to plan, and to plan both the content and the method of instruction for that session. The method should be directly related to the procedures learned in the in-service workshops (to the extent that the staff is participating in a change project) and should embody the principles of the new method. The plan must mention the resources to which the students will have access, how these resources will be obtained, where they will be located during the class session, and whose responsibility it is to make sure that the resources are made available as planned. If the class is to conduct its work outside the classroom or the school, details must be set out in the plan.

3. Setting criteria for observation. A short list of criteria, usually not more than four or five items, for observing the teacher and the students should be composed collaboratively by the team. These criteria are to direct the attention of the two teachers who will observe the third teacher conduct the class to the most important acts (verbal and nonverbal) that the teacher must perform if the method is to be implemented according to plan. If the criteria are overly general and abstract ("the lesson is interesting" or "the teacher was nervous"), identifying them will be difficult and reporting them to the observed teacher will not be helpful. The criteria must be observable in some way, although reporting the general atmosphere prevailing in the classroom can be important if the observers can put their finger on some manifestations of behavior that express what they felt. Formulation of criteria for observation requires practice and will undoubtedly improve in the course of time as teachers gain experience with this approach.

There is no substitute for feedback based on direct observation. Most teachers are unaccustomed to having other adults in the classroom during a lesson, and initially this element in the mutual assistance team's operation can arouse resistance. Our experience is that once teachers become accustomed to having colleagues in their class, especially colleagues with whom they planned the lesson and with whom they collaborated in determining the criteria by which they will be observed, they come to appreciate the enormous benefits they derive from this situation. These benefits are clearly perceived by teachers to be related to the fact that they no longer feel alone "behind the classroom door," for all the seeming autonomy that state of affairs appears to allow (Sharan, Gal, and Stock,

1984; Sharan and Hertz-Lazarowitz, 1982). Teachers' resistance to being observed by colleagues is largely neutralized by the mutuality inherent in the entire
process. The teacher being observed now will serve as an observer of the other
teachers during the next two lessons. This mutuality should also affect the manner in which teachers address each other after the conclusion of the lesson. Since
the entire procedure of mutual assistance and observation is predicated on each
member's trust that the others are acting in good faith, the method simply will
not work when staff members have bad feelings toward and/or are in conflict
with one another.

The teacher who is to be observed conducting the class should prepare a self-
report observation sheet to be filled out immediately following the end of the
class session. That self-report can be compared to the observations made by the
two observers.

The mutual assistance team is another example of how the school can make
significant steps toward improving its functioning by establishing intercollegial
communication, instead of continuing the prevailing pattern of the "one class,
one teacher" organizational model.

4. *Conducting the observations.* After the preparations have been completed,
three cycles of "teaching-observing-giving and receiving feedback-replanning"
begin, wherein each team member, in whatever order the team decides, serves
as the "teacher" of the class and the other two as observers. The "teacher"
then carries out the team's plan. The "observers" certainly may participate in
conducting the class during the time they are not observing, if that is part of
the plan.

There are many ways to conduct observations. Teachers could simply record
their global impressions for each criterion on the list at regular times during the
class session. A potentially more effective approach is when observers agree in
advance to make a recording at specific intervals, such as once every two or
three minutes for the first ten, the middle ten, and the last ten minutes of the
class. If it is a long class, observations could be limited to the first hour only
and be made three or four times during the hour, as indicated. It is helpful to
have a recording sheet prepared in advance that has the requisite number of
spaces in which to make a check or any other agreed-upon sign that a particular
form of behavior was or was not observed.

5. *Giving and receiving feedback.* Team members should meet for the feedback session as soon as possible after conclusion of the lesson, while classroom
events are fresh in their memory, even though they have written records to help
them. It is recommended that an agenda for the feedback session be drawn up
before the observations take place, as well as several basic rules as to how the
meeting is to be conducted. The teachers who was observed should speak first,
presenting how he or she perceived the lesson, the students' behavior, the progress of their work during the class, and comments about his or her management
of the class and of student learning. Afterwards, the two observers make their
comments using their notes and formulating their comments, to the extent pos-

sible, on "objective" information rather than on inferences about what people thought or felt. The observed teacher can compare his or her comments with those of the observers. Behavior, on the part of the teacher or the students, that was not consistent with the plan for the lesson (although not "a lesson plan" in the traditional sense)—such as students who seemed unable to cooperate with others, or the teacher spending a lot of time lecturing to students seated in groups, some with their backs turned—should be discussed and clarified. Questions to be answered could include:

• Is there any clear connection between what the teacher did and how students performed?
• What can be done to be more effective the next lesson?

Various problems can arise during the feedback session. Some teams are hypersensitive to the danger of hurting a teacher's feelings by making negative comments about the lesson. The net result can be that the teacher does not benefit much from the feedback because problems are glossed over in favor of maintaining good relations. Other teams may manifest very different behavior, voicing negative comments in a way that arouses defensiveness in the observed teacher, who also does not benefit from the observers' comments, but for the opposite reason. After some practice, the fact that the feedback session is intended to draw the team members' attention to behavior that is inconsistent with the teaching plan and with the teaching method they wish to implement, will eventually result in a constructive relationship based on mutual trust and not in overly protective or overly critical interaction. Obviously, the giving and receiving of feedback is somewhat of an art, albeit an art that can be learned and mastered with a little effort. We elaborate on this topic later in this chapter.

It is possible that the team will not have time during the feedback session to plan the next class session to be conducted by some other member of the team. In that case, another meeting will be required.

6. *Summarizing results.* At the end of the entire cycle, after all of the three teachers in the team have been observed, a summary session can prove valuable. What, if any, were the similarities between the three sessions that were observed in terms of the teachers' and students' behavior? Can any conclusions be reached about the differences between teachers' self-evaluations and the observations made by the observers? Perhaps the team will have some thoughts about long-term planning of curriculum and/or the teaching method that can improve the quality of students' learning experiences.

Giving and Receiving Feedback: Some Necessary Skills

There are a number of communication skills that all professional people need if they work in close contact with colleagues. As these skills have been presented and discussed in many publications, we will not undertake to repeat them here

(Schmuck and Runkel, 1985, 1994). However, the set of skills related to giving and receiving feedback is critical to many of the kinds of teamwork and interaction patterns suggested in this book in general and for the success of mutual assistance teams in particular. Some additional comments on this topic might be of assistance to educators.

The many contributions feedback can make to personal, professional, and institutional development have been documented in numerous research studies, religious texts, psychological treatises, and the like. All of these potential benefits cannot be realized unless the feedback is offered in a manner that is acceptable and useful to the receiver, and only if the receiver knows how to make use of it. If not, it is wasted. Hence, both the giving and receiving of feedback determine whether it will be productive.

When giving feedback to the teacher whose work was observed by colleagues, it is all too easy to make the receiver defensive about his or her behavior in the classroom, even when the information cited by the observers is merely the numerical frequency with which the observed teacher performed a particular kind of act. The feedback session must be conducted in an atmosphere of cooperation in a collective undertaking, not in a situation where the observed teacher is an individual target for comments by independent observers who are not personally involved. The mutual assistance team is not an instance of scientific research, but rather one of collective responsibility by all members of the team for the education of a class of students. Team members are there to help one another. That general principle applies to many situations of giving and receiving feedback.

In addition to this fundamental principle, a number of more specific features and skills for communicating feedback can be mentioned.

Giving Feedback

1. *The person observed is willing to receive the feedback.* Giving feedback to someone is meaningful only when that person is willing to relate to it. That person must be prepared to listen actively to the feedback. The person giving the feedback can contribute a great deal toward creating the proper atmosphere for this purpose, as discussed in the preceding section.

2. *Provide descriptive, nonjudgmental information.* The information provided during the feedback session should depict a given situation as it was observed, with little or no interpretation of the situation's meaning or implications on the part of the observer. The person observed can request such interpretations if he or she so wishes, or suggest that the observing teachers and the one observed interpret the situation together. However, observers should refrain from doing so on their own initiative.

3. *Provide feedback close to the events.* It is advisable to conduct the feedback session as soon after the conclusion of the lesson as possible, preferably immediately afterwards. If so, the observed teacher is more likely to recall the precise behavior being discussed, whether the teacher's or the students'. It is also important to recall, if possible, the feelings that accompanied the events as

they unfolded in the classroom, which is less likely if several hours have elapsed between the end of the class session and the team feedback meeting.

4. Relate to phenomena that can be changed. Observers giving feedback should restrict their comments to behavior or events that can be changed in the future. It is senseless to discuss phenomena or behavior that the observed teacher cannot control in any way. This consideration should be given much thought during the preparation of the list of criteria for use during the classroom observations, but it is of even greater significance if the observers do not use a prepared observation schedule to direct their work. On the other hand, there is a wide range of behavior, her or his own as well as that of the students, that the observed teacher definitely can control or change. For example, a teacher's vocabulary is not easily changed, if at all, by feedback from observers. Hence, it is inadvisable to refer to a phenomenon of that kind during the feedback session, especially since it is unlikely that the team members agreed in advance to observe that topic. Talking in a loud voice or in a voice so soft that no one can hear can be corrected. Too many teachers damage their vocal cords during teaching and create an unpleasant atmosphere in the class by yelling. Learning to approach groups at work and ask pointed questions about their progress is a pattern of behavior that can be acquired by teachers who are reminded that such acts are important during cooperative group study.

5. Provide focused information in reasonable quantity. It is important not to drown the observed teacher in a sea of comments and to give a limited but effective quantity of feedback. Not everything that *can* be said about a classroom session necessarily *should* be said. People are able to absorb a relatively limited amount of information at a given time, especially when that information refers to their behavior and how to improve it. One way to make reception of feedback more likely is by dividing the session into two separate meetings, one for giving and receiving feedback, the other for planning the next session. When the team is relieved of pressure to accomplish all of its goals at one meeting, team members can be more relaxed to do well what they can during the time allotted.

6. Observers and the observed teacher should share feelings about their work. When observers share their impressions, feelings, and thoughts about their own teaching behavior with the teacher who was observed, that contributes to eliminating any sense of inferior status for the observed teacher. The fact that all the team members are teachers in the same school and operate on the basis of total mutuality usually is sufficient to preclude any sense of inferior status on the part of the observed teacher. Nevertheless, as such feelings can arise and interfere with the team's work, it is recommended that steps to share feelings should be taken.

7. Formulate feedback in specific rather than in general terms. Observers are urged to employ quotations from the students' or teacher's talk during the class session to make their comments more specific, and not to rely on only general impressions. The broader the statements made about classroom events, the more explanations they require for their meaning to be understood.

Receiving Feedback

1. Help observers express their observations. The person receiving their feedback can assist the observers by encouraging them to express their thoughts or
observations by giving specific examples of what they are referring to. The
receiver should not be a passive listener only.

*2. Try to clarify the observers' comments by using various communication
skills.* The receiver can paraphrase the observers' comments in order to be certain that their meaning is understood clearly. It is natural for the receiver to
anticipate being criticized by the observers, even if they did not intend any
criticism in their comments. It is of some importance to reach a full understanding of the observers' remarks so that no misunderstandings remain. The observers' comments are best understood by linking them to specific events that
occurred in the classroom.

*3. The receiver should tell the observer how he or she reacts to their com-
ments.* To encourage the observers and to maintain an atmosphere of mutual
understanding and assistance in the team, the receiver should tell the observers
now and then how he or she is reacting to the findings being reported. It is
instructive for the observers to learn which comments the receiver finds helpful
and which are not helpful. Knowledge of that kind can help the team construct
the set of observation criteria to be use in the next lesson. No one wants to
make observations of a teacher who finds no interest in what the observers have
to say.

Clearly, the observers learn as much if not more from their observations as
does the teacher who is observed. Those who offer feedback can derive as much
benefit from it as those who receive it. It is instructive to learn what *not* to do
or what leads to unwanted consequences, not only what *should* be done, which
is what is learned in the workshop. Furthermore, planning the next lesson in
light of the observations reported during the feedback session should be of equal
value to all team members. It encourages all of them to relate their plans to
what actually happens in the classroom with the students, to try to think about
cause-and-effect relationships in terms of their behavior and that of their students. This kind of team is probably one of the few settings, in which teachers
feel free to offer and receive such specific feedback about their teaching behavior. The mutual assistance team determines the social conditions under which
this kind of communication can occur productively in schools, without exposing
teachers to unsolicited criticism coming from persons in authority who do not
help teachers improve their professional work. Peer cooperation is a unique
medium for creating conditions for professional growth (Carkhuff, 1969; Devita,
1963; Egan, 1975; Gorman, 1969; Hopkins, Ainscow, and West, 1994, 97–98;
Horwitz, 1960; Johnson, 1974; Joyce and Harootunian, 1967; Jung, Howard,
Emory, and Pino, 1972).

Chapter 7

The Nonlinear Curriculum

Our school systems today are challenged by a complex and dynamic social reality where a wide range of information is readily accessed by anyone who so wishes. It challenges how we think about education and how the conclusions we reach arc applied in the schools. Postmodern appraisal of contemporary education raises many questions about the educational, social, and academic effects that schools have on society, in light of innovations that influence our approach to knowledge in general, and in particular to the knowledge we have gained regarding processes of learning (Wertch and Shomer, 1955; Collins and Ferguson, 1993; Morrison and Collins, 1995; Smagorinsky, 1995).

For schools to be relevant within a postmodern context, our approach to education must undergo a fundamental change. This change must embrace a fresh set of beliefs concerning the goals of schooling. Technical or quantitative change is certainly not the answer, nor is any solution that proposes applying "more of the same." Our old models hamper us in our struggles to understand the realities of the present and to set visions for the future. Clearly, tomorrow's challenges will not be met through control of yesterday's knowledge, and teaching and learning methods that attempt to impose stability upon a dynamic environment will only prove ineffective (Langer, 1993; Levine and Nevo, 1997a).

The situation is no different from that described by Kuhn (1970), who noted that revolutions in physics were primarily the consequence of conceptual change—the renunciation of old theoretical systems for new ones—and not necessarily of an accumulation of empirical evidence. In other words, scientific developments most often occur despite existing theories, not because of them (Thomas, 1997). In education, too, as we enter the twenty-first century, the option of updating existing approaches is no longer valid, and a conceptual change is required. It is thus a time for a major paradigm shift in education.

The curriculum is the conceptual framework that guides schools and schooling. It embraces decisions regarding educational goals and objectives, the selection and organization of meaningful contents, and the design of learning and teaching processes. It also embraces teacher and student roles and the design of experiences in the learning environment. As such, the curriculum reflects the educational conception of the human being, of knowledge and its acquisition. Thus, a conceptual change in curricular thinking can contribute to the redesign of schools to be meaningful social, educational, and academic organizations.

THE CONTEMPORARY SCHOOL AND PRESENT-DAY REALITY

Schools have often been accused of being detached from meaningful life events (Resnick, 1987; Sarason, 1983). Both educators and researchers have described the contemporary school as an introverted culture, detached from the authenticity and contextuality that characterize reality (Brown, Collins, and Duguid, 1989; Rugg and Shumaker, 1969; Sizer, 1993). According to this group of researchers, learning in the typical contemporary or normative school characteristically is rigid, uses absolute language and rule-based explanations, and offers clear-cut solutions to well-defined problems. It also attaches fixed meaning to absolute concepts and emphasizes personal success or failure. School learning is thus founded on a static concept of knowledge: facts are presented as unequivocal truths, disregarding context or perspective (Langer, 1993), while creating the illusion of cultivating individual learning. School learning is on the whole a far cry from the authentic learning experienced in daily life and in the professional work of experts, where learning entails ill-defined or emergent problems, causal explanations, conceptual situations, contextual interpretations, interim as opposed to unequivocal problem-solving, negotiable meaning, and socially constructed understanding.

Scholarly debate on the nature of the curriculum in the postmodern era has improved both qualitatively and quantitatively. Yet, its effect on our schools has remained minuscule. Schools largely remain preoccupied with repetition, practice, and a well-structured approach to curriculum, which, out of metaphysical loyalty to absolute certainty, employs sequential or linear thinking and views learning solely as the outcome of instruction (Doll, 1993). Such an approach to learning contradicts the notion of "mindfulness" in education, which emphasizes the need of an individual to be open to view a situation or environment from multiple perspectives, to create new observations, to examine facts or data from a variety of situational contexts, and to appreciate social context as a means of facilitating learning (Langer, 1993; Salomon, 1991).

The term "curriculum" stems from the Latin root meaning "to run." In our schools it has acquired the connotation of a "running track" in the sense of a unidirectional, pre-planned, uniform, well-structured track, along which teachers and students travel to a predetermined finishing line. This view of the curriculum is consistent with the conservative approach to education, which sees knowledge, culture, and man in a formalistic, unidimensional, standardized, and quantifiable fashion, whose goal is uniformity in learning. To reconceptualize curriculum for the school of tomorrow, we need to understand the antecedents of this absolutist, standardized, and linear approach. We also need to discuss what considerations are necessary if we are to achieve the desired change in approach to the curriculum.

EPISTEMOLOGICAL FOUNDATIONS OF CURRICULAR THINKING

Deliberations concerning the curriculum and its design are closely related to epistemological perceptions. Epistemology is the branch of philosophy that examines the nature of human knowledge and knowing. It is a subject of interest to psychologists and educators interested in exploring such questions as: "How does a person construct knowledge?" "What are his or her theories and beliefs concerning knowledge?" and "How do these theories affect the cognitive processes involved in thinking and reasoning?" (Hofer and Pintrich, 1997). Thus, attempts to understand our conception of curriculum involves an inquiry into its epistemological origin, that is, how the curriculum views the nature of knowledge and the process of its acquisition.

The prevalent school curriculum is fostered by an epistemological worldview that dominated the social sciences and education until the 1970s. The basic premise of the so-called positivist epistemology is that there is no essential difference between the scientific methodology required for the human and social sciences and the approach used in the natural sciences. This outlook denotes absolute faith in a scientific approach that relies on empirical evidence and "certainty." It assumes that objective reality exists outside ourselves, waiting to be discovered. It also views human beings as subject to or governed by the laws of nature, and thus represents a deterministic scientific approach. The positivist approach also contains the notion of objectivity, according to which the objective and independent world, usually represented in facts, is totally separate from the expectations, desires, or values that motivate our behavior. This is a view that Kuhn (1970) terms the "rationalistic mythology" of the scientific approach to research.

According to the positivist approach, knowledge is certain and absolute, and it is organized within an established framework of closely bound, unidirectional details. Knowledge is thus conceived as a well-defined object that can be seized, preserved, controlled, and manipulated. According to this view, knowledge is a mental representation of reality itself, independent of human consciousness. Thus, human knowledge becomes a kind of replica of the external world, and knowledge acquisition is a process of receiving and internalizing this world. The role of the human cognitive mechanism is thereby reduced to replicating reality as accurately as possible, absorbing and internalizing the objective world.

Another striking characteristic of the positivist viewpoint is its adoption of scientific methodology that led educators to think in linear models. A linear model is simple and convenient and lends itself to graphic representation as a straight line. Linearity implies maintaining a constant proportion between one variable and another, and sometimes between cause and effect. Conceptually, it is simple to understand a linear relationship since its message is that greater input inevitably leads to greater output, for example, "greater effort, greater results," "spend more time, be more successful." Linearity, which permits prediction, is often associated with a stable relational system incorporating efficiency and, to a great extent, immediacy of outcome (Caine and Caine, 1997).

However, this view fails to account for a reality that is obviously not so straightforward. No wonder therefore that the linear model fails to represent real life in such contexts as health, justice, or education (Caine and Caine, 1997). Goemer (1994) crystallized this point with his observation that eight aspirins are not eight times more effective in reducing a headache than one aspirin and that, furthermore, swallowing painkillers before you feel pain does not immunize you against pain in the future. Clearly, greater input does not necessarily yield greater output. On the contrary, often a small input yields a large output. For example, a few motivational words, a sign of empathy, a word indicating trust in one's ability to cope, can bring about greater effort by someone to accomplish a task, to be more involved, and to succeed.

Thinking in linear models boasts a further asset, modularity of systems, which means that a system can be dismantled and reassembled when all the parts can be placed back in exactly the same way. This way of thinking reflects the stability of a system that considers the whole as equal to the sum of its parts and values the parts of the system above the system as a whole. It is a mechanistic approach characterized by an affinity to parts, to their exact identification, classification, and functioning. In the past two decades, chaos scientists have highlighted the limitations of the accepted scientific linear view of the world, criticizing the classical scientific habit of ignoring difficult nonlinear problems. In fact, they claim that the science of chaos, as representative of a new way of thinking, requires a return to long-shelved data found to lack consistency within its system of linear connections. Scientists, it is suggested, need to retrace their steps and examine phenomena that were explained in the past by simple, even simplistic, systems. There is also disagreement regarding particle theory, or the reductive view of classical science, as demonstrated by Gleick (1987), who claimed that there is a kind of pretentiousness in physics that understands the world by continuing to break it into its elements until allegedly the truly basic elements are reached. Then you assert that anything left that is not understood is just detail.

According to Gleick, many scientists have come to recognize the sterility of an approach that examines the parts while ignoring the whole and to see that chaos theory heralds the demise of the reductionist approach to science. Many researchers have felt that the compartmentalization of science impedes their work. No wonder therefore that chaos, a science that recognizes the comprehensive quality of systems, has succeeded in establishing a common ground for different, barely related scientific fields. It is a science that seeks to tear down boundaries between different scientific disciplines. It is the science of process, of becoming, not of being (Gleick, 1987). It emphasizes the complexity of phenomena and thereby strengthens the need to perceive societal and human issues as interdisciplinary or transdisciplinary.

The complexity approach as opposed to the linear and particles approach is rooted in the principles of systems theory. It deals with the meaning of the whole and the interrelationships of its parts. In fact, it views a system as "a global/the total complexity," between whose elements mutual and dynamic links are found (Kauffman, 1980; see Chapter 1 of this book). This means that an element in isolation from the other elements will lack meaning. Therefore, a change in one element will modify the entire system. This approach implies that (a) the whole is greater than the sum of its parts and (b) items with a particular meaning in one system would have a different meaning in another.

Complexity theory therefore emphasizes the connections between systems and examines events in which subsystems form larger, more complex systems. Thus, any system currently considered independent is in fact made up of internally linked subsystems, each with its unique attributes and integrity. At the same time, any system will represent a subsystem within a larger system with its own uniqueness, diversity, and integrity. For example, according to the complexity approach, each individual is at one and the same time a totality, part of a separate totality, and a collection of other totalities (Davis and Sumara, 1997). It is important to emphasize that, according to the complexity approach, complex systems are adaptive, undergo spontaneous self-organization, and in this process form a new entity (Waldrop, 1992). Complexity theory is taking the place of the linear scientific approach (Caine and Caine, 1997). Lack of linearity, previously believed to represent instability, inefficiency, and complications within systems, is now gaining an increasing foothold with respect to man and society. Natural, social, and psychological reality are considered systems that constantly reorganize themselves at different levels of complexity. Interestingly, many principles of complexity theory exist in dialectic philosophy, according to which man is an active subject in shaping, affecting, and being affected by his environment, rather than a passive object of external forces. Man actively constructs knowledge following interaction between external, objective reality and internal cognitive structures and knowledge. These constructs enable our active participation in comprehending, interpreting, and constructing our knowledge of reality. According to the new approach, people actively construct knowledge, but this construction is personal and unique. So we find that social and individual causality are interactive, multidimensional, and multidirectional.

The dialectic view fosters an appreciation of contradictions and conflicts as normal phenomena, essential to the process of development and change. Thus, approaches anchored in the dialectic conception do not seek to maintain equilibrium in the sense of preserving that which exists. Rather they suggest that interference with equilibrium provides a stimulus for growth. This coincides with Feyerabend's (1993) and Holton's (1995) view, which suggests that theories are rigid frameworks that define boundaries to knowledge and limit scientific thinking and development. According to Feyerabend, cognition evolves from a maze of connections: It can occur incidentally and is often the consequence of an examination of contrasting and conflicting notions prompted by curiosity. Development of thinking is nonlinear and most often evolves by juxtapositions of events or ideas. Foucault too (1981) suggests that knowledge develops more in an anarchical way than systematically and is an outcome of diverse, unconventional ideas and curiosity. Thinking, according to Foucault, is the result of critical reference to the existing and develops through ideological confrontation. The shift from a positivist perception of reality as something external, objective, and independent of human cognitive activity to a dialectic philosophy and complexity theory does indeed represent a revolution in epistemology. Knowledge has come to be considered as context-contingent information. Or as Postman (1992) notes, knowledge is information that expresses an opinion or a point of view. A fact, for example, is not perceived anymore as neutral because it can be interpreted differently in different conceptual frameworks (Vygotsky, 1978). Knowledge is perceived as contextual, relative and alterable—constructed by everyone, everywhere. Knowing is therefore a process of generating interpretation. According to Perry (1981), this perceptual revolution offers us a novel view of man, who was once "the holder of meaning" and has now become "a creator of meaning."

The two approaches to knowledge that influence the way we think about the desired and the prevailing curriculum are summarized in the first part of Table 7.1: linearity versus complexity; absolute and certain versus open-ended, skeptical, relative, and interpretative; and elitist versus pluralistic. The two views of knowledge obviously lead to different ways of thinking about curriculum, its structure and construction.

LEARNING AND DEVELOPMENT THEORIES AND THE CURRICULUM

For many years, the behaviorist approach dominated school instruction and learning. This approach links knowledge and knowledge acquisition to external stimuli. Behaviorists consider the human brain an empty vessel that external forces gradually fill. Human responses are controlled by reinforcement and stimulus, and knowledge acquisition is a process of receiving, whereby the specific action of external forces gives rise to new behavior or performance. According to this approach (Thorndike, 1914; Skinner, 1961), human behavior can be predicted, controlled, and shaped by applying certain well-defined rules. It is not surprising therefore that behaviorist influence on curriculum organization and structure is identifiable in such concepts as reinforcement, programmed learning,

Table 7.1
Epistemological Assumptions of Current and Desired Curricula

	Current Curriculum	Desired Curriculum
Knowledge	Objective.	Subjective.
	Well-defined.	Open-ended.
	Unequivocal.	Complex and fuzzy.
	Linear conception, simple, and simplistic.	Contextual conception appreciating complexity.
	Absolute and fixed.	Fluid.
	Created only in academic institutions (elitist).	Created everywhere by everyone (pluralistic).
Learning	Accumulation of information. Receiving knowledge.	Knowledge construction. Mental activity/dialogue.
	A preplanned process aimed at a defined product. A responsive activity.	A spontaneous and active process; learning occurs anywhere at any time; the process is a product.
	Standardized and measurable process.	A unique and qualitative process.
	Separating knowledge from thinking.	Holistic conception.
	Emphasis on rationale and logical thinking.	Multiple intelligence and integration of cognitive, emotional, and social attributes.
People	People are products of culture (fragmented and mechanistic approach).	People are creators of culture (integrative, humanistic, and dialogical approach).
		People are active in their development.

practice, and guided practice. It represents a desire to achieve automatic response control (Darling-Hammond and Snyder, 1992) and an unequivocal description of so-called effective instructional sequences.

According to basic behaviorist theory, the process whereby the student learns and becomes an expert involves the transference and accumulation of behaviors. The characteristics of accumulation are expressed by the term ''more'': more speed, more facts, more assignments, more improvement, and so on (Thorndike, 1914). Behaviorist theory also implies that the teacher is required to apply pre-determined rules and principles uniformly. Thus we have a conception of the teacher as a production-line technician (Darling-Hammond and Snyder, 1992) who applies a structured, uniform, well-defined, and quantifiable curriculum.

The behavioral approach may be contrasted with later approaches whose roots lie in cognitive and developmental psychology. Whereas classical learning theories reduce ''development'' to accumulated learning, and learning itself to the narrowest context, Piaget's (1970) theory of development sees human cognition as a complex, dynamic reflective system, which experiences phases of balance and imbalance as it develops (Papert, 1980; Case, 1993). The neo-Piagetian view contributed to education what other learning theories could not: a perception of the student as an active participant in the developmental process occurring within a personal, social, and cultural context (Case, 1993).

A range of theories has emerged based on conceptions related to a cognitive and developmental psychology. Despite the differences among the various theories (Strauss, 1993) of relevance here is their common ground, namely, their regard for the individual as a being who develops via physical and mental interaction with the external environment (Piaget, 1970). According to these theories, knowledge stems from both internal and external sources. Reality is not really seen, but rather perceived and interpreted as we build our worlds out of experiences, observations, and knowledge that we have gathered or gleaned from others. Learning is therefore the product of disequilibrium and cognitive dissonance between an external and an internal situation. Such a mechanism of learning creates a positive tension, one that allows for the restructuring of an individual's conception of both himself and the outer world. In this process the individual is aware of the changes he or she experiences and undertakes. Learning is thus an expression of both qualitative and quantitative change in an individual.

Cognitive-developmental theories have affected curriculum theory and practice. They have major implications for the processes involved in selecting contents and skills, in designing learning activities, and in the organization of these activities. Based on the assumption that people gradually develop cognitive constructs that allow them to organize and apply knowledge and that during the process of development individuals select new information and integrate it with their existing knowledge, developmental theories have encouraged the recognition of the need for active learning. They also promoted the concept of the self-directed learner and of the importance of a rich learning environment. Supporters of these conceptions have contributed significantly to focusing curriculum planning on different interest domains of learners and to ensuring that learning experiences correspond to individual developmental and intellectual phases. As a result of this focus, the concepts of experiential and discovery learning have emerged and matured.

The contribution of cognitive developmental theories to curricular thinking lies also in its focus on the importance of developing thinking and learning strategies. From this viewpoint, thinking structures receive greater emphasis than content, and structural and conceptual connections receive greater accent than isolated skill (Ausubel, 1963; Wertheimer, 1959). This conception provided the ground for designing learning situations concentrating on general organizing ideas in the form of themes, concepts, principles, or values that are believed to help students learn and develop through mapping of information and linking old and new knowledge—for example, to identify key concepts or principles in a problem or to identify and discuss issues and values implied from a scientific experiment, a story, or a journal article.

The cognitive scientific approach makes a unique contribution to curriculum planning by focusing on the cognitive structures *created* by the individual, rather than on the structures of the discipline studied (Darling-Hammond and Snyder, 1992). Cognitive theories conceive of the mind as using intellectual structures for organizing knowledge. According to this conception, learning is not affected only by how a task is presented or what information it contains or by the structure or scheme used to understand and process information. It is also affected by our search for meaning—our desire to understand the purpose of learning, to interpret new situations according to perception, and to make a conscious use of prior knowledge and learning strategies. In contrast to the conditioning and response approach at the heart of the behaviorist conception of education, constructivism forms the basis of the approaches to learning and development derived from cognitive theory. It considers learning as an internal, personal, complex, and mostly unobserved process, one in which the individual actively constructs his own world of knowledge in a personally unique and meaningful way. This conception emphasizes the importance of both personal resources and the environment supplying the learning stimuli. The learning process is therefore regarded as a complex interactive process, a dialogue between individuals and the environment and between individuals and themselves.

According to this theory, learning takes place anywhere and everywhere during an individual's lifetime. Knowledge a person constructs about the world and himself takes different shape, is changed and renewed, and develops both quantitatively and qualitatively. Schematically represented, knowledge undergoes construction and reconstruction. Although knowledge construction processes are dynamic in themselves, the schemes are stable only if they explain the world logically for the individual (Briscoe, 1996). The constructivist approach therefore supports a curriculum that enables students to organize knowledge in different and diverse ways, using learning activities that require personal interpretation and integration of knowledge. As such, the constructivist approach enhances the importance of situations or contexts in the learning process.

The second section of Table 7.1 summarizes two views of the learning process that serve as the basis for discussion on the current and the desired curricula. Thus we find accumulation versus construction, product versus process, absorption versus dialogue, uniformity versus uniqueness, diversity versus totality.

These two different views of learning represent different points of departure for the curriculum, with totally different implications for educational goals and practices.

As we have seen, the premises regarding knowledge and knowing represent two different world views regarding the nature of people. The conservative, mechanistic view conceives of people existing *within* a well-defined reality who are, therefore, a product of culture. In contrast, the organic view conceives of human thought as complex, nonlinear, and constructivist, which is especially appropriate to a dynamic environment the individual is a systems-oriented being, an active *part* of reality profoundly involved in shaping both himself or herself and the environment. This organic view looks at the individual in terms of rational, emotional, social, and intuitive systems—as playing an effective and affective role in the dynamic process of interaction within a number of referential contexts (systems). A person is also the creator of culture, not just its product.

This more novel approach to knowledge, learning, and man require educators and curriculum developers to ask questions different from those asked heretofore. Instead of asking "What is it?" and "Is it right or accurate?" we need to ask, "How can we interpret it?" "What could it be?" "How does our knowledge connect with it?" or "What does it tell me?" For example, instead of asking "What is a power?" we should rather ask, "What can power mean?" "How can we interpret the concept of power?" "Which concepts, ideas, events, values, or emotions are related to power?" The vital questions concerning man have also changed. A pair of questions: "What is a person capable of becoming?" and "What effect can a person have?" has replaced the single question currently in focus: "How can man survive in a given reality?"

ESSENCE AND STRUCTURE OF THE CONTEMPORARY AND DESIRED CURRICULUM

In positivist terms, technically speaking the curriculum is a way to organize content and educational methods. It is conceived as an instrument of society that combines administrative and pedagogical elements. It conceives of organizational structure as subordinate to a supreme need for order and control in the educational process (Hamilton, 1989). Accordingly, organizational structure is determined largely by external authorities as a means of controlling educational processes within schools. In practice, this means that preselected programs are introduced into a tight, well-defined structure that students and teachers must follow.

Figure 7.1 is a schematic presentation of the linear curricular-pedagogic model used in most schools. The model is hierarchical and reductive, and its nature is reflected in its funnel shape. The model shows the relative positions held by the teacher and the student in a closed, well-defined reality. The curriculum in this model is determined by academic experts with a unidimensional, disciplinary

Figure 7.1
The "Funnel" Model: The Linear Reductive Model

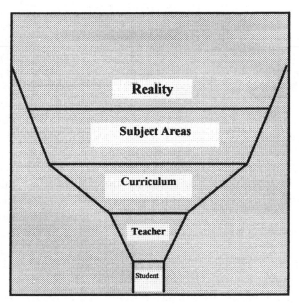

view of reality. The authority of the experts who select curriculum contents from existing knowledge domains (''material'') is transmitted to the teacher who receives the material and passes it on to the students. The process is hierarchical: expert > teacher > student; and reductive: reality > disciplines (knowledge domains) > planned curriculum materials > selected materials or programs.

The model does not allow teachers and students to make free choices based on personal interest. On the contrary, it reflects a system of control, whereby each authority dominates subordinates lower in the hierarchy. It also emphasizes the onus on the teacher and the weight of responsibility for processes that others have designed and selected. We also see the burden placed on the teacher and the student. Moreover, the narrow perspective through which they are viewed is no less serious than the narrow expectations set for them. The linear curriculum as seen from the model in Figure 7.1 is extremely simple and firmly structured, artificial, tightly bound and limited, context alienated, and detached from real life.

In contrast, the complexity view, which is based on systems, on dialectical and constructivist theories, conceptualizes the curriculum as a channel for personal and cultural development that enables teachers, students, and experts to examine the world from different and diverse points of view (Greene, 1993; Cross, 1995). Based on this conception, we should regard the curriculum not as ''a running track,'' but rather in the sense of ''running along a track,'' with emphasis on the activity of the runner who is searching for meaning and finds it through interpretation and dialogue (Doll, 1993). Such a curriculum focuses on the search for meaning, culture, and society and addresses issues and problems related to everyday life (Dewey, 1902, 1956).

A curriculum anchored in the principles of complexity theory is conceived as a dynamic and creative process in which information and knowledge are being related in various ways. It is designed "here and now," in every school and classroom, prompted by their unique qualities and needs (Levine and Nevo, 1997a). The basic premise underlying such a curriculum is freedom for teachers and students to choose what they wish to clarify, explore, develop, apply, and create (Rogers, 1973). It does not represent boundaries or means of control. Instead, it is a creative endeavor that encourages breaking through the limits of human ability and the world of knowledge.

This new conception of curriculum represents complexity theory and the integrative and systems approaches, which are the fundamentals of the science of chaos. It involves movement away from a mechanistic, linear, and, in the opinion of some, technocratic approach toward a nonlinear, system-oriented, more complex approach. This is a curricular approach that we characterize as dialogical, humanistic, and social.

The model shown in Figure 7.2 represents the curriculum based on the complexity approach to learning. It is clearly rather complex: open, flexible, dynamic, context-contingent, time-dependent, and tied to reality. Reality itself is far from an unequivocal totality; it is a dynamic system whose boundaries, like those of its components, are constantly changing. One indication of the temporary and dynamic nature of reality is represented by the "empty structures" waiting to be filled. We therefore entitled the model "Learning Space" (Levine and Nevo, 1997a). The concept of learning space expresses multidimensionality (length, breadth, depth, and time), openness, and flexibility with dynamic goals, processes, and partners who are involved in its design. According to this model, teacher and students are constituents of a reality that embraces experience, development, and change and encompasses not only their development but also the development and change of experts, knowledge, and the disciplines.

The model depicts a complex reality with related conventional knowledge domains, as well as other contextual structures such as concepts, issues, and values that cross boundaries between structures usually perceived as well-defined. For example, the model describes relationships between languages, mathematics, social studies, the sciences, art, and humanistic studies. Some of the relationships are direct and some indirect. When they are related through concepts, problems, or values they represent indirect relationships.

For example, development is a basic concept that helps understand different societies and cultures. However, it is also highly important in facilitating scientific thinking, technology, and different approaches to the arts. Moreover, the concept of development is essential in coping with ethical issues, for example, the question of whether development is always desired, good, or helpful. How are people affected by technological developments, and how do we face such

Figure 7.2
The Complex Interactions Model: A Learning Space

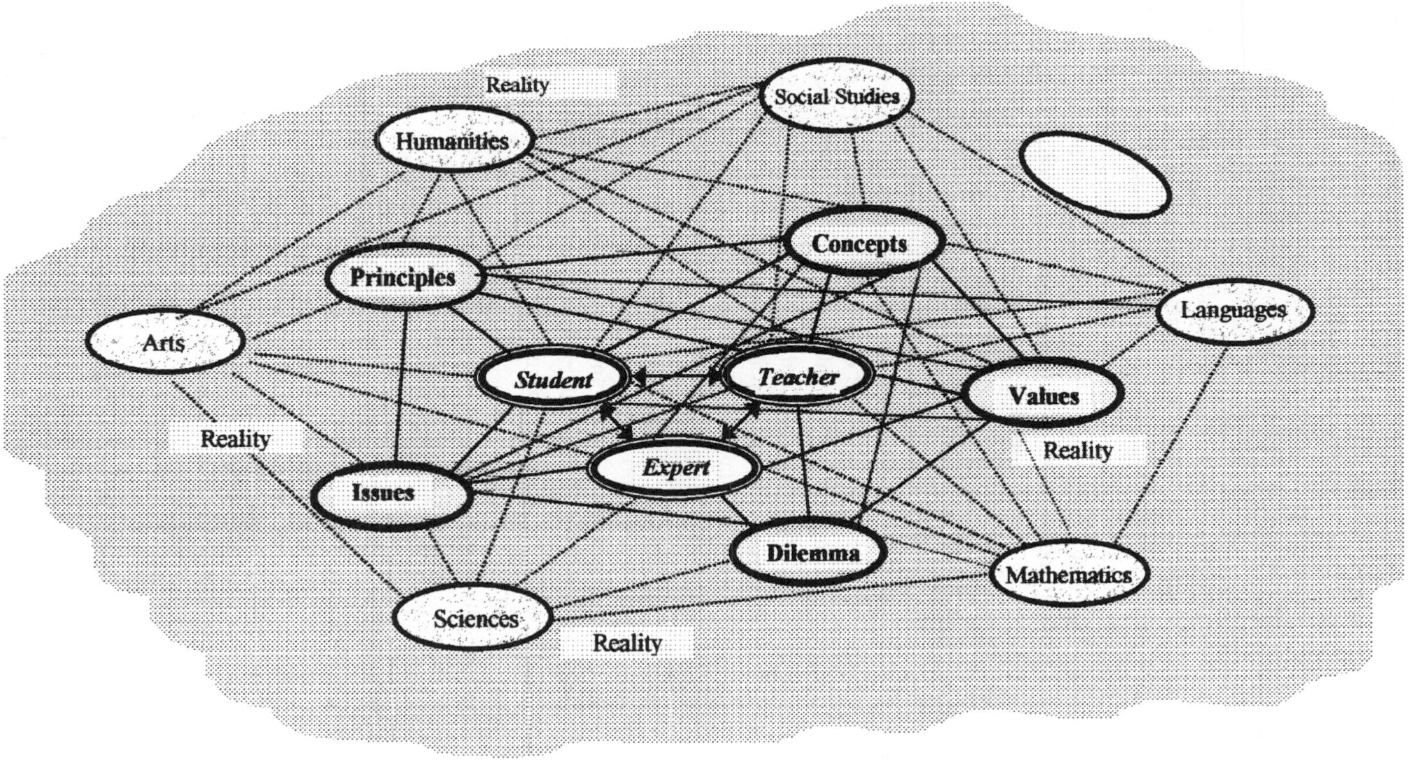

developments? Dealing with such questions in the classroom requires the use of knowledge and thinking strategies that are traditionally connected to many different disciplines or domains of knowledge.

Inside the learning space, knowledge domains serve as important social, cultural, and intellectual data bases, which are constantly changed and updated. They also serve to enrich the process of student development, cognition, and concern to help clarify issues under discussion. That is, contents in the learning space are dealt with in contexts that are relevant to the learners, teachers, experts, and issues under public discussion. Languages, mathematics, and history are tied to matters of significance. The specific contents are no more or less than a serviceable "tool box" that the culture provides for its members (teachers and students) to help them develop as human beings who are sensitive, aware of their heritage and culture, creative, and self-directed and whose aim is to understand and influence the personal and social worlds they occupy.

The learning space represents the ideas embedded in the science of chaos, this time in the field of education. It breaks the boundaries among different fields of study; it values the multiplicity and diversity that exist in our society, acknowledges the dynamic and fluid nature of knowledge, and emphasizes contextuality and the complexity of the human being. It therefore strongly supports the freedom of students, teachers, and experts to explore any question that fascinates and encourages thinking and imagination as well as emotion.

The responsibility for planning the learning space is distributed among all members of the teaching team, the students and the curriculum advisors or other experts such as scientists, artists, principals, or industrialists. All parties contribute, and all provide sources of enrichment and inspiration for one another. Because of their uniqueness, such an approach to curriculum allows the originality and authenticity that exist everywhere, and in everyone, to be expressed. Indeed, the goal of the learning space is to cultivate individuals (teachers, students, and experts) who are creative, growing, and changing, who have developed values, who examine their own environment, who are aware of different interpretations and points of view, and who influence the nature of the universal world of knowledge. Involving experts at the heart of the learning space reflects and expands their role in education. They not only contribute but also develop as the process of learning evolves.

It is apparent from the description of the two models that their differences are manifested not only in their basic structures linear versus complex (system), but also in three significant processes involved in curriculum planning: (1) *knowledge conceptualization*, (2) *knowledge organization*, and (3) *knowledge selection* (Schrag, 1992).

Conceptualizing the World of Knowledge

Knowledge conceptualization in the prevailing curriculum is based on the academic approach, one of five recognized approaches (Eisner and Vallance,

1974). According to this view, the curriculum is a tool allowing existing knowledge structures to be presented in an arrangement known as disciplines. These disciplines represent a primary curricular goal and are easily definable forms of knowledge organization (Hirst, 1972). However, this method of organizing knowledge and information is not necessarily appropriate in the classroom, and it certainly does not represent the only way of organizing concepts, ideas, skills, or content.

A hundred years ago, Dewey strongly criticized disciplinary organization on the grounds that problem solving in different areas of life does not fall into neatly organized structures representing different subject areas. He noted that disciplinary organization had taken on a mystic form, which exists, inexplicably, in schools and only in schools (Mayhew and Edwards, 1965). If knowledge is trapped within a discipline founded on a conception of linearity and hierarchical organization of knowledge, our freedom to ask and respond to questions, to create and solve problems of concern to society, will be severely limited, since most of the world's problems cannot be defined or resolved within the confines of a single knowledge domain. On the contrary, the issues we encounter in our lives are mostly interdisciplinary or multidisciplinary (Rugg and Shumaker, 1969).

Therefore, a curriculum based only on disciplines or well-defined knowledge domains reflects a monolithic approach in that (a) it offers a single conceptualization of knowledge organization sanctioned by an academic elite that fails to represent the thinking and views of other agencies or social institutions that deal with knowledge; (b) it could represent only the dominant culture, with little room for minority cultures within a given society; and (3) it fails to facilitate dialogue between representatives of different knowledge domains and between these representatives and teachers and students.

In contrast to the monopolistic or exclusive disciplinary view of knowledge are the integrative approaches. Here, knowledge domains are studied in their cultural contexts, and content is defined on the basis of general topics (themes), problems, issues, values, and interests of those involved in the learning process (teachers, students, and experts). The integrative approaches have an up-to-date conception of knowledge, even though the knowledge structures in a given domain cannot represent the most updated changes in the world of knowledge. Since information undergoes constant change and regeneration, it cannot be absolute, but transient, nonobjective, and contextual, with knowledge domains diverging and joining in a dynamic process. Therefore, exclusive reliance on knowledge domains or disciplines is contrived and limiting (Levine and Nevo, 1997a).

Supporters of integrative approaches see them as pedagogically effective in both qualitative and quantitative terms. In exposing the learner to comprehensive situations in all their complexity, they treat the learner as a whole, taking into account the complexity of his or her nature within a pluralistic environment and society. These approaches are contextual, relevant, and responsive to the constant flow of information and to the individual's learning processes within the academic or home environment. That is, integrative approaches provide an opportunity for a less fragmented and a more relevant and stimulating experience for learners. It helps students foster a range of perspectives that would help them in the real world. No wonder therefore that integrative approaches are considered responsive to educational goals in the knowledge era by helping shape ideas regarding "what is important to learn" by implementing constructivist, holistic, and authentic learning processes.

Among the integrative models proposed for knowledge conceptualization the most noteworthy are the multidisciplinary model, the interdisciplinary model, and the transdisciplinary model (Jacobs, 1989; Fogarty, 1991; Petrie, 1992; Drake, 1993). These three models are sensitive to the learner's developmental needs and represent a different level of commitment toward knowledge domains or disciplines and toward the degree of freedom in curriculum planning.

The multidisciplinary model views the world through the lens of a discipline that includes content from other disciplines, in order to increase relevance. It asks, "What is important to learn within different disciplines?" It is therefore considered firmly discipline-oriented. Throughout the process of addressing an issue or topic, each discipline maintains its uniqueness and explains the issue from its own point of view. The discreteness of the procedures of the discipline is kept intact by a teacher who approaches the task from his or her own specialization. The effect of a multidisciplinary approach is therefore additive rather than integrative.

The interdisciplinary model starts off discipline-bound, but it seeks to break through the fences that separate knowledge domains by focusing on what is shared and relevant in any given issue, mostly thinking skills and strategies. That is, here the content and procedures of individual disciplines are transcended.

The transdisciplinary model offers the greatest degree of freedom in terms of dynamic, flexible, interactive planning since it is based on information and knowledge relevant to real life and the creation of unique social, cultural, and intellectual contexts at any time or place and in any classroom, for any teacher or student (Drake, 1993). The question in the transdisciplinary mode of integration shifts to, How we can prepare students to be creative and productive human beings? Disciplines are transcended, and the emphasis is on meaning and relevance through a life-centered approach. Specific discipline-based contents are not considered intrinsically important but rather dependent on the themes, concepts, problems, or values selected for learning. Integration in the transdisciplinary approach is therefore almost limitless.

For example, multidisciplinary integration can be easily implemented in the classroom because it requires relatively slight adjustments to the existing curriculum. It can be designed to allow teachers to sequence their lessons to correspond to lessons of the same topic or issue in other disciplines. Thus, if the concept "system" is considered meaningful to different subject areas or disciplines, it can be taught from a multidisciplinary perspective by teaching biological, social, ecological, economical, or physical systems in each subject class separately. In each subject area or classroom the unique attributes of the specific system would be emphasized and the relationships between the different systems can be discussed. In a biology class, students would learn about the blood system and the reproductive system and would most likely compare and contrast these two systems while exploring possible relationships between them. In a physics class, students could learn whether, why, and how the sun as a system is affected by the galaxy, which itself is affected by its neighbors. They could also study the relationships between the earth and the moon and its effects on the tides.

Interdisciplinary integration, however, shifts from an emphasis on applying themes to subject areas to focusing on conceptual commonalities across disciplines (Drake, 1993). Thus, for example, the use of the concept "system" in an interdisciplinary curriculum mode would imply dealing thoroughly with the concept itself while discussing other related concepts or phenomena such as feedback, subsystem, mutual relationships, equilibrium, and systems boundaries. Different kinds of systems, mentioned earlier, would be used only as means to understand the more basic concepts, principles, or thinking skills.

In the interdisciplinary mode of integration, the emphasis is on the similarities between the exemplary systems and on the possible links between them. For example, one could explore the possible effects of magnetic activity on the sun (viewed as a system) on the behavior of human beings (a social system) or examine the effects of a solar eclipse on life on earth or on the relationships between changes in climate and systems of life, with an emphasis on the evolution of these relationships from the past through the present and on into the future.

In a transdisciplinary context, however, any example is more tentative and speculative. The concept of system would be selected for the curriculum only if it were found important and meaningful to enhance relevant issues for students and teachers and only if it would have the potential to serve as a means to trigger ideas, principles, values, and insights of significance to life. The concept itself would be explored by using related concepts, problems, and dilemmas suggested by the students and the teacher, not necessarily in any link to a discipline or a traditionally accepted knowledge domain.

In our example of the concept "system," it is most likely that concepts like stability, complexity, and dependency could emerge and be explored. It is also possible that curriculum activities that could emerge would relate to the stability of a system—its advantages and disadvantages, the implications of systems flexibility, the distinction between a system and a structure—or elaborate on conditions that assist or interfere with a system development. In the transdisciplinary curriculum the emphasis is thus on meaning and relevance through a life-centered approach. Its origin is in no way discipline-based but rather context-related or context-based. It is reasonable, however, that discipline-based knowledge would serve as a data base for both students and teachers in studying specific issues and problems related to the concept.

Knowledge Organization

In the contemporary curriculum, knowledge organization is conceptualized as an organization of information in the sense of knowledge packaged in a closed, predefined structure ready to be transferred to the student in a structured, linear fashion: from concrete to abstract, from the simple to the complex, or on the basis of chronological sequence of a phenomenon's events. These sequences are defined by the knowledge structures pertaining to a particular discipline or, to be more precise, on the basis of how disciplinary experts perceive the appropriate sequencing. The underlying principle for this type of organization is the dissection of a complex topic into smaller, simpler units, which are then taught in sequence. Linear, predetermined disciplinary organization is therefore based on analyzing knowledge to its logical components. The logic used does not necessarily suit the needs of every student, nor does it reflect the order or direction that occurs in knowledge development (Wiggins, 1995). Such an approach to curriculum organization results in planning and implementing simplistic, shallow, and repetitive curricula (Olson, 1994; Jakwerth, 1996), or as Schmidt and colleagues (1996) put it, a curriculum that is "a mile long and an inch deep."

Indeed, considerable criticism of this approach to knowledge organization has been offered by the contemporary curriculum. The criticism of knowledge organization can be summarized by paraphrasing the words of Sizer (1984), "more means less." Emphasis on coverage and on breadth rather than depth resulted in fostering superficiality and encouraged the use of curricular activities that require attention to specific contents rather than to cognition or metacognition. It also entails activities that weary students rather than challenge them, by asking them, for example, to perform exercises and memorization tasks lacking relevance to their learning. Neither the activities or the standards they set provide a challenge for students. Westbury (1992) believes that such an approach to knowledge and curriculum organization is a major cause of school failure.

Traditional pedagogical beliefs are also partially responsible for the preplanned and highly sequential characteristics of knowledge organization in contemporary curriculum. For example, the commonly held belief that elementary school children think "concretely" and that they are not yet sufficiently developed to engage in abstract and complex cognition motivated educators and curriculum developers to base elementary school curriculum primarily on linear progression and demonstration. Considering these limitations, learning sequences should be well-planned and designed to progress from the specific to the general, from the concrete to the abstract, from what is considered familiar and "close" to the student's world to the unfamiliar. This widely accepted view has been severely criticized by a number of researchers and theoreticians, who regard learning and complex cognitive processes as essential elements in the development of young students (Doll, 1993; Case, 1993; Papert, 1980; Gardner, 1995; Levine and Nevo, 1997b).

The professional literature on the integrative curriculum suggests different models for organizing knowledge. Brady's (1995) idea of knowledge organization, for example, is based on a view of reality as "supradisciplinary," involving five factors: time, environment, action, actors, and motives. According to Brady, these five areas and their relationships form an integrated conceptual structure that encompasses and organizes all of reality, not only all that lies within the boundaries of the disciplines. The model makes it clear that specific instructional content is merely a means to the larger end of building conceptual structures and also ensures that the curriculum constantly evolves. Brady believes that the exploration of the relationships among these five components provides students with a powerful intellectual tool that alters in fundamental ways the nature and thrust of schooling and would ultimately expand human cognitive capabilities.

Boyer (1995) proposes a different approach to knowledge organization, which he labels "the core commonalities" of the world of information. By core commonalities he means universal experiences shared by all cultures on the planet. This idea suggests that the common core of human experience is defined by eight categories: life cycle, language, the arts, time and space, groups and institutions, work, the natural world, and the search for meaning. Drake (1996), a supporter of the transdisciplinary curriculum, presents yet another framework. She proposes a two-dimensional framework for knowledge organization, which she calls the story model of education. One dimension refers to three different levels of experience that characterize one's life: the self, society, and the world. The second dimension refers to time: past, present, and future. In contrast to Boyer's framework, Drake does not suggest a list of knowledge domains considered important for learning, but rather suggests the use of concepts and principles that stem from students' interests and prior knowledge. The student is therefore challenged by specific concepts linked to the three sociocultural spheres with reference to time frames.

Such a conceptual framework enhances meaningful learning of worthwhile and significant issues, viewing them from both personal and cultural perspectives and relating them to change and development over time. Therefore, when using concepts and students' ideas, one can learn much about a variety of life domains such as politics, law, social issues, history, business, media, technology, and science including science fiction.

A different approach to knowledge organization, not restricted to disciplinary organization, naturally leads to a different approach to curriculum development. In today's disciplinary and stable curriculum, its development is associated with carefully controlled planning procedure. The assumption is that it is possible to predict and plan scenarios and thereby incorporate order, stability, content, and meaning into the curriculum. This conception of planning is a further expression of the present curriculum's unequivocal linear orientation. However, "planning" in the sense of establishing an absolute and compulsory order is actually antagonistic to dynamism, that is, it is anti-change, it overlooks updated and actual events and opportunities, and it acts to discourage spontaneity and wonder.

Curriculum planning in the context of complexity theory means an open, flexible, and tentative path, which can branch out in new and unexpected directions. Here, knowledge and information organization will naturally give rise to development, growth, and dynamic flow. It is not organized around content-oriented frameworks or discipline-based ideas or principles, but rather on fundamentals, often called organizing ideas, that provide opportunities to break through the boundaries of thinking to diverse contexts. These might be concepts, themes, dilemmas, problems, or values that are not required to be disciplinary, or even drawn from a single discipline. The organizing ideas are actually rooted in the reality of life itself.

This is an additional manifestation of the nonlinear or the complexity approach to knowledge organization. Such an approach reflects the idea of a system's state of disequilibrium, its capability to spontaneously and contextually adjust and restructure itself, and the fact that one cannot predict phenomena with absolute certainty. Knowledge organization is therefore an open, flexible, and emergent process that adapts to changing situations or contexts. It is likely to be autonomous, creative, and unique to a specific school or class.

A conception of knowledge organization open to diverse points of view fits the idea of mindfulness (Langer, 1993), which emphasizes the importance of observing the environment through more than one perspective and of creating new categories of knowledge. Spiro (Spiro et al., 1991) suggests that ability to present information in different conceptual frameworks is one of the characteristics of cognitive flexibility. According to Gardner (1995), almost all information can be dealt with in different ways and in different contexts. Therefore organization that affords multidirectional exposure to concepts, principles, and methods will assist all partners in the process—students, teachers, and educational experts—to develop new understanding and reflective capabilities about their own cognition and that of others.

Knowledge Selection

With the contemporary curriculum, the process of knowledge selection and organization rests in the hands of authorities outside the school. These are scholars involved in different knowledge domains, psychologists and educators concerned with applying pedagogical principles, and selected teachers representing the practical aspects of teaching. Even sources of knowledge and information are controlled, whether by scholars, teachers, books, or specially produced materials (worksheets, for example). The curriculum is thus supported by a linear-hierarchical organizational structure, ultimately controlled by the classroom teacher.

Selection of knowledge involves filtering the content, principles, and skills considered important for each of the disciplines. Selection takes place prior to implementing the curriculum and sharply defines the boundaries of and information in terms of what is preferred and/or considered possible to be learned. The selection process usually reflects an approach favoring compartmentalization of knowledge according to unambiguous identification of knowledge domains or disciplines. In the selection process, differentiation is made between knowledge and cognition, placing great emphasis on facts and memorization and less on thinking. Moreover, if cognition is taken into account, the emphasis is almost exclusively on logical and rational thinking.

Westbury (1992) labels such selective knowledge selection as "inappropriate coverage." He proposes that schools have failed to achieve their goals, not only because they fail in their conceptualization of knowledge but also because of a mindless choice of knowledge and information. He believes that the common school curriculum does not contain up-to-date, universally important knowledge. Apple (1995) too criticizes prevailing selection processes, suggesting that preoccupation with procedural models concerned with linear algorithms has diverted focus from such questions as "What should be learned and why?" In this sense, prevailing knowledge selection processes have failed to justify the knowledge chosen for the curriculum. As a consequence, political and scientific pressure groups have influenced the selection of monocultural knowledge and monodimensional literacy. Thus for example, the curriculum does not usually relate to social factors such as life conditions for different ethnic groups and groups with different religious beliefs. Also, in selecting knowledge within the current curriculum, not enough emphasis is given to the psychological needs of individuals and groups, such as attitudes, relationships, dependency, identity, and self-confidence (Stedman, 1997), despite the fact that these elements are meaningful to our lives.

Obviously therefore, an approach to curriculum development that amalgamates knowledge selected from different life domains and seeks to adapt to changing needs will not be institutional, well structured, or finalized without the involvement of experts, teachers, and students. It will not comprise contents detached from life outside school, or artificial material estranged from the real world. This approach ties in with Cremin's ecological approach (1976), according to which the school is one among many educational agencies. Therefore, selecting knowledge associated with problems, issues, data, and examples should be connected to a range of educational situations expressed in different educational institutions.

Although it is important for knowledge selection and organization to take place in the school, it is mostly one-time planning, appropriate to the "here and now," to specific teachers, students, and experts in specific life circumstances. Planning should therefore be initiated by school teams, with consideration given to changing needs identified by the school and its community. They must construct and develop the curriculum, design the learning environment, and plan classroom activities, materials, and instruments. The outcomes of choice cannot be known in advance. Such curriculum planning demands openness and courage on the teachers' part, coupled with a high degree of flexibility and the ability to manage ongoing dialogue with students and with experts whose knowledge, attitudes, and ideas will serve as the building blocks of the evolving curriculum in the classroom.

It is especially important to emphasize that this approach to curriculum involves students in knowledge selection and curriculum planning no less than the teachers and experts. According to Kohn (1993), although we have made it possible nowadays to choose which school to go to, not enough is being done to allow students to exercise choice within the classroom, even though we believe that individuals should be partners in deciding what happens in their lives. Involving students in the choice of learning goals and educational processes is not only functional but also an indication of respect for their current needs. It also reflects a dual view of the school as an organization seeking both to nurture the intellect and to facilitate the growth of a personality that is responsible, considerate, and capable of decision making and problem solving. According to Apple (1995), all too often, the contemporary curriculum relates to the student as an "input" within a broader formula. We should be alert to the function of the curriculum as a channel for individual development (Kliebard, 1986) of both teachers and students because without the personal aspect, the significance of the curriculum is lost.

Table 7.2 is a summary of current curriculum attributes versus those of the desired curriculum. It outlines the following critical factors: goal, structure, planning process, knowledge organization, methods, evaluation, and sources of learning.

The contemporary linear curriculum, with its foundations in the mechanistic approach, allows no space for the teacher or student to grow and develop freely. It seeks to preserve the existing control of schools by central authorities. It is represented as a definite product reflecting a uniform, stable, and distinct worldview. It fails to provide students or teachers the freedom to think and create. It represents a worldview lacking respect for a person's uniqueness and potential to create and influence. Such a conception of curriculum also represents a fragmented approach to the person, reflected in its clearcut separation between learning goals related to the mind and those involving "emotion," faith, and attitude. The linear curriculum reflects an approach that sees the unexpected, the unknown, or the different as some sort of mistake requiring adjustment. It is monolithic, in terms of content selection, form of organization, and classroom implementation.

On the other hand, a curriculum founded on a complex worldview represents a partially planned and tentative process, which develops in unexpected directions as the process of learning evolves (Doll, 1993). Its emphasis is on authentic learning processes, supported by contextual thinking, openness, and creativity

Table 7.2
Descriptions of Current and Desired Curricula

	Current Curriculum	Desired Curriculum
Essence	Organizational and standardized pedagogical structure; external control of authority.	A dynamic emergent process, unique, time and place dependent.
Goals	Mastery of discipline-based knowledge and skills.	Dynamic learning and development processes. Higher-order thinking skills and creativity.
	Unidimensional literacy.	Multidimensional literacy.
	Transmission of accepted values.	A wide range of universal values.
	Well-defined expectations.	A variety of outcomes and emphasis on processes.
	Standardized and well-defined outcomes.	Appreciation of variability and uniqueness.
Structure	Well-defined instructional units. Emphasis on specific contents.	Motivating conceptual frameworks: concepts, ideas, values, problems, etc.
	Discipline-based contents. Basic skills.	Themes and processes. Personal and collective knowledge.
	Non-authentic/artificial instructional and learning materials.	A variety of knowledge resources/ authentic sources and activities.
Planning Process	External: directed and controlled by experts.	Internal: a multilateral dialogue between learning partners.
	Pre-planning of all details.	Evolving and context-based.
	The process consists of: design, experimentation, correction, and well-defined product.	An evolving process which develops in spontaneous and unexpected ways. One-time and unique use.
Organization	A linear process: simple to complex, concrete to abstract, chronological sequencing.	Unexpected: depends on specific circumstances, contexts, and classroom situations, and students' knowledge and interests.
	Compartmentalized by knowledge domains.	Integrative.
	Repetitive.	Dynamic and creative.
Methods	Hierarchical and authoritative.	Interactive and dialogical; supports knowledge construction.
	Quantitative emphasis.	Emphasis on quality.
	Verbal emphasis.	Multimedia and multimodal.
	Direct instruction and standardized implementation.	Cooperative learning and creative instruction.

Table 7.2 (*continued*)

	Current Curriculum	Desired Curriculum
	Absolute/fixed instruction.	Context dependent.
Materials	Well-elaborated and specific.	Original, based on personal and collective knowledge.
	Artificial, nonauthentic.	Selection of materials is a component in the design.
Evaluation	Specific activities, differentiating evaluation from learning.	A natural process of learning and instruction.
	A teacher evaluates students.	Teacher and students are partners in evaluation.
	Unequivocal and standardized criteria.	Multiple and context-dependent criteria.
	Judgmental; relative and absolute.	Searching to understand complexities and development.
	Evaluating pre-planned outcomes.	Spontaneous and contextual evaluation depends on the process.

(Brown et al., 1989; Resnick, 1987; Papert, 1980). It fulfills the requirements of mindful learning, which deals with contextual, situation-dependent knowledge that can be interpreted from different points of view (Langer, 1993; De Bono, 1990). It acknowledges personal, cultural, and social divergence and provides an impetus for learning enrichment (Gardner, 1995). It is integrative, dynamic, and interactive (Levine and Nevo, 1997a). In this connection, Briscoe (1996) sees the teacher as a learner who constructs a personal curriculum, choosing resources and deciding on their use as a vehicle for personal learning. According to this view, the student and the teacher are partners in designing the curriculum, selecting and organizing knowledge, planning their learning, and thinking reflectively about it. Such an approach to curriculum is more like a personal and social voyage as reflected by Schubert's (1986) note, that ''you should live your life as if it were a curriculum for others.''

CHARACTERISTICS AND EVALUATION OF LINEAR AND NONLINEAR CURRICULUM

The transition from the linear, stable and discipline-based curriculum to a system-oriented, contextual, and dynamic one is not at all simple. Such a transition from the old to the new means abandoning long-held beliefs, attitudes, expectations, habits, and terminology while learning to cope with completely new assumptions, attitudes, expectations, thought processes, and modes of action. Moreover, the very attributes that shaped curricular development and evaluation become irrelevant or take on new meaning. Descriptions of these attributes in terms of the different curricular approaches are shown in Table 7.3. The focus is on ten characteristics pertaining to the contemporary and the future curriculum. Some characteristics represent dimensions used to evaluate the linear curriculum; others are drawn from significant, unique ways of evaluating the nonlinear curriculum, or "learning space," as it is labeled here.

For example, for many years the curriculum was assessed in terms of its level of coherence. This practice arose from the assumption that the curriculum is not an arbitrary collection of contents or knowledge but rather an organized body of knowledge connected in a way that creates a unity or completeness that can be characterized and evaluated. The questions usually asked with regard to co-herence are "Does the sequence of objectives and activities form a structure that reflects the structure of the discipline or knowledge domain?" "Is there a relationship between different subject areas?" "Are prerequisites for one do-main learned in other domains 'covered' by the curriculum, or must they be acquired separately?" "Are new programs and information integrated into the existing curriculum, and if so, how is this achieved?" In other words, checking for coherence means reliance on an "external," "objective" framework dictated by the discipline or knowledge domain.

Thus, evaluating curriculum coherence is mostly based on teachers and expert opinion, it can be carried out prior to introducing the curriculum into the school system, and it can be done once in several years. Beane (1995), however, notes that in every school today the curriculum appears as a disconnected collection of elements. The lack of coherence results from the fact that the world outside the school, with all its experience, has no bearing on the emphases found in the school curriculum. The meaning of coherence thus changes when we discuss the dynamic, system-oriented and context-related curriculum.

The fact that the curriculum is defined as an emerging process and not as a *final product* means that the level of coherence cannot be assessed prior to learning. On the contrary, because coherence becomes contextual, it is shaped and constructed during the learning process and involves an examination and clarification of meaningful contexts. Coherence is thus *being constantly examined* and can only be judged in retrospect.

Moreover, coherence is not assessed in the light of an external framework, such as a subject area or knowledge domain, but in the light of the relationship between the world outside the school and the students' and teachers' internal worlds. It is a relationship, in the sense of both connection and meaning, on the part of the individual (internal) and reality (external). It is important to note that a curriculum replete with attractive, challenging activities that fail to reflect any personal connection to students and teachers would be regarded as lacking a high level of coherence. Integration of content, concepts, or activities across knowledge domains will also not necessarily lead to a high degree of coherence. Coherence would be achieved if we succeed in establishing connections between what is meaningful to students and their teachers and real-life phenomena and events.

Table 7.3
Curriculum Attributes and Means for Evaluation

	Contemporary Curriculum	**Desired Curriculum**
Coherence	Artificial, external framework, discipline-based.	Organic, a meaningful organizing anchor enhancing thinking and creativity.
	Relationships among different disciplines.	Coherence between internal and external worlds produced spontaneously through contexts.
	One-time appraisal prior to introduction.	Emerging and being appraised at every moment and retrospectively.
Validity	Assessed on basis of "scientific" reliability and accuracy.	Assessed using skeptical scientific approach.
	Academic-logical in nature.	Validity based on intellectual, social, cultural, academic, and justified personal perceptions.
	External requirement of fairness toward different groups.	Fairness is a crucial aspect of pluralism.
	Formal pedagogical considerations: appropriate/ inappropriate.	Unique pedagogical considerations: significance, interest, productivity (richness).
Relevance	Means of demonstrating and stimulating interest. Scientific-academic updating.	Significant point of departure and critical condition: source of generating meaning for man and society and for broadening interest domains.
Authenticity	Episodic (authentic tasks). Loyalty to external sources.	Significant resource: important source for ongoing curricular development.
Flexibility	Choosing from existing repertoire while focusing on well-defined sequences.	Maximal freedom and minimal (only when essential) compulsion.
	Predetermined structure, congruence with external objectives.	Dynamic, unpredictable.
	Guided by outside authority.	Autonomy.
	Unequivocal outcomes (predetermined criteria).	Unique outcomes (using contextual criteria).
Clarity	Absolute, certain, unequivocal, concrete, unidimensional, simple, external.	Evolving, complex, loosely defined, internal dynamism on a clear-fuzzy scale.
Creativity	Provides diversity, entertainment, "decorative" assignments.	Vital element in the evolving curriculum.

Table 7.3 (*continued*)

	Contemporary Curriculum	Desired Curriculum
Congruence between Planning and Implementation	Material coverage, perfect performance.	Evolving, flexible, and unique planning. Continuous interaction between teachers, students, and experts, due to a constructivist philosophy of knowledge, learning, and development.
Potential for Renewal	Limited due to closed and linear structure. Easier to repeat than to renew.	High potential owing to recursive processes. Curriculum evolves based on needs defined "here and now."
Measures of Success	Student attainment of skills, contents, and attitudes.	Teacher and student development: knowledge construction, intellectual development, inner satisfaction, ability to tolerate ambiguity, cognitive and metacognitive development.
	Congruence with goals.	Links school to real world/life.

Curricular *coherence* is related to curricular *relevance*. The important questions here are: "To what degree is the curriculum relevant to students and teachers?" "Why is it important for me teach or learn this?" For a dynamic curriculum based on a dynamic contextual, system-oriented conception, relevance is the point of departure and critical requirement; it is the basis for its planning process and structure. Relevance in the contemporary curriculum is sporadic and to a great extent artificial, occurring chiefly in "special" activities, most of which aim to provide information in an effort to raise interest levels. For example, we may explore how a certain curricular topic is linked to famous people or elaborate on the relationship between a given topic and an important scientific development. Such types of relevance are mainly academic-scientific in character. They respond to a need to explain how the constituents of a knowledge domain relate to real life, a kind of desire to animate and legitimize a subject. In contrast, the contextual, learning-space curriculum seeks answers to the question, "How do I/we/others view and understand important matters that have a bearing on our lives?"

The concept of *validity* too has completely different meanings when applied to the two different curricula. For the contemporary curriculum, assessment of content authenticity is based on adherence to standards of accuracy and obedience to recognized scientific norms. Validity in the contemporary curriculum is therefore academic and logical in character. In contrast, the dominant approach in the curriculum proposed here is one of healthy skepticism. The questions asked are more in the vein of "Is this feasible?" or "Under what conditions will X be feasible?" rather than "Has X been proved?" Reliance on academic findings embraces the gamut of social, intellectual, cultural, and personal perceptions, all of which are legitimate if convincingly justified.

The notion of validity differs in the pedagogical sense as well. When dealing with the contemporary curriculum, we assess the degree to which content, activities, and skills are compatible with formal pedagogical considerations, such as the "age appropriate" or "group appropriate" nature of the topic. With the system-oriented curriculum, however, the main considerations are how interesting is the subject, concept, or dilemma and how meaningful is it for students, teachers, and experts? Examining the appropriateness of the contents to the students reflects an authentic and dynamic process.

The dynamic systems orientation to curriculum is also characterized by authenticity and originality, in that teachers and students select issues, problems, and topics that are meaningful to them. Authenticity is thus an important resource representing the backbone of curriculum development. On the other hand, in a linear curriculum context, even when it includes some authentic tasks such as "Write a paper about a subject which interests you," there is usually a compulsory element. Such limitations often serve to obscure the meaning of authenticity. Task dimensions designed to cultivate creativity are also present in the contemporary curriculum. However, these are typically defined as optional and are usually few in number. On the other hand, within the dynamic, system-oriented curriculum, creativity is regarded as a primary consequential factor in shaping the curriculum, in terms of both the individual and the entire class or group. It is the very point of departure, and its cultivation is the prime objective.

Flexibility is the core attribute of the system-oriented, constructivist curriculum. It is an organic part of a process founded on continuous interactions among teachers, students, and experts. Flexibility is reflected in individual and group selection of useful topics and contents, the freedom to affect the learning process in different directions (in the sense of various contexts), and in acknowledging the importance of diverse and unique learning outcomes. In the linear curriculum, however, flexibility is conspicuous by its absence. It is indeed difficult to introduce flexibility into well-planned procedures determined by external authorities. It is even harder to introduce flexibility into learning and teaching procedures designed as well-defined sequences and reinforced by content coverage. When contemporary curriculum provides choice, it is typically very limited; therefore, when some flexibility exists in the contemporary linear curriculum, it is most apparent in the liberty to choose enrichment activities.

For many years, *clarity* has been a primary criterion used to evaluate curriculum content (goals, material, activities, teaching manual, etc.). Questions pertaining to the clarity of curricular elements are "Is the task clear to the student?" "Is it unambiguously phrased or simply designed? Can it be solved?" or "Has the student's task been clearly defined?" "Does the problem provide enough data for the student to be able to answer?" Such questions indicate a view of knowledge as unequivocal, unambiguous, complete, and simple. In contrast, the proposed approach to curricular thinking is concerned with tasks whose design leaves boundaries open, that is, they leave room for individual interpretation and promote novel thought processes and contexts. Such tasks call for research and in-depth inquiry to search for information, organize it, and elaborate on it. Rather than ask for confirmation of the "known," these tasks set thought-provoking questions that engender creativity. They deliberately leave boundaries undefined, thus allowing diverse possible "answers." They possess an inner dynamism, which means they can be uniquely "designed" and continue to evolve during learning (Y. Sharan and S. Sharan, 1992 Levine and Nevo, 1997b).

In a changing and complex reality, the *potential for curriculum renewal* is vital to our appreciation of the curriculum as a dynamic and constructivist process. It is an evaluation index often used for assessment of computerized courseware (Levine, 1994). As expected of a closed, linear curricular structure, it has little potential for renewal. The rigid and hierarchical sequences of learning and instruction and the well-defined prerequisite knowledge structure impede any attempt to easily update the curriculum in any meaningful way. However, the constructivist curriculum that emerges anew in response to specific circumstances of students and teachers in the classroom has by definition a high potential for renewal (Ben-Peretz, 1975).

It is not at all surprising that the criterion of congruence between curriculum planning and implementation, the notion of fidelity, is fundamentally different in the two curricular approaches. The conservative curriculum typically looks for precise implementation in the sense of accuracy, coverage, and outcomes. This is an unambiguous and clear criterion of congruency. In contrast, the dynamic, constructivist curriculum interprets congruence between planning and implementation in terms of the quality of the *process of construction*: its degree of uniqueness, the depth of ideas, the cognitive and emotional flexibility indicated, and the degree to which the process enhances learning and development of students and teachers. Inevitably, therefore, success will be measured differently by these curricula. If today success is measured in terms of defined and measurable attainment (skills, knowledge, and content), then ability to link school to real life is the dominant measure of the constructive, contextual curriculum. Success, in terms of growth and learning of teachers and students, is assessed in terms of developing the level of awareness and understanding about the self, society, and culture.

DEVELOPING A LEARNING SPACE

When planning a curriculum as a learning space, it is up to each school to establish how teachers and the student population perceive education. This process will involve the entire teaching team, teachers of different grade levels as well as teachers of different subject areas. Teachers must deliberate together, which inevitably involves interaction between representatives of different worlds that have points of intersection as well as ambiguous boundaries. This is the first phase of planning a learning space. It is therefore important that the initial design utilize selected frameworks similar to those proposed by Boyer, Drake, and Brady, as discussed earlier, or construct a unique conceptual framework that ultimately can be represented in a diagram like that shown in Figure 7.2 (the learning space). This is how the curriculum-mapping specific to a school begins. This approach replaces the process of formulating general objectives that so many schools still use today.

At this planning stage, decisions are made concerning disciplinary knowledge domains to be learned and the domains or contents to be addressed via inter-disciplinary or transdisciplinary approaches. At the same time, decisions are made concerning values in need of clarification, themes requiring investigation, issues and problems for exploration and consideration, and abilities and skills in need of cultivation. At this point, teachers deal with knowledge conceptual-ization and with an initial selection of knowledge. For example, a teaching team may decide to deal with mathematics and foreign languages via a disciplinary approach, while culture, relationships, time, and power will serve as the under-lying concepts for a transdisciplinary curriculum. The school may make other decisions and select mainly important issues, such as the influence of beliefs on individuals and society in different cultures, technological development and its effect on the quality of human existence, and the meaning of research and its ethical and moral implications.

At this stage, options for organizing a nonlinear curriculum should consider forming multiple-grade-level groups. The premise is that when students' inter-ests, problems, dilemmas, values, or disciplinary-based issues form the basis for the curriculum, no strong justification exists for keeping the traditional study groups limited to a single age.

The design of the learning space infrastructure is an ongoing process, chal-lenging and fascinating. Ideas and issues are assessed on the basis of values, content and pedagogical considerations that each teacher contributes as an in-dividual playing the role of both a professional teacher and a learner. At this point it is important to bring in an assortment of disciplinary experts, curriculum advisors, and relevant professionals. The school engages in identifying re-sources, sources, and venues to provide relevant learning environments both within and outside school. Thus, for example, it is important to investigate re-search institutes, industry, museums, and other venues that the teachers and students can use as sites for learning. Alternative sources of information should be identified and contact be established with experts whose involvement will extend beyond the planning stage. It is important for the teaching team also to develop data bases of alternative, multifaceted, and multimodal learning activ-ities, based on a broad range of methods, means, materials, and tools.

Having established the learning space infrastructure and a comprehensive range of activities, the development process is ready for the individual teacher and students to begin the learning at the classroom level. The learning space must remain open ended and only tentatively planned if it is to be meaningful, relevant, and replete with opportunities for authentic learning. While some activities will prove satisfactory in achieving their goals, inadequate ones may be modified or discarded. As new activities arise, new ideas for additional activities will ensue. Thus a dynamic learning space develops from activity to activity and idea to idea, where the teacher perceives the broader picture without being able to predict how the learning space will develop or what surprises and experiences wait along the path of discovery.

When working with a *process-oriented* curriculum the teacher should be open, flexible, sensitive, and resourceful. Ideas and materials introduced by students, colleagues, and experts are integrated into the learning space to enrich the dynamic process that unfolds. We are discussing a process that places great emphasis on students' existing knowledge and their interest domains, on critical and creative thinking, on alternative interpretations of issues seen from different angles, and on the cultivation of values, reflective processes, and self-awareness. The developmental process of the learning space at the classroom level is open and dynamic and refers to many information sources and ways of knowledge presentation. It encourages experimentation with and creative use of many channels for expression and communication. Dialogue-oriented learning occurs in large and small groups and through personal research projects.

From experience gained in operating the constructivist transdisciplinary curriculum for some years, we find that a learning space formed by using concepts (e.g., concepts of boundary, of relations, or of power) contains contents drawn from many knowledge domains. Some of these are part of the regular curriculum materials, but some were drawn or developed from less conventional contexts that are highly contemporary or were previously considered "inappropriate due to its difficulty level." A coherent link between the contents was formed, as they were the means that allowed teachers and students to deal with meaningful questions, dilemmas, or important ideas. The transdisciplinary approach provided a rich and fruitful basis for developing students' high-level thinking skills and learning strategies and enhanced meaningful learning experiences while exploring issues related to values of interest to individuals and to their environment.

For example, by cultivating a learning space using the concept of boundary (Levine and Nevo, 1997b), students addressed issues concerned with breaking the boundaries of knowledge, distinguishing between physical and abstract boundaries, examining equitable relational systems, investigating the implications of technological inventions, and creating alternative solutions to conflicts. During their learning, many more concepts and issues were discussed, such as the concepts of equality, difference, racism, nationalism, friendship, tolerance, concession, exploitation, flexibility, time, universe, and love. Students and teachers operated at the concrete and the abstract, looked at the self and at others, minority and majority groups, their own country and other countries, the past and the present.

Schools that implemented the proposed curricular approach show the learning space to be open and flexible, allowing the incorporation of changes and additions on the basis of the varied suggestions and initiatives provided by students. As learning takes place, a large amount of content knowledge is acquired that had not been resolved in advance or defined as a primary objective. The vehicles for expression used by students were open ended and varied and included drawing, free writing, concept mapping, formulating sayings, role playing, model construction, and working with texts. Different types of texts from different sources were used and included current events, texts written by students, and scientific texts.

To sum up, the learning space discussed in this chapter represents a very different view of the curriculum than the linear approach in current use. Learning space is not only a theoretical conception; despite its complexity and demands, it can be applied in schools. Learning space is conceptualized and shaped by the principal, teachers, and students. It is no simple matter to plan the space anew each time, especially when new parameters have to be taken into consideration because of new ideas and needs, changes in the local community and in society at large, and developments in culture and science. Nevertheless, it seems that a number of principles for planning the learning space remain constant. These are openness, dynamism, relevance, curiosity, creativity, reflective thinking, self-awareness, commitment to developmental processes, and in the main, recognition of the centrality of interaction between members of the student population and among students, teachers, experts and sources of information.

The teachers' role in planning and developing a learning space is not simple or straightforward. On the contrary, it is complex and deep and opens up many different alternatives in answer to needs and choice. It is action replete with deliberation and hesitations, but it is empowering and rewarding. It enhances a sense of responsibility and autonomy, enriches interest and encourages growth, and offers gratification and engagement for teachers seeking professional and individual growth. In the words of one of the teachers, after two years' experience with the transdisciplinary curriculum: "My experience as a teacher has been interesting, unusual, and difficult. I learned a lot throughout the process; it is enriching and opens up horizons. I can never return to the kind of teaching I used to practice. We have touched on our lives and found them not to be absolute, black and white, but full of diversity and often fuzziness."

Chapter 8

Restructuring Time in Schools

Understanding the nature and use of time continues to occupy human thought and practice today in many walks of life, as it has throughout the ages. Prophets, physicists, philosophers, poets, biologists, mathematicians, and artists have devoted their minds and talents to depicting, analyzing, prescribing, planning, and studying the concept of time. How people conceive of, experience, and use time remains one of life's perennial and profound questions.

The many ways society, particularly institutions within society, is affected by different conceptions of time have been illuminated by many insightful works. They call attention to the significance of time in the conduct and regulation of our mental, social, and organizational lives (Fraser, 1966; Progogine and Stengers, 1984; Zerubavel, 1981, 1985). The conception of time typical of a given religion, social group, or organization probably embodies the core ideas or beliefs of that group or setting. The conception of time affects how the group or setting will enact and order its life and the lives of its members. Precisely because the conception and use of time stem from the fundamental beliefs and values prevailing in any particular setting or group, an attempt to change the way in which time is allocated inevitably encounters serious obstacles.

Schools are no exception. They too express some of their most fundamental values, ideas, and beliefs about education and how it is to be conducted through the way in which they organize and utilize the time societies allocate to them. In the deepest sense, how schools have decided to use their time conveys what they have decided that teachers and students should do with that portion of their lives lived in schools and indeed with their own "lives," so to speak, as educational institutions. Like many individuals and public organizations (though *not* like private groups), schools have successfully resisted for generations any genuine change in the principles by which they order their lives or portion their time (Jenkins, 1996; Sarason, 1982, 1990; Sizer, 1993; Wilson and Daviss, 1994).

Readers interested in learning what contemporary scholars have observed about the various ways schools understand and deal with time can refer to several informative publications (Anderson, 1984; Anderson, Ryan, and Shapiro, 1989; Anderson and Walberg, 1993; Berliner, 1990; Connelly and Clandinin, 1990; Fisher and Berliner, 1985; Sarason, 1982; Wilson and Daviss, 1994). The study of time and its uses in school has produced many critical comments on current organizational and instructional practices. The substance of these comments is that classroom learning is conducted in a fashion that results in very poor use of time. One study found that, on average, close to 17 percent of classroom time is spent on non-instructional activities (with a range of 7 percent to 24 percent) (Anderson, 1993). However, other authors report far more serious conditions prevailing in schools: "Barely 25% of the typical school day is spent with students learning successfully" (Hutchins, 1990, 2).

More important than the amount of time devoted to teaching and learning is what the time is used for: "a great deal of time in many high school classrooms is allocated to the memorization of facts and the rote application of rules ... much time is spent by students repeating almost verbatim what their teacher says or what is found in textbooks. Far less time is spent helping students express and defend their opinions about the subject matter" (Anderson, 1993, 19). It has been pointed out that

temporal regularity [e.g., uniform class periods], when it reaches high levels as it does in schools, is an enemy of spontaneity. . . . People seem to dance like marionettes on the cog wheels of the clock. Although life as a whole is experienced cyclically, school cycles are almost entirely without natural reference. Life cycles appear to be given, normal and natural, but school cycles are artificial. They are "made up" . . . Students, for example, may be in the middle of a lesson when the class bell signals the end of a period. When students return the next day, the intellectual intensity of the lesson may have dissipated and be further affected as class start-up routines take place. By the time students "get up to speed," the class period may be over. (Connelly and Clandinin, 1993, 11–12)

It seems clear that, contrary to many educators' claims, schools are organized around teachers' work, and their work schedule is set out according to the standard plan of the school as a bureaucracy. Schools are not really designed around the needs of learners.

If learning were truly the focus today, no one would set up a classroom with 30 to 40 students, for five, six or seven periods a day, within a rigidly set time schedule. Neither could one seriously suggest that this many students can learn the same way during the same amount of time, or for that matter learn much at all in such a setting. (Banathy, 1991, 102)

Equally poignant are the comments of Fenwick W. English (1993, 24):

the school schedule assumes a perfect mechanical cycle that leaves out human will, any experience that is unique, and all that is known about how humans learn. It epitomizes the school as a dull, repetitive, lifeless place, devoid of any purposive inquiry. . . . it views the school as an agency of social control. It links factory to school as near mirror images: the concepts of one are reflected in the other.

School schedules must become more human centered and built around support of teachers and learners and their interaction, not around the requirements of uniformity dictated by an antiquated conception of institutional organization. Our concept of the sectioning of time will undergo distinct change when the learning process is recognized as one of inquiry and the *pursuit of knowledge by students*, rather than one of teachers' delivery of information to students. How can schools of the future use time more productively than today's schools? We focus on the problem of restructuring the way schools allocate blocks of time to the various functions they wish to carry out.

CAN SCHOOLS RESTRUCTURE TIME FOR TEACHERS AND STUDENTS?

Schools must perform several basic functions. These are organizing (clarifying, planning, decision making, etc.) and facilitating (teaching) students' pursuit of knowledge (curriculum). One goal of the restructuring effort is to coordinate these three subsystems of the school (staff organization, curriculum, and instruction) in novel and more flexible ways than generally practiced heretofore. The restructuring of time in schools is needed to support a series of changes in the school's operation that were identified and explained in this book, namely:

• to implement planning and teaching by teams of teachers;
• to have students study an integrated, multidisciplinary or transdisciplinary curriculum;
• to emphasize an inquiry form of learning, often in cooperative small groups.

The realization of these goals is contingent upon a fundamental restructuring of the school's teaching schedule, or a basic change in how it uses time (Cambone, 1995; Goodlad, 1984; Jenkins, 1996, 1996; Schaefer, 1967; Shachar and Sharan, 1995; Y. Sharan and S. Sharan, 1994; Sizer, 1993; Wilson and Daviss, 1994).

The typical bureaucratic approach to school organization sets up a uniform schedule for all classes in the school, to the effect that all classes meet for the same amount of time and start and end at the same time. That schedule is usually intended to be in force for an entire academic year, and frequently remains essentially unchanged for many years. Such uniformity is considered by many administrators or governing boards of educational institutions to be a necessary component of a rational system of control and accountability (Goodlad, 1984; Chubb and Moe, 1990).

By contrast, the systems approach to organization and change in schools described here is more consistent with a flexible form of scheduling for classes and teachers. ("Flexible scheduling" at one time referred to individualized study programs for students.) Flexible scheduling seeks to accommodate a range of temporal rhythms that vary as a function of subject matter, of the place in which learning occurs (not necessarily in a classroom), and of the teaching method employed. The latter is determined by the nature of the task, such as inquiry into a complex problem or mastery of material and the pace with which students are able to cope with the task. A uniform teaching schedule for an entire school that cannot be changed for a long period of time, such as an academic year, embodies a totally different conception of education than does a flexible schedule (Cambone, 1995; Jenkins, 1996; Schaefer, 1967; Schlechty, 1990). Each conception certainly requires an altogether different organizational scaffolding to support it.

However, the uniform character of the typical teaching schedule is only one manifestation of the bureaucratic heritage that still survives in schools. Another premise, no less resistant to change than other elements in school organization, is that teachers' work is identified solely with the hours they teach and that only one teacher is to be scheduled with a class for a given session, whatever its temporal duration. Many schools are governed by the premise that a teacher who is not teaching a class is not working: "One class, one teacher, one subject" is the conceptual foundation on which rests the organization of many schools' teaching schedule (Sarason, 1982). This overarching rule of school organization has been called "temporal tyranny" (Wilson and Daviss, 1994, 123), and it rules not only schools but the teachers themselves, who have thoroughly internalized its message. They too have come to believe that they are working only when teaching a class. The undesirable features of the long teaching day (six hours a day for five days a week, or five hours a day for six days a week) typical of schools in many countries have long been lamented by education's thinkers and researchers, thus far with less than a spectacular response from educators in the field (Goodlad, 1984, see in particular pages 194–195; Schaefer, 1967).

Some countries have escaped this particular "tyranny," though they may have others. In Japan, for example, teachers might have larger classes than in the United States, but they teach fewer hours per day even though they spend more hours per day in the school than teachers in the United States. Much of nonclass time is spent in the company of other teachers discussing how to teach (Goodlad, 1984; Stevenson and Stigler, 1992). A study in the United States found that schools where teachers met daily to discuss their teaching were more successful in reaching underprivileged students than were schools where teachers met less frequently and spent their time together discussing subjects other than their own teaching, particularly what was wrong with the students or their families, which allegedly explained their poor work in school (Little, 1982; McLaughlin, 1993).

The present discussion does not treat the question of *what* teachers talk about when they meet, even though that is an important issue. Rather, we wish to address the more basic problem of scheduling time so they can meet. In regard to the problem of changing the bureaucratically organized schedule of classes, the decision about *when* precedes the question of *what*. The first challenge is to achieve the goal of restructuring time by adopting the principle that teachers' work is far more multifaceted than just the time they spend in the classroom. Teachers' work includes, among many other tasks and duties, arranging for and obtaining constant feedback about the conduct of teaching in school and maintaining consultations among colleagues about their work and about the organizational conditions in which it takes place (Goodlad, 1984). Teachers' work cannot be limited to the delivery of classroom instruction, no more than a hospital would claim that a surgeon works only during the time spent in the operating room. Yet, that is precisely the situation current in a very large number of schools in different countries. School systems must acknowledge that the official role of teachers includes (a) the ongoing assessment of their work and the work of the school, (b) receiving and utilizing feedback about these processes, and (c) planning their work for the future and that these activities are frequently performed by teachers working together in teams. The challenge of just how teachers will utilize the time given them to work together in teams is a topic that has been dealt with at length in many works about group dynamics and organizational development (Schmuck and Runkel, 1985).

Finally, another goal of the restructured school refers to an integrated curriculum that must be planned, developed, and implemented by multidisciplinary teams of teachers. Achieving that goal requires a change in the premise that only one teacher can be assigned to a given class during a particular class session. School systems interested in genuine restructuring must accept the practice, along with its budgetary implications, that groups of two, three, or four teachers can and should work together when teaching a class. Students can be engaged for relatively long periods of time (two hours, for example, or more, as the case may be) in doing research in teams on a problem that bridges or incorporates several disciplines. The presence or availability of several teachers as resource persons and guides for student teams is vital for maintaining that kind of instruction (Petrie, 1992).

"The division into subjects and periods encourages a segmented rather than integrated view of knowledge. Consequently, what students are asked to relate to in schooling becomes increasingly artificial, cut off from human experiences subject matter is supposed to reflect" (Goodlad, 1984, 266). The restructured schedule that allows for teams of teachers to collaborate on directing students' efforts to conduct serious inquiries into various intellectual/social/scientific problems seems to be the most promising way to finally overcome the atomization of knowledge and learning decried countless times over the past century (Doll, 1993; Petrie, 1992).

The big question, then, is can schools succeed in restructuring time for students and for teachers when they are still locked into organizational and pedagogical premises that function as powerful obstacles to change? Change agents, whether from inside or outside the school, will have to take all aspects of this problem—organizational, pedagogical, curricular, and budgetary—into consideration when assisting schools seeking to restructure themselves. No wonder serious students of educational reform can predict with a disturbingly high degree of certainty that reform efforts will fail unless all of the major obstacles are accounted for that potentially can derail the change effort (Sarason, 1990; Wilson and Daviss, 1994).

THE VARIABLES OF SCHEDULING

Several large school restructuring projects in the United States offer suggestions about how schools can restructure their teaching schedules to achieve basic goals of contemporary schooling. It is eminently worthwhile to study these programs, which embody many desirable features. However, before examining these suggestions for their use of time, we wish to examine the more salient variables that affect teaching schedules in schools in general. When teachers and principals meet to plan how time can be restructured in their school, it can be advantageous to experiment—mentally if not in practice—with alternative plans, rather than trying to adopt those prepared for other schools with different circumstances. A convenient point of departure for discussing a restructured schedule is to consider which major variables can be included in the plan. Once these are identified, the question becomes what values or quantities for these variables will provide the desired flexibility in scheduling that supports the curricular and instructional needs of the restructured school.

The following list of variables does not exhaust all possibilities, nor could it include variables that are unique to conditions in different localities. No list prepared by people removed from a given school will encompass all of the variables affecting the schedule of that school. That task remains for a problem-solving team comprised of teachers who work in the school and have a thorough acquaintance with its conditions. Variables that can be altered to restructure the schools' teaching schedule include the following:

- the duration of a class session (lesson),
- the duration of recess periods or other intervals between classes,
- teachers' free periods during the day or week,
- the length of the school day,
- the division of the school year into sections (semesters, trimesters, two-month modules, etc.),
- the number of courses and/or subjects that the school offers,
- the number of courses or subjects that a student is required to study at a given time or during the course of an academic year,
- the number of class sessions taught by each teacher,

- the number of students participating in a given class session, and
- the total number of hours per week devoted to different subjects.

Another variable, not included in this list, that each school will have to consider is the days of the week when different teachers are not required or do not wish to be in school. Not every country or school district allows teachers to work four (out of five) or five (out of six) days a week instead of every day. That is one variable that has many local variations and constitutes an important element in planning the school schedule.

A team of teachers and/or a principal wishing to restructure a school's teaching schedule can make changes in one or a combination of the variables listed. The possible number of such variations is very large and offers an enormous degree of adaptability to the needs of different schools.

CHANGING THE LENGTH OF LESSON AND INTERCLASS INTERVALS

A popular and relatively limited change derives from the simultaneous alteration of two variables, namely, the length of the recess along with the length of the class session. Schedule changes such as the following do not necessarily entail profound rethinking of the school's pedagogical mission, but they could lead to some desired goals.

Before Changes	*After Changes*
1. uniform class sessions of 45 minutes	1. classes of 35, 50, and 70 minutes
2. bell rung at beginning and end of each class	2. bell rung twice a day, at start and end of school day
3. ten-minute intervals between classes	3. no interval or five-minute interval between classes
4. 30-minute recess after three 45-minute sessions	4. 30-minute recess after two 70-minute sessions or after three 50-minute sessions

These changes in the schedule appeal to schools taking their first steps toward restructuring. They are very cautious steps that will not drastically disrupt the status quo. The length of the school day remains fixed, and there are classes which are both shorter (35 minutes) and longer (70 minutes) than the standard 45-minute unit.

THE DOUBLE SESSION BLOCKING APPROACH

The double session blocking method is, perhaps, the most prevalent change taking place at this time in the restructuring of high school teaching schedules.

Some schools begin by doubling the length of a single lesson. Many schools have experimented with introducing the double-length session once or twice a week, while leaving other sessions untouched (Jenkins, 1996). In this case, students would attend five different classes on a given day, plus lunch. The double session can be rotated so that a different class is doubled the following week on the next day, and so on (i.e., one week there is a double session on Monday, the next week on Tuesday, etc.). Or, the double session can be introduced every day for a different class, if that is desired.

A more encompassing application of the blocking method is the "4 by 4" semester block schedule, where students have four courses each semester, each course for about 90 minutes a day. This schedule and an alternative block schedule that emphasizes a "language immersion" program during the second semester appear in Figure 8.1 (Canady and Rettig, 1995; Jenkins, 1996).

It is anticipated that teachers will change their instructional style during the longer classes, since longer periods do not lend themselves to the typical lecture method. However, this method of changing the school schedule does not strive to achieve an interdisciplinary curriculum, even in part. Its primary goal is to allow teachers to employ alternative styles of teaching and learning, if they have the skills required for using such methods. If they don't, the change in schedule will ignite a great deal of conflict and resistance (Cambone, 1995). Teachers should be given an opportunity to master several alternative teaching methods before double session blocking is initiated. Nevertheless, a block schedule can make it possible for teachers to use alternative teaching methods and to implement cross-disciplinary integration in the curriculum, if the school decides to adopt such a policy.

The blocking schedule provides for substantial changes in scheduling variables including length of lesson, number of courses taken by students, number of courses taught by teachers, cross-disciplinary integration of curriculum, and so forth. To this extent, this program shares several basic features with Sizer's Essential School program, discussed later in this chapter.

On the other hand, this program does not display much flexibility, although that feature can be introduced at will by the appropriate organizational arrangements. One suggestion is that a team of teachers can serve as a scheduling committee that accepts requests from teachers to alter the schedule at given times during the year or after some specified advance notice. Teachers can then implement innovative projects when the students' work would benefit from them. In that case, the schedule is only a foundation on which teams of teachers build their classroom study programs with the expectation that they have the leeway to alter this program as the class proceeds with its studies.

Let us turn to the number of classes offered by the school. A school that wishes to reduce the number of subjects studied at any given time can do so by changing its course offerings and requirements. Students can be required to complete eight semester-long courses during an academic year, four per semester plus physical education and music/art on different days, but not every day. Given

Figure 8.1
4 by 4 Blocking Schedules

		Semester 1	Semester 2
P	1	Course 1	Course 5
	2		
E			
R	3	Course 2	Course 6
	4		
I	5	Course 3	Course 7
	6		
O			
D	7	Course 4	Course 8
	8		

Blocks	Fall Semester	Spring Semester
Block 1 (90 min.)	Course 1	French 2-4
Block 2 (85 min.)	Course 2	
Lunch (35 min.)	Lunch	Lunch
Block 3 (90 min.)	Course 3	French 2-4
Block 4 (90 min.)	Course 4	

that the length of the school day remains unchanged (say from 8:30 A.M. to 3:00 P.M. including lunch), each course could last 90 minutes, or there could be several very long courses and several short ones. Then again, perhaps a particular course would meet only three times a week, each time for 90 minutes, while on the other two days the students would spend the remaining portion of the day in the library, in the laboratory, or doing fieldwork. In this latter instance, the restructured schedule has altered three variables simultaneously, namely, the number of course offerings by the school was changed to permit students to study eight semester courses per year, and the duration of each class session was changed accordingly, as was the number of classes taught by a given teacher. The lengthening of the class session automatically involves a reduction in the number of different classes to be taught by a particular teacher.

Also, it might be possible to change the length of the school day as often as twice a week, so that teachers can schedule planning time together as part of the regular workday. Twice a week students could work in libraries, laboratories, or the field, as suggested, with the guidance of a few teachers or paraprofessional personnel. The majority of teachers will be free to engage in planning the curriculum for the coming week based on feedback received from the current or past week's teaching. This approach changes four variables simultaneously, the three just discussed plus the length of the school day.

Of course, this approach is predicated on the assumption that the school district or system grants the school sufficient autonomy to make changes of this kind. Some school systems mandate the number of hours per week that must be devoted to specific subjects. The greater the number of such constraints, the more difficult it will be for a school to accomplish any genuine restructuring effort. While school districts often realize that authority to make such curricular changes must be delegated to schools if restructuring is to be more than a catchword, proclaiming support for a restructuring policy and relinquishing power and control over the curriculum are frequently "decoupled" from one another. As expected, the consequences are that restructuring is limited to a cosmetic change that leaves the situation exactly as it was.

This is one of the crucial points at which school restructuring connects into the larger system of which it is a part and where the restructuring process at the microlevel of the school is not completely autonomous. School administrators will have to negotiate this topic with district authorities.

CARROLL'S COPERNICAN PLAN

Joseph Carroll, author of the Copernican Plan, decided that a revolution was needed in the field of how high schools scheduled classes. Carroll named his plan for changing the structure of teaching and learning in high schools after the sixteenth-century astronomer Nicolaus Copernicus, who in his book *The Revolution of the Heavenly Orbs* asserted that the planets revolved around the sun, and that the sun did not revolve around the earth, as everyone thought. Carroll points out that the term "revolution" came to mean social upheaval (in addition to revolving around) from the time of Copernicus (Carroll, 1989, 15). Carroll's main goal in restructuring the teaching-learning schedule is for students to have time to master the various facets of complex issues in the contemporary world, as well as to provide an opportunity for students to pursue their personal interests related to learning (Carroll, 1990, 1994).

Carroll emphasizes repeatedly that the frontal lecture method is much overused in high schools, and the new distribution of time blocks provides the framework for alternative forms of instruction (Figure 8.2). Two plans were suggested, one for students who enroll for a single 226-minute course each day for 30 days, the other for those who enroll in two 110-minute courses (with six minutes between classes) each day for 60 days. Students would enroll in six such courses per year for a total of 24 courses in four years of high school. Naturally, the precise duration of each of these long courses is subject to change at the local level. Schools can choose to offer both courses, the 30-day and the 60-day courses, simultaneously. In addition, on some days a seminar is held in the afternoon (alternating with music and physical education) to provide assistance to students to "integrate knowledge across traditional disciplinary lines" (Carroll, 1990, 361). Many schools begin their day at 8:30 A.M., not at 7:45 A.M. as appears in Carroll's schedule, but they conclude the day at 3:15 P.M., rather than at 2:45 P.M. Those are minor adjustments, dependent upon local preferences.

There are many other features of the Copernican plan, particularly those concerning new grading and credit systems, that we cannot discuss here in the context of the topic of restructuring time. However, one observation made by Carroll about the meaning of how time is used in schools deserves serious attention from educators anywhere, not only in the United States. He wrote:

Americans typically view teenagers as hyperactive, frenetic individuals who are difficult to understand. The American high school deals with this hyperactivity by placing teenagers in a state of perpetual motion and interrupted attention. Today, typical high school students are in seven different classes, a homeroom, a cafeteria. . . . in a 6½ hour day. In addition, if they have physical education, these young people may change clothes twice and shower once. This is certainly not a schedule that fosters deep reflection. (Carroll, 1990, 364–365)

We think that the high school program current in several countries actually contributes to the "perpetual motion" character of young people today, fostered first and foremost by the mass media and maybe by the computer age as well (a topic worthy of careful research). The rapid succession of subjects and classes to which countless high school students are subjected fits well with the mentality of the TV frame, which allows for and is directed at an attention span of seconds, at best. Schooling is not a counterbalance to the flight of ideas and scenes typical of the mass media, but only an extension of it.

To evaluate the effects of the Copernican plan, an independent team of evaluators from Harvard University administered a variety of measures in seven high schools, including achievement tests, questionnaires to teachers, students, and parents, and interviews, over a two-year period beginning when the students

Figure 8.2
Two Proposed Schedules for the Copernican Plan

Time	Schedule A	Schedule B
7:46		
		Macroclass I (110 min.) for 60 days
9:36	Macroclass (226 min.) for 30 days	
		Passing (6 min.)
9:42		
		Macroclass II (110 min.) for 60 days
11:32		
	Passing (6 min.)	
11: 38		
	First Lunch (35 min.)	Seminar I /Music/Phys. Ed. (70 min.)
12:13		
12:48	Seminar II /Music/Phys. Ed. (70 min.)	Second Lunch (35 min.)
1:23		
	Passing (6 min.)	
1:29		
	Preparation/Help/Study/Phys. Ed/Music (70 min.)	
2:39		
	Departure (6 min.)	
2:45		
	Activities/Sports (135 min.)	
5:00		

were in the ninth grade (Carroll, 1994). Some of the findings, particularly those specifically related to the restructuring of class duration, are of interest here. Both students and teachers responded enthusiastically to the "macroclasses" of two (clock) hours. Students displayed great flexibility in moving from longer to shorter classes, although they preferred the longer ones, and teachers "felt rejuvenated and believed they were teaching students more productively than ever" (Carroll, 1994, 108). Students from the Copernican plan also measured significantly better than students from traditional classes on higher-order thinking, one of the goals of the Copernican plan. However, the fact that the Copernican plan is not sufficiently comprehensive limits its ability to serve as a blueprint for school restructuring. One of the main subsystems of the school, the organization of the staff, is not treated in any depth by the Copernican plan.

Empirical data show positive effects on students' learning from several outstanding methods of school organization and instruction that remain peripheral to most schools and to students' experience. The source of this major gap between what we know to be effective and what is practiced is a complex issue that some authors have elaborated on (Sarason, 1982, 1996b, 1996c; Wilson and Daviss, 1994). One salient reason for this gap is that plans for school reform ignore decisive elements comprising the organization and operation of the school. It's as if aeronautic engineers were to plan the fuselage of a new plane but fail to specify what fuel the engines will require. When the plan is almost complete, someone discovers that the specific fuel needed for this plane has not been invented. The time teachers require to work together to plan their instruction, from all points of view, must be included in any serious plan for the reform of instruction (Cambone, 1995). If that is not done, the plan simply won't "fly," no matter how effective the instructional method may have been proven to be (Sarason, 1990; Shachar and Sharan, 1995). The restructuring of the use of time and alternative methods of instruction are inseparable in reality, regardless of how well-meaning educators are who separate them in thinking about improving schools.

SIZER'S ESSENTIAL SCHOOL PROGRAM

Carroll's Copernican plan shares several elements with Sizer's model schedule for the Essential Schools program (see Figures 8.3–8.5). These include the distinct extension of the class period, the marked reduction in the number of courses students study at any given time (although Sizer's program permits double the number of courses called for by Carroll's plan), and the the need to exchange the lecture method for alternative pedagogical methods. Despite their common characteristics, the differences between the two programs justify a separate presentation here of Sizer's model schedule (which schools belonging to the Coalition of Essential Schools are free to modify).

The suggestion for a weekly schedule published by Sizer (1993, 226) entails a change in every variable in our earlier list of scheduling variables. A basic

Figure 8.3
House 1, Team A—Master Schedule

Time	Monday	Tuesday	Wednesday	Thursday	Friday
7:00 Special #1	Band, choir, other activities	Band, choir, other activities	Band, choir, other activities	Band, choir, other activities	Band, choir, other activities
8:00 Period One	Math-Science History-Philosophy Arts (Generalist has prep time)	History-Philosophy Arts Generalist (Math-Science has prep time)	Math-Science Arts Generalist (History-Philosophy has prep time)	Math-Science History-Philosophy Generalist (Arts has prep time)	The schedule is a 4-day rotation. The Monday schedule would start again here.
9:55 Period Two	Math-Science History-Philosophy Generalist (Arts has prep time)	Math-Science History-Philosophy Arts (Generalist has prep time)	History-Philosophy Arts Generalist (Math-Science has prep time)	Math-Science Arts Generalist (History-Philosophy has prep time)	
11:45 Periods Three, Four and Five	Lunch Advisory Tutorial: History-Philosophy Arts/Generalist (Math-Science prep)	Lunch Advisory Tutorial: Math-Science Arts/Generalist (History-Philo. prep)	Lunch Advisory Tutorial: Math-Science History-Philo./Gener. (Arts prep)	Lunch Advisory Tutorial: Math-Science/Arts History-Philosophy (Generalist prep)	
1:45 Period Six	Math-Science Arts Generalist (History-Philo. prep)	Math-Science History-Philosophy Generalist (Arts has prep time)	Math-Science History-Philosophy Arts (Generalist prep)	History-Philosophy Arts Generalist (Math-Science prep)	
3:30	Team meeting for staff	Team meeting for staff	Team meeting for staff	Team meeting for staff	Team meeting for staff
4:00-6:00 Special #2	Band, choir, other activities	Band, choir, other activities	Band, choir, other activities	Band, choir, other activities	Band, choir, other activities

assumption of this program is that teachers who participate in the Essential Schools program will radically change their pedagogical approach, particularly since the program calls for extensive use of alternative evaluation through student-prepared exhibitions to substitute for paper-and-pencil tests. Obviously, the preparation of exhibitions by individuals or by small groups of students cannot take place in a lecture-style classroom. Nevertheless, unlike Carroll, who endorsed mastery learning as the preferred pedagogical approach (albeit without excluding other approaches such as cooperative learning), Sizer does not undertake to describe or recommend pedagogical methods that appear to be essentially related to his general educational conception. On the other hand, Sizer's program calls for far-reaching restructuring of all the major subsystems of the school and their coordination in ways that depart considerably from current practice (Sizer, 1993).

The division of the school, numbering approximately 1,300 students, into houses with approximately 200 students and a staff of thirteen teachers per house, creates the organizational conditions where responsibility for ongoing planning, implementation, evaluation, feedback on progress, and replanning is placed squarely on the shoulders of the house staff, along with the authority to make and carry out their decisions. Guidelines for house-based policy are most likely coordinated with the school principal, but each house within the school retains a degree of freedom needed to respond to the educational needs and interests of its students. The subsystem of the "house" is not constrained to implement a predetermined plan or curriculum set by the school as a whole or by district administrators.

To this extent, each "house" is decoupled from the others in the school, and the scheduling of the teachers' instructional time is not affected by the scheduling constraints mandated by teachers' needs in the other houses. The considerable autonomy of the individual house makes flexible scheduling more feasible than in larger organizational units. The house structure can be viewed as a unique combination of loose coupling between units, with relatively tight coupling within units. It is a widely adopted method for achieving the benefits of relatively small high schools (less that 400 students) while not requiring that communities abandon large school buildings. Research demonstrates clearly that large schools (900 or more students) contribute to many distinctly negative consequences, social and academic, for teachers and students alike (Fowler and Walberg, 1991; Lee and Smith, 1995, 1996).

The thirteen or so teachers assigned to a given house constitute a multidisciplinary team whose primary mandate is to design and implement a multidisciplinary curriculum. The team can also decide how to divide the instructional time and how to distribute students to classes within the structure of the house according to their interest, progress, and the like. The house structure permits cross-grade or nongraded classes, the formation of subgroups of students with special interests, and the pacing of learning by student teams engaged in investigating problems derived from the intersection of disciplines.

One scheduling problem not resolved satisfactorily in the Essential School plan is the allocation of sufficient time to teachers for planning curriculum and instruction. If the process of instruction is to be planned on the basis of ongoing feedback and is not to repeat the old model of implementing a given program, then teachers need several hours each week to engage in collective planning. Ostensibly, these hours could be made available on Fridays from 10:00 A.M. to 3:30 P.M. if most of the students would conduct their studies in the field on that day or perform other work with the guidance of adjunct personnel. Recent suggestions for scheduling by the Essential School project provide a four-hour planning session (8:00 A.M. to noon) for teachers once a week, while students are to work on community-based projects (Figure 8.4). Or, multidisciplinary teams could meet on alternating days for 90 minutes each time, because their class meets only twice or three times a week (Figure 8.5).

If properly coordinated with the students' studies during the week, fieldwork could be an exciting, highly motivating, and highly instructive complement to the regular academic program, not a ''field day'' disconnected from the rest of the students' learning experiences. It could achieve another of the restructured school's major goals of establishing a strong and clear link in the students' experience between real life and school learning (Dewey, 1938; Goodlad, 1984; Sarason, 1983).

Arranging for groups of students to carry out study projects in the community poses a host of problems for today's schools, which are boarded up behind administrative and legal barriers that prevent them from taking students out into the world for sustained study. This legacy of insulation from the community will have to be overcome by tomorrow's schools, probably by enlisting the close involvement of the parents and other bodies of the local government (Lee, Bryk, and Smith, 1993; Sarason, 1995a).

To structure the school schedule to add time for teachers to plan their work together and time for students' study projects in the community, the school will need the help of its problem-solving team or teams. They can consider systematically the forces that will help or hinder the implementation of such a program and evolve a viable scheduling system for their school. The staff of the school or of the specific houses will have to work out how to integrate different subjects in the multidisciplinary curriculum, who the members of the different instructional teams will be, and so forth. The suggestions offered here demonstrate that many potential solutions to this problem can be evolved by teacher teams in accordance with the overall policy and organization of their school (Canady and Rettig, 1995).

COMBINING ELEMENTS FROM DIFFERENT PROGRAMS

The models of school schedules presented here provide a number of alternatives from which elements appropriate to the needs of different schools can be selected. It may be advisable to construct a schedule that has borrowed parts

Figure 8.4
Plan C Schedule

	MONDAY	TUESDAY	WEDNESDAY	THURSDAY	FRIDAY
8:00 - 9:00	Language	Language	Community Service	Language	Language
9:00 - 11:00	Humanities	Humanities		Humanities	Humanities
11:00-12:00	Advisory	Advisory		Advisory	Advisory
12:00 -1:00	Lunch/Options	Lunch/Options	Lunch/Options	Lunch/Options	Lunch/Options
1:00 - 3:00	Math/Science	Math/Science	Math/Science or Humanities	Math/Science	Math/Science
3:00 - 5:00	Electives/Library	Electives/Library	Electives/Library	Electives/Library	Electives/Library

Figure 8.5
Alternative Plan A

	MONDAY	TUESDAY	WEDNESDAY	THURSDAY	FRIDAY
8:30 - 8:49	Home room	Home room	Home room	Home room	Home room
8:53 - 9:41	Science	Math	Science	Math	Science
9:45 - 10:33					
10:37 - 11:35	History	English	History	English	History
11:29 - 12:16					
12:21 - 12:46	Lunch	Lunch	Lunch	Lunch	Lunch
12:50 - 1:38	Study	Physical Education	Study	Physical Education	Study
1:42 - 2:30	Elective	Elective	Elective	Elective	Elective

from different programs. A two-hour class, as suggested by the Copernican plan, can be followed by one 45-minute class, then a lunch period and one 90-minute class on one day. The next day could have a different combination, depending on the team of teachers responsible for a given group of students and the topics that will be studied. The source of the scheduling idea is not important. What matters is how the schedule is integrated with teachers' planning time and the nature of the teaching-learning process that the school wishes to employ. How much time do students need to pursue a topic in depth and become genuinely involved in the problems inherent in the topic, so their interest stems from their curiosity and not just from the goal of obtaining a good grade? The answer to that question should guide the process of instruction!

These alternative schedules seek to enable students to delve deeply into a few topics, devoting their minds and energies to those problems without distraction by a myriad of other topics. However, long periods of time to work on a single topic on any given day is only one necessary condition for accomplishing this goal. Another required feature of the schedule is continuity in the pursuit of a study goal (such as a group research project) over a period of days, weeks, or months long enough that the students can complete their projects. Too often schools bombard students and teachers with many activities of all sorts, in addition to an overburdened curriculum. While many of these activities are intended to enrich the students' lives, they often interrupt students' concentration and progress because they are not integrated into the students' learning projects.

Figure 8.6
Three 100-Minute Classes per Day

MON.	TUES.	WED.	THURS.	FRI.
Class 1 105 min.	Class 2 105 min.	Class 1 105 min.	Class 2 105 min.	Class 1 105 min.
Advis. Team	SSR*	Advis. Team	SSR	Break
Break	Break	Break	Break	Class 3 100 min.
Class 3 100 min.	Class 4 100 min.	Class 3 100 min.	Class 4 100 min.	Lunch, 30 m.
Lunch, 30 m.	Lunch, 30 m.	Lunch, 30 m.	Lunch, 30 m.	Class 5 100 min.
Class 5 100 min.	Class 6 100 min.	Class 5 100 min.	Class 6 100 min.	Team Plng.

*SSR = Sustained Silent Reading.
Source: Cushman, 1995, p. 3.

The notion of the curricular module, whereby students concentrate on a few topics intensively for a period of six or eight weeks and then proceed to other subjects, is one approach that can focus student attention without permitting interruptions for a host of reasons external to the academic program. Another version is to have students study six knowledge domains for an entire year without change in the program. A program of that kind appears in Figure 8.6 (Cushman, 1995).

There may never be a totally satisfactory resolution of the tension between an intensive approach and an extensive approach to the design of school study programs. The conception offered here seeks to provide one solution to this dilemma, namely, the multidisciplinary, integrated curriculum that also includes an inquiry approach to learning. When this curriculum is coupled with a measure of field study and the application of knowledge to a "practical" goal (such as the preparation of some product that incorporates the essence of the study project), perhaps a balance can be found between the two poles, allowing students to experience in-depth study along with a reasonable degree of breadth of horizon. In that manner it may be possible to avoid both superficiality and premature specialization by young people.

References

Abbot, M. and Caracheo, F. (1988) Power, authority and bureaucracy. In N. Boyan (Ed.), *Handbook of research on educational administration*. New York: Longman, 239–257.

Amir, Y. and Sharan, S. (Eds.) (1985) *School desegregation*. Hillsdale, NJ: Erlbaum.

Anderson, L. (1993) What time tells us. In L. Anderson and H. Walberg (Eds.), *Timepiece: Extending and enhancing learning time*. Reston, VA: National Association of Secondary School Principals (NASSP), 15–22.

Anderson, L. (Ed.) (1984) *Time and school learning*. London: Croom Helm.

Anderson, L., Ryan, D. and Shapiro, B. (Eds.) (1989) *The IEA classroom environment study*. Oxford: Pergamon Press.

Anderson, L. and Walberg, H. (Eds.) (1993) *Timepiece: Extending and enhancing learning time*. Reston, VA: National Association of Secondary School Principals (NASSP).

Apple, M. W. (1995) Facing reality. In J. A. Beane (Ed.), *Toward a coherent curriculum*. Yearbook of the Association for Supervision and Curriculum Development (ASCD). Alexandria, VA: ASCD, 130–138.

Arends, R. and Arends, J. (1977) *Systems change strategies in educational settings*. New York: Human Sciences Press.

Argyris, C. (1992) *On organizational learning*. Oxford: Blackwell.

Argyris, C. and Schon, D. (1978) *Organizational learning*. Reading, MA: Addison Wesley.

Ausubel, D. (1963) *The psychology of meaningful verbal learning: An introduction to school learning*. New York: Grune and Stratton.

Banathy, B. (1971) *A systems view of education*. Belmont, CA: Fearon.

Banathy, B. (1991) *A systems view of education*. Englewood Cliffs, NJ: Educational Technology Publications.

Banathy, B. (1992) *Systems design of education*. Englewood Cliffs, NJ: Educational Technology Publications.

Barker, R. and Gump, P. (1964) *Big school, small school.* Palo Alto, CA: Stanford University Press.

Barker, R. and Schoggen, P. (1973) *Qualities of community life.* San Francisco: Jossey-Bass.

Barnes, D. (1976) *From communication to curriculum.* Harmondsworth, England: Penguin.

Barr, R. and Dreeban, R. (1983) *How schools work.* Chicago: University of Chicago Press.

Barth, R. (1980) *Run school run.* Cambridge, MA: Harvard University Press.

Beane, J. A. (Ed.) (1995) *Toward a coherent curriculum.* Yearbook of the Association for Supervision and Curriculum Development (ASCD). Alexandria, VA: ASCD.

Ben-Peretz, M. (1975) The concept of curriculum potential. *Curriculum Theory Network,* 5(2), 151–159.

Berlak, A. and Berlak, H. (1981) *Dilemmas of schooling.* London: Methuen.

Berliner, D. (1990) What's all the fuss about instructional time? In M. Ben-Peretz and R. Bromme (Eds.), *The nature of time in schools.* New York: Teachers College Press, 3–35.

Berman, P. (1981) Educational change: An implementation paradigm. In R. Lehming and M. Kane (Eds.), *Improving schools.* Beverly Hills, CA: Sage, 253–286.

Berman, P. and McLaughlin, M. (1977) *Federal programs supporting educational change, Vol. 7: Factors affecting implementation and continuation.* Santa Monica, CA: Rand Corporation.

Berman, P. and McLaughlin, M. (1978) *Federal programs supporting educational change. Vol. 8: Implementing and sustaining innovations.* Santa Monica, CA: Rand Corporation.

Bidwell, C. (1965) The school as a formal organization. In J. March (Ed.), *Handbook of organizations.* Chicago: Rand McNally, 972–1022.

Bidwell, C. and Quiroz, P. (1991) Organizational control in the high school workplace: A theoretical argument. *Journal of Research on Adolescence,* 3, 211–229.

Boyer, E. L. (1995) The educated person. In J. A. Beane (Ed.), *Toward a coherent curriculum.* Yearbook of the Association for Supervision and Curriculum Development (ASCD). Alexandria, VA: ASCD, 16–25.

Brady, M. (1995) A supradisciplinary curriculum. In J. A. Beane (Ed.), *Toward a coherent curriculum.* Yearbook of the Association for Supervision and Curriculum Development (ASCD). Alexandria, VA: ASCD, 26–33.

Brisco, C. (1996) The teacher as learner: Interpretations from a case study of teacher change. *Journal of Curriculum Studies,* 28(3), 315–329.

Brown, J. S., Collins, A. and Duguid, P. (1989) Situated cognition and the culture of learning. *Educational Researcher,* 18, 32–42.

Bryk, A. and Driscoll, M. (1988) *The school as community: Theoretical foundations, contextual influences, and consequences for students and teachers.* Madison, WI: National Center on Effective Secondary Schools, University of Wisconsin.

Bryk, A., Lee, V. and Smith, J. (1990) High school organization and its effects on teachers and students: An interpretative summary of the research. In W. Clune and J. Witte (Eds.), *Choice and control in American education: Vol. 1. The theory of choice and control in American education.* Philadelphia: Falmer Press, 135–226.

Caine, R. N. and Caine, G. (1997) *Education on the edge of possibility*. Alexandria, VA: Association for Supervision and Curriculum Development (ASCD).

Caldwell, B. and Spinks, J. (1988) *The self managing school*. Lewes, U.K.: Falmer Press.

Cambone, J. (1995) Time for teachers in school restructuring. *Teachers College Record*, 96, 512–543.

Campbell, R., Fleming, T., Newell, L. and Bennion, J. (1987) *A history of thought and practice in educational administration*. New York: Teachers College Press.

Canady, R. and Rettig, M. (1995) *Block scheduling: A catalyst for change in high schools*. Princeton, NJ: Eye on Education.

Carkhuff, R. (1969) *Helping and human relations*. Vols. I and II. New York: Holt, Rinehart and Winston.

Carroll, J. (1989) *The Copernican plan: Restructuring the American high school*. Andover, MA: The Regional Laboratory for Educational Improvement of the Northeast and Islands.

Carroll, J. (1990) The Copernican plan: Restructuring the American high school. *Phi Delta Kappan*, 71, 358–365.

Carroll, J. (1994) The Copernican plan evaluated: The evolution of a revolution. *Phi Delta Kappan*, 76, 105–113.

Case, R. (1993) Theories of learning and theories of development. *Educational Psychologist*, 28(3), 219–233.

Cawelti, G. (1994) *High school restructuring: A national study*. Arlington, VA: Educational Research Service.

Chubb, J. and Moe, T. (1990) *Politics, markets and America's schools*. Washington, DC: Brookings Institute.

Clark, D. (1985) Emerging paradigms in organizational theory and research. In Y. Lincoln (Ed.), *Organizational theory and inquiry: The paradigm revolution*. Newbury Park, CA: Sage, 43–78.

Clifford, G. and Guthrie, J. (1988) *Ed school: A brief for professional education*. Chicago: University of Chicago Press.

Cohen, D. and Spillane, J. (1992) Policy and practice: The relations between governance and practice. *Review of Research in Education*, 18, 3–49.

Cohen, E. (1994) *Designing groupwork: Strategies for the heterogeneous classroom* (2nd edition). New York: Teachers College Press.

Collins, A. and Ferguson, W. (1993) Epistemic forms and epistemic games: Structures and strategies to guide inquiry. *Educational Psychologist*, 28, 25–42.

Connelly, F. and Clandinin, D. (1990) The cyclic temporal structure of schooling. In M. Ben-Peretz and R. Bromme (Eds.), *The nature of time in schools*. New York: Teachers College Press, 36–63.

Connelly, F. and Clandinin, D. (1993) Cycles, rhythms, and the meaning of school time. In L. Anderson and H. Walberg (Eds.), *Timepiece: Extending and enhancing learning time*. Reston, VA: National Association of Secondary School Principals (NASSP), 9–14.

Cook, W. (1988) *Strategic planning for America's schools*. Arlington, VA: American Association of School Administrators.

Corcoran, T. (June 1995) Helping teachers teach well: Transforming professional development. *CPRE* (Consortium for Policy Research in Education) *Policy Briefs*, 1–11.

Cremin, L. A. (1976) *Public Education*. New York: Basic Books.

Cross, B. (1995) The case for a culturally coherent curriculum. In J. A. Beane (Ed.), *Toward a coherent curriculum*. Yearbook of the Association for Supervision and Curriculum Development (ASCD). Alexandria, VA: ASCD, 71–86.

Cushman, K. (1995) [Alternative schedules for essential schools.] *Horace* (November).

Dalin, P. and Rolf, H. (1993) *Changing the school culture*. London: Cassell.

Darling-Hammond, L., Bullmaster, M. and Cobb, V. (1995) Rethinking teacher leadership through professional development schools. *Elementary School Journal*, 96, 87–106.

Darling-Hammond, L. and Snyder, J. (1992) Curriculum studies and the traditions of inquiry: The scientific tradition. In P. W. Jackson (Ed.), *Handbook of research on curriculum*. New York: Macmillan, 41–78.

Davis, B. and Sumara, D. J. (1997) Cognition, complexity and teacher education. *Harvard Educational Review*, 67(1), 105–125.

Deal, T. and Petterson, K. (1990) *The principal's role in shaping school culture*. Washington, DC: U.S. Department of Education.

DeBono, E. (1990) *I am right—you are wrong*. Harmondsworth, U.K.: Penguin Books.

Devita, J. (1963) A stimulating technique: Teachers observe other teachers. *Clearing House*, 37, 549–550.

Dewey, J. (1902) *The child and the curriculum*. Chicago: University of Chicago Press.

Dewey, J. (1922) *Human nature and conduct*. New York: Henry Holt. Also: The nature of aims, reprinted (1964) in R. Archambault (Ed.), *John Dewey on education: Selected writings*. Chicago: University of Chicago Press, 70–80.

Dewey, J. (1933) *How we think: A restatement of the relation of reflective thinking to the educative process*. New York: D.C. Heath.

Dewey, J. (1938) *Experience and education*. New York : Macmillan.

Dewey, J. (1939) The continuum of ends-means. Reprinted (1964) in R. Archambault (Ed.), *John Dewey on education: Selected writings*. Chicago: University of Chicago Press, 97–107.

Dewey, J. (1956) *The child and the curriculum: The school and society*. Chicago: University of Chicago Press.

Dewey, J. and E. Dewey (1915) *Schools of tomorrow*. New York: E. P. Dutton (reissued, 1962).

Doll, W. (1993a) *A post-modern perspective on curriculum*. New York: Teachers College Press.

Doll, W. (1993b) Curriculum possibilities in a "post"-future. *Journal of Curriculum and Supervision*, 8(4), 277–292.

Dornbusch, S. and Scott, R. (1975) *Evaluation and the exercise of authority*. San Francisco: Jossey-Bass.

Doyle, W. (1983) Academic work. *Review of Educational Research*, 53(2), 159–199.

Drake, S. (1993) *Planning integrated curriculum: The call to adventure*. Alexandria, VA: Association for Supervision and Curriculum Development.

Drake, S. (1996) Towards a new story in education. *Orbit*, 27(1), 1–3.

Egan, G. (1975) *The skilled helper*. Monterey, CA: Brooks/Cole.

Eisner, E. W. and Vallance, E. (1974) *Conflicting conceptions of the curriculum*. Berkeley, CA: McCutchan.

Elmore, R. and Associates (1991) *Restructuring schools: The next generation of educational reform*. San Francisco: Jossey-Bass.

English, F. (1993) Changing the cosmology of the school schedule. In L. Anderson and

H. Walberg (Eds.), *Timepiece: Extending and enhancing learning time*. Reston, VA: National Association of Secondary School Principals (NASSP), 23–29.

Feyerabend, P. (1993) *Against method* (3rd edition). London: Verso/New Left Books.

Fine, M. (1994) *Charting urban school reform*. New York: Teachers College Press.

Firestone, W. (1982) Prescriptions for effective elementary schools don't fit secondary schools. *Educational Leadership*, 40, 51–53.

Fisher. C. and Berliner, D. (1985) *Perspectives on instructional time*. New York: Longman.

Fogarty, R. (1991) Ten models of integrating curriculum. *Educational Leadership*, 49, 61–65.

Foucault, M. (1981) Questions of method: An interview with Michel Foucault. *Ideology and Consciousness*, 8, 3–14.

Fowler, W. and Walberg, H. (1991) School size, characteristics and outcomes. *Educational Evaluation and Policy Analysis*, 13, 189–202.

Fraser, J. (Ed.) (1966) *The voices of time*. New York: George Braziller.

Fullan, M. (1993) *Change forces*. London: Cassell.

Fullan, M. and Miles, M. (1992) Getting reform right: What works and what doesn't. *Phi Delta Kappan*, 73, 744–752.

Fullan, M., Miles, M. and Taylor, G. (1980) Organization development in schools: The state of the art. *Review of Educational Research*, 50, 121–183.

Fullan, M. and Stiegelbauer, S. (1991) *The new meaning of educational change*. New York: Teachers College Press.

Gali, Y. (1983) The administrative behavior of secondary school principals. *Studies in Education (Iyunim B'chinuch)*, 37/38, 287–305. (in Hebrew).

Gardner, H. (1995) Reflections on multiple intelligence: Myths and messages. *Phi Delta Kappan*, 77(3), 200–209.

Getzels, J. and Guba, E. (1957) Social behavior and the administrative process. *School Review*, 65, 423–441.

Getzels, J., Lipham, J. and Campbell, R. (1968) *Educational administration as a social process*. New York: Harper and Row.

Gleick, J. (1987) *Chaos: Making a new science*. Penguin: New York.

Glickman, C. (1993) *Renewing America's schools*. San Francisco: Jossey-Bass.

Goemer, S. J. (1994) *Chaos and the evolving ecological universe*. Langhome, PA: Gordon and Beach.

Goodlad, J. (1984) *A place called school*. New York: McGraw-Hill.

Goodlad J. (1990) *Teachers for our nation's schools*. San Francisco: Jossey-Bass.

Goodlad, J. Soder, R. and Sirotnik, K. (Eds.) (1990) *Places where teachers are taught*. San Francisco: Jossey-Bass.

Gorman, A. (1969) *Teachers and learners: The interactive process of education*. Boston: Allyn and Bacon.

Grant, G. (1988) *The world we created at Hamilton High*. Cambridge, MA: Harvard University Press.

Greene, M. (1993) The passions of pluralism: Multiculturalism and the expanding community. *Educational Researcher*, 22 (1), 1–18.

Griffiths, D. (1964) Administrative theory and change in organizations. In M. Miles (Ed.), *Innovation in education*. New York: Teachers College Press, 425–436.

Griffiths, D. (1988) Administrative theory. In N. Boyan (Ed.), *Handbook of research on educational administration*. New York: Longman, 27–51.

Grossman, P. and Stodolsky, S. (1994) Considerations of content and the circumstances of secondary school teaching. *Review of Research in Education*, 20, 179–221.

Hackman, R. and Oldham, G. (1980) *Work redesign*. Reading, MA: Addison-Wesley.

Hall, R. (1962) The concept of bureaucracy: An empirical assessment. *American Sociological Review*, 27, 295–308.

Hall, G. and Hord, S. (1984) *Change in schools: Facilitating the process*. Albany, NY: State University of New York Press.

Hamalainen, K., Oldroyd, D. and Haapenen, E. (Eds.) (1995) *Making school change happen*. Helsinki: University of Helsinki.

Hamilton, D. (1989) *Toward a theory of schooling*. London: Falmer.

Hargreaves, A. (1993) Individualism and individuality: Reinterpreting the teacher culture. In J. Little and M. McLaughlin (Eds.), *Teachers' work: Individuals, colleagues and contexts*. New York: Teachers College Press, 51–76.

Hargreaves, A. and Dawe, R. (1990) Paths of professional development: Contrived collegiality, collaborative culture and the case of peer coaching. *Teaching and Teacher Education*, 6, 227–241.

Herriot, R. and Firestone, W. (1984) Two images of schools as organizations: A refinement and elaboration. *Educational Administration Quarterly*, 20, 41–57.

Hertz-Lazarowitz, R. and Calderon, M. (1994) Facilitating teachers' power through collaboration: Implementing cooperative learning in elementary schools. In S. Sharan (Ed.), *Handbook of cooperative learning methods*. Westport, CT: Greenwood, 300–317.

Hirst, P. H. (1972) Liberal education and the nature of knowledge. In R. F. Dearden, P. Hirst and R. S. Peters (Eds.), *Education and the development of reason*. London: Routledge and Kegan Paul, 391–414.

Hofer, B. K. and Pintrich, P. R. (1997) Epistemological theories: The development of beliefs about knowledge and knowing and their relation to learning. *Review of Educational Research*, 67(1), 88–140.

Holton, G. (1995) The controversy over the end of science. *Scientific American*, 273(4), 168.

Hopkins, D., Ainscow, M. and West, M. (1994) *School improvement in an era of change*. London: Cassell.

Horwitz, M. (1960) Feedback processes in classroom groups. In N. Henry (Ed.), *The dynamics of instructional groups* (59th yearbook of the National Society for the Study of Education). Chicago: University of Chicago Press, 218–224.

House, E. (1981) Three perspectives on innovation: Technological, political and cultural. In R. Lehming and M. Kane (Eds.), *Improving schools*. Beverly Hills, CA: Sage, 17–41.

Hoy, W. and Miskel, C. (1987) *Educational administration: Theory, research and practice* (3rd edition). New York: Random House.

Huberman, M. (1993) The model of the independent artisan in teachers' professional relations. In J. Little and M. McLaughlin (Eds.), *Teachers' work: Individuals, colleagues, and contexts*. New York: Teachers College Press, 11–50.

Huberman, M. and Miles, M. (1984) *Innovation up close: How school improvement works*. New York: Plenum.

Hutchins, L. (1990) *A+ chieving excellence*. Aurora, CO: Mid-Continent Regional Laboratory.

Jackson, P. (1968) *Life in classrooms*. New York: Holt, Rinehart and Winston.

Jacobs, H. H. (1989) *Interdisciplinary curriculum: Design and implementation.* Alexandria, VA: Association for Supervision and Curriculum Development.

Jakwerth, P. (1996) *U.S. curriculum analysis report.* Report No. 6. East Lansing, MI: U.S. National Research Center.

Janis, I. and Mann, L. (1977) *Decision making.* New York: Free Press.

Janowitz, M. (1969) *Institution building in urban education.* New York: Russell Sage.

Jenkins, J. (1996) *Transforming high schools: A constructivist agenda.* Lancaster, PA: Technomic.

Johnson, D. and Johnson, R. (1987) *Learning together and alone.* Englewood Cliffs, NJ: Prentice-Hall.

Johnson, D., Maruyama, G., Johnson, R., Nelson, D. and Skon, L. (1981) The effects of cooperative, competitive and individualistic goal structures on achievement: A meta-analysis. *Psychological Bulletin,* 89, 47–62.

Johnson, S. (1990) The primacy and potential of high school departments. In M. McLaughlin, J. Talbert and N. Bascia (Eds.), *The contexts of teaching in secondary schools: Teachers' realities.* New York: Teachers College Press, 167–186.

Johnson, W. (1974) The fateful process of Mr. A. talking to Mr. B. In R. Cathcart and L. Samovar (Eds.), *Small group communication* (2nd edition). Dubuque, IA: Brown, 237–258.

Joyce, B. and Harootunian, B. (1967) *The structure of teaching.* Chicago: Science Research Associates.

Joyce, B., Hersh, R. and McKibbin, M. (1983) *The structure of school improvement.* New York: Longman.

Joyce, B. and Showers, B. (1988) *Student achievement through staff development.* New York: Longman.

Joyce, B., Weil, M. and Showers, B. (1992) *Models of teaching* (4th edition). Boston: Allyn and Bacon.

Joyce, B., Wolf, J. and Calhoun, E. (1993) *The self renewing school.* Alexandria, VA: Association for Supervision and Curriculum Development.

Jung, C., Howard, R., Emory, R. and Pino, R. (1972) *Interpersonal communication* (Leaders' Manual). Portland, OR: Northwest Regional Educational Laboratory.

Katz, D. and Kahn, R. (1978) *The social psychology of organizations* (2nd edition). New York: Wiley.

Kauffman, D. L. (1980) *Systems 1: An introduction to systems thinking.* Minneapolis, MN: S. A. Carlton.

Kaufman, R. (1972) *Educational system planning.* Englewood Cliffs, NJ: Prentice-Hall.

Kaufman, R. and Herman, J. (1991) *Strategic planning in education.* Lancaster, PA: Technomic.

Kliebard, H. (1986) *The struggle for the American curriculum.* New York and London: Routledge.

Kohn, A. (1993) Choices for children: Why and how to let students decide. *Phi Delta Kappan,* 75 (September), 8–20.

Kolb, D. (1984) *Experiential learning: Experience as the source of learning and development.* Englewood Cliffs, NJ: Prentice-Hall.

Kolb, D. and Fry, R. (1975) Towards an applied theory of experiential learning. In C. Cooper (Ed.), *Theories of group processes.* London: Wiley, 33–57.

Kolb, D. and Lewis, L. (1986) Facilitating experiential learning: Observations and reflections. In L. Lewis (Ed.), *Experiential and simulation techniques for teaching adults*. San Francisco: Jossey-Bass, 99–107.

Kruse, S., Louis, K. and Bryk, A. (1994) Building professional community in schools. *Issues in Restructuring Schools*, Report 6, Spring. Madison, WI: Center on Organization Restructuring of Schools, University of Wisconsin, 3–6.

Kuhn, T. (1970) *The structure of scientific revolutions* (2nd edition). Chicago: University of Chicago Press.

Ladwig, J. and King, M. (1992) Restructuring secondary social studies: The association of organizational features and classroom thoughtfulness. *American Educational Research Journal*, 29, 695–714.

Langer, E. J. (1993) A mindful education. *Educational Psychologist*, 28(1), 34–50.

Lawrence, P. and Lorsch, J. (1986) *Organization and environment*. Boston: Harvard Business School Press.

Lee, V., Bryk, A. and Smith, J. (1993) The organization of effective secondary schools. *Review of Research in Education*, 19, 171–267.

Lee, V. and Smith, J. (1995) Effects of high school restructuring and size on early gains in achievement and engagement. *Sociology of Education*, 68, 241–270.

Lee, V. and Smith, J. (1996) High school size: Which works better and for whom? Unpublished paper. (http://www.edexcellence.net/research/ressizel.html) University of Michigan, Ann Arbor.

Leithwood, K. (1989) School system policies for effective school administration. In M. Holmes and D. Musella (Eds.), *Educational policy for effective schools*. Ontario, Canada and New York: OISE Press and Teachers College Press, 73–92.

Levine, T. (1994) Courseware evaluation. In *International Encyclopedia of Education* (Eds. H. Thurstone and N. Postlethwaite) (2nd edition). Oxford: Pergamon Press, 1170–1175.

Levine, T. and Nevo, Y. (1997a) The elementary school of the future. In S. Zahar (Ed.), *The current school: From complex reality to a challenging future*. Ministry of Education, Jerusalem (in Hebrew).

Levine, T. and Nevo, Y. (1997b) *Facilitating children's and teachers' thinking via transdisciplinary and dynamic curriculum*. Ministry of Education, Jerusalem (in Hebrew).

Lieberman, A. (1988) *Building a professional culture in schools*. New York: Teachers College Press.

Lieberman, J. (1970) *The tyranny of the experts: How professionals are closing the open society*. New York: Walker.

Lightfoot, S. (1983) *The good high school: Portraits of character and culture*. New York: Basic Books.

Lincoln, Y. (Ed.) (1985) *Organization theory and inquiry: The paradigm revolution*. Newbury Park, CA: Sage.

Litterer, J. (1969) *Organization: Systems, control and adaption* (2nd edition). Vol. 2. New York: Wiley.

Little, J. (1982) Norms of collegiality and experimentation: Workplace conditions of school success. *American Educational Research Journal*, 19, 325–340.

Little, J. (1995) Contested ground: The basis of teacher leadership in two restructuring high schools. *Elementary School Journal*, 96, 47–63.

Louis, K. (1994) Beyond "managed change": Rethinking how schools improve. *School Effectiveness and School Improvement*, 5, 2–24.

Louis, K., Kruse, S. and Associates (Eds.) (1995) *Professionalism and community: Perspectives on reforming urban schooling.* Thousand Oaks, CA: Corwin Press.

Louis, K. and Miles, M. (1990) *Improving the urban high school: What works and why.* New York: Teachers College Press.

Lounsbury, J. and Clark, D. (1990) *Inside grade eight: From anxiety to excitement.* Reston, VA: National Association of Secondary School Principals (NASSP).

Malen, B. and Ogawa, R. (1988) Professional patron influence on site based governance councils: A confronting case study. *Educational Evaluation and Policy Analysis,* 10, 251–270.

Mayhew, K. and Edwards, A. (1965) *The Dewey school: The laboratory school of the University of Chicago 1896–1903.* New York: Atherton Press.

McCarthy, R. (1985) Technology, time and participation: How a principal supports teachers. *Education and Urban Society,* 17, 324–331.

McLaughlin, M. (1993) What matters most in teachers' workplace context? In J. Little and M. McLaughlin (Eds.), *Teachers' work: Individuals, colleagues and contexts.* New York: Teachers College Press, 79–103.

McNeil, L. (1986) *Contradictions of control: School structure and school knowledge.* New York: Routledge and Kegan Paul.

Meyer, J. and Rowan, B. (1977) Institutionalized organizations: Formal structure as myth and ceremony. *American Journal of Sociology,* 83, 440–463.

Miles, M. (1964) On temporary systems. In M. Miles (Ed.), *Innovation in education.* New York: Teachers College, Columbia University, 437–490.

Miles, M. (1967) Some properties of schools as social systems. In G. Watson (Ed.), *Change in school systems.* Washington, DC: National Training Laboratories, 1–29.

Miles, M. (1983) Unravelling the mysteries of institutionalization. *Educational Leadership,* 41(3), 14–19.

Miles, M. (1986) Research findings on the stages of school improvement. New York: Center for Policy Research. Unpublished manuscript.

Miles, M., Ekholm, M. and Vandenberghe, R. (Eds.) (1987) *Lasting school improvement: Exploring the process of institutionalization.* Leuven, Belgium: Association of Child Care Offices.

Miles, M. and Khattri, N. (1995) *Thinking about restructuring: The maps in our minds.* New York: National Center for Restructuring Education, Schools and Teaching, Teachers College, Columbia University.

Milstein, M. and Belasco, J. (1973) (Eds.) *Educational administration and the behavioral sciences: A systems perspective.* Boston: Allyn and Bacon.

Morgan, G. (1986) *Images of organization.* Newbury Park, CA: Sage.

Morrison, D. and Collins, A. (1995) Epistemic fluency and constructivist learning environment. *Educational Technology,* 35 (Sept.–Oct), 39–45.

Murphy, J. (1991) *Restructuring schools.* New York: Teachers College Press.

Murphy, J. and Hallinger, P. (1993) *Restructuring schooling: Learning from ongoing efforts.* Newbury Park, CA: Corwin Press.

Murphy, J. and Louis, K. (Eds.) (1994) *Reshaping the principalship: Insights from transformational reform efforts.* Newbury Park, CA: Corwin Press.

National Education Commission on Time and Learning (1994) *Prisoners of Time.* Washington, DC: U.S. Government Printing Office.

Neale, D., Bailey, W. and Ross, B. (1981) *Strategies for school improvement: Cooperative planning and organization development.* Boston: Allyn and Bacon.

Newman, F. and Oliver, D. (1967) Education and community. *Harvard Educational Review*, 37, 61–106.

Newman, F. and Wehlage, G. (1995) *Successful school restructuring.* Madison, WI: Center on Organization and Restructuring of Schools, University of Wisconsin–Madison.

Newman, F., Wehlage, G. and Lamborn, S. (1992) The significance and sources of student engagement. In F. Newman (Ed.), *Student engagement and achievement in American secondary schools.* New York: Teachers College Press, 11–39.

Oliver, D. and Gershman, K. (1989) *Education, modernity and fractured meaning: Toward a process theory of teaching and learning.* Albany, NY: State University of New York Press.

Olson, L. (1994) International math and science study finds U.S. covers more in less depth. *Education Week*, June 22, p. 10.

O'Neil, J. (1995) On technology and schools: A conversation with Chris Dede. *Educational Leadership*, 53, 6–12.

Papert, S. (1980) *Mindstorms, children, computers, and powerful ideas.* New York: Basic Books.

Pedersen, J. and Digby, A. (Eds.) (1995) *Secondary schools and cooperative learning.* New York: Garland.

Perry, W. G. (1981) Cognitive and ethical growth: The making of meaning. In A. Chickering (Ed.), *The modern American college.* San Francisco: Jossey-Bass, 76–116.

Petrie, H. (1992) Interdisciplinary education: Are we faced with insurmountable opportunities? *Review of Research in Education*, 18, 299–333.

Piaget, J. (1970) *Science of education and the psychology of the child.* New York: Penguin Books.

Pink, W. and Hyde, A. (1992) *Effective staff development for school change.* Norwood, NJ: Ablex.

Postman, N. (1992) *Technopoly.* New York: Alfred A. Knopf.

Powell, A., Farrar, E. and Cohen, D. (1985) *The shopping mall high school: Winners and losers in the educational market-place.* Boston: Houghton Mifflin.

Prigogine, I. and Stengers, I. (1984) *Order out of chaos: Man's new dialogue with nature.* New York: Bantam Books.

Raywid, M. (1995) Professional community and its yield at Metro Academy. In K. Louis and D. Kruse (Eds.), *Professionalism and community: Perspectives on reforming urban schools.* Thousand Oaks, CA: Corwin Press, 45–75.

Resnick, L. (1987) Learning in school and out. *Educational Researcher*, 16(9), 13–20.

Rogers, C. (1973) *Freedom to learn.* Columbus, OH: Charles E. Merrill.

Rosenblum, S., Louis, K. and Rossmiller, R. (1994) School leadership and teacher quality of work life. In J. Murphy and K. Louis (Eds.), *Reshaping the principalship: Lessons from restructuring schools.* Newbury Park, CA: Corwin Press.

Rosenholtz, S. (1989) *Teachers' workplace: The social organization of schools.* New York: Teachers College Press.

Rowan, B. (1990) Commitment and control: Alternative strategies for the organizational design of schools. *Review of Research in Education*, 16, 353–389.

Rugg, H. and Shumaker, A. (1969) *The child-centered school: An appraisal of the new education.* Yonkers-on-Hudson, NY: World Book.

Runkel, P., Schmuck, R., Arends, J. and Francisco, R. (1978) *Transforming the school's capacity for problem solving*. Eugene: College of Education, University of Oregon.

Rutter, M., Maughan, B., Mortimore, P., Outson, J. and Smith, A. (1979) *Fifteen thousand hours: Secondary schools and their effects on children*. Cambridge, MA: Harvard University Press.

Salomon, G. (1991) Learning: New conceptions, new opportunities. *Educational Technology*, 31, 41–44.

Sarason, S. (1971) *The culture of the school and the problem of change*. Boston: Allyn and Bacon. (2nd edition, 1982).

Sarason, S. (1974) *The psychological sense of community: Prospects for a community psychology*. San Francisco: Jossey-Bass.

Sarason, S. (1976) *The creation of settings and the future societies*. San Francisco: Jossey-Bass.

Sarason, S. (1981) *Psychology misdirected*. New York: Free Press.

Sarason, S. (1982) *The culture of the school and the problem of change* (2nd edition). Boston: Allyn and Bacon.

Sarason, S. (1983) *Schooling in America: Scapegoat and salvation*. New York: Free Press.

Sarason, S. (1985) *Caring and compassion in clinical practice*. San Francisco: Jossey-Bass.

Sarason, S. (1990) *The predictable failure of educational reform*. San Francisco: Jossey-Bass.

Sarason, S. (1993) *The case for change: Rethinking the preparation of educators*. San Francisco: Jossey-Bass.

Sarason, S. (1995a) *Parental involvement and the political principle*. San Francisco: Jossey-Bass.

Sarason, S. (1995b) *School change*. New York: Teachers College Press.

Sarason, S. (1996a) Power relationships in our schools. In S. Sarason, *Barometers of change*. San Francisco: Jossey-Bass, 239–263.

Sarason, S. (1996b) *Barometers of change*. San Francisco: Jossey-Bass.

Sarason, S. (1996c) *Revisiting "The culture of the school and the problem of change."* New York: Teachers College Press.

Sarason, S. (1997) *How schools might be governed and why*. San Francisco: Jossey-Bass.

Sarason, S., Carroll, C., Maton, K., Cohen, S. and Lorentz, E. (1977) *Human services and resource networks*. San Francisco: Jossey-Bass.

Sarason, S. and Lorentz, E. (1979) *The challenge of the resource exchange network*. San Francisco: Jossey-Bass.

Schaefer, R. (1967) *The school as a center of inquiry*. New York: Harper and Row.

Schein, E. (1988) *Process consultation. Vol. 1: Its role in organization development* (2nd edition). Reading, MA: Addison-Wesley.

Schlechty, P. (1990) *Schools for the twenty-first century*. San Francisco: Jossey-Bass.

Schmidt, W., McKnight, C., Raizen, S. et al. (1996) *A splintered vision: An investigation of mathematics and science teaching in six countries*. London: Kluwer Academic Publishers.

Schmuck, R. and Miles, M. (Eds.) (1971) *Organization development in schools*. Palo Alto, CA: National Press Books.

Schmuck, R., Murray, D., Smith, M., Schwartz, M. and Runkel, M. (1975) *Consultation for innovative schools: OD for multi-unit structure.* Eugene: College of Education, University of Oregon.

Schmuck, R. and Runkel, P. (1970) *Organizational training for a school faculty.* Eugene: University of Oregon.

Schmuck, R. and Runkel, P. (1972) *Handbook of organization development in schools.* Palo Alto, CA: National Press.

Schmuck, R. and Runkel, P. (1985) *Handbook of organization development in schools* (3rd edition). Palo Alto, CA: Mayfield.

Schmuck, R. and Runkel, P. (1994) *The Handbook of organization development in schools and colleges* (4th edition). Prospect Heights, IL: Waveland Press.

Schrag, F. (1992) Conceptions of knowledge. In P. W. Jackson (Ed.), *Handbook of Research on Curriculum.* New York: Macmillan, 268–301.

Schubert, W. H. (1986) *Curriculum: Perspective, paradigm, and possibility.* New York: Macmillan.

Senge, P. (1990) *The fifth discipline: The art and practice of the learning organization.* New York: Doubleday.

Sergiovanni, T. (1994) *Building community in schools.* San Francisco: Jossey-Bass.

Shachar, H. (1996) Developing new traditions in secondary schools: A working model for organizational and instructional change. *Teachers College Record*, 97(4), 549–568.

Shachar, H. and Sharan, S. (1994) Talking, relating, achieving: Effects of cooperative learning and whole class instruction. *Cognition and Instruction*, 12, 313–353.

Shachar, H. and Sharan, S. (1995) Cooperative learning and the organization of secondary schools. *School Effectiveness and School Improvement*, 6, 47–66.

Sharan, S. (1980) Cooperative learning in small groups: Recent methods and effects on achievement, attitudes and ethnic relations. *Review of Educational Research*, 50, 241–271.

Sharan, S. (Ed.) (1990) *Cooperative learning: Theory and research.* New York: Praeger.

Sharan, S. (Ed.) (1994) *Handbook of cooperative learning methods.* Westport, CT: Greenwood.

Sharan, S. (1995) Group Investigation: Theoretical foundations. In J. Pedersen and A. Digby (Eds.), *Secondary schools and cooperative learning: Theories, models and strategies.* New York: Garland, 231–277.

Sharan, S., Gal, I. and Stock, S. (1984) Mutual assistance teams in schools. *Studies in Education (Iyunim B'chinuch)*, 39, 73–88 (in Hebrew).

Sharan, S. and Hertz-Lazarowitz, R. (1978) *Cooperation and communication in schools.* Tel-Aviv: Schocken Publishing House (in Hebrew).

Sharan, S. and Hertz-Lazarowitz, R. (1982) Effects of an instructional change project on teacher's behavior, attitudes and perceptions. *Journal of Applied Behavioral Science*, 18, 185–201.

Sharan, S., Hertz-Lazarowitz, R. and Sharan, Y. (1981) The "It can be done this way too" project: Planning, organization and implementation. In S. Sharan and R. Hertz-Lazarowitz (Eds.), *Teachers and students in the process of change.* Tel-Aviv: Ramot-Tel-Aviv University, 81–111 (in Hebrew).

Sharan, S., Kussell, P., Hertz-Lazarowitz, R., Bejarano, Y., Raviv, S. and Sharan, Y. (1984) *Cooperative learning in the classroom: Research in desegregated schools.* Hillsdale, NJ: Erlbaum.

Sharan, S. and Shachar, H. (1994) Cooperative learning and school organization: A theoretical and practical perspective. In S. Sharan (Ed.), *Handbook of cooperative learning methods.* Westport, CT: Greenwood, 318–335.

Sharan, S. and Sharan, Y. (1991) Changing instructional methods and the culture of the school. In N. Wyner (Ed.), *Current perspectives on the culture of schools.* Cambridge, MA: Brookline Books, 143–164.

Sharan, S. and Shaulov, A. (1990) Cooperative learning, motivation to learn, and academic achievement. In S. Sharan (Ed.), *Cooperative learning: Theory and research.* New York: Praeger, 173–202.

Sharan, Y. (1995) Music of many voices: Group investigation in a cooperative high school classroom. In J. Pedersen and A. Digby (Eds.), *Secondary schools and cooperative learning: Theories, models and strategies.* New York: Garland, 313–339.

Sharan, Y. and Sharan, S. (1987) Training teachers for cooperative learning. *Educational Leadership,* 45, 20–25.

Sharan, Y. and Sharan, S. (1992) *Expanding cooperative learning through group investigation.* New York; Teachers College Press.

Sharan, Y. and Sharan, S. (1993) What do we want to study? How should we go about it? Group Investigation in the cooperative classroom. In R. Stahl (Ed.), *Cooperative learning in the social studies: A handbook for teachers.* Menlo Park, CA: Addison-Wesley, 257–276.

Sharan, Y. and Sharan, S. (1994) Group investigation in the cooperative classroom. In S. Sharan (Ed.), *Handbook of cooperative learning methods.* Westport, CT: Greenwood Press, 97–114.

Shedd, J. and Bacharach, S. (1991) *Tangled hierarchies: Teachers as professionals and the management of schools.* San Francisco: Jossey-Bass.

Siskin, L. (1991) Departments as different worlds: Subject subcultures in secondary schools. *Educational Administration Quarterly,* 27, 134–160.

Siskin, L. and Little, J. (1995) *The subjects in question: Departmental organization and the high school.* New York: Teachers College Press.

Sizer, T. (1984) *Horace's compromise: The dilemma of the American high school.* Boston: Houghton-Mifflin.

Sizer, T. (1993) *Horace's school: Redesigning the American high school.* Boston: Houghton-Mifflin.

Skinner, B. F. (1961) *Cumulative Record.* New York: Appleton-Century-Crofts.

Slavin, R. (1983) *Cooperative learning.* New York: Longman.

Slavin, R. (1989) PET and the pendulum: faddism in education and how to stop it. *Phi Delta Kappan,* 70, 752–758.

Slavin, R. (1990) *Cooperative learning: Theory, research and practice.* Englewood Cliffs, NJ: Prentice-Hall.

Slavin, R., Sharan, S., Kagan, S., Hertz-Lazarowitz, R., Webb, C. and Schmuck, R. (Eds.) (1985) *Learning to cooperate, cooperating to learn.* New York: Plenum Press.

Smagorinsky, P. (1995) The social construction of data: Methodological problems of investigating learning in the zone of proximal development. *Review of Educational Research,* 65, 191–212.

Smylie, M. (1994) Redesigning teachers' work: Connections to the classroom. *Review of Research in Education,* 20, 129–177.

Sousa, D. and Hoy, W. (1981) Bureaucratic structure in schools: A refinement and synthesis in measurement. *Educational Administration Quarterly,* 17, 21–40.

Spiro, R. J., Feltovich, P. J., Jacobson, M. J. and Coulson, R. L. (1991) Cognitive flexi-
    bility, constructivism, and hypertext: Random access instruction for advanced
    knowledge acquisition in ill-structured domains. *Educational Technology*, 31
    (May), 24–33.
Stedman, L. C. (1997) International achievement differences: An assessment of a new
    perspective. *Educational Researcher*, 26(3), 4–15.
Stevenson, H. and Stigler, J. (1992) *The learning gap: Why our schools are failing, and
    what we can learn from Japanese and Chinese education.* New York: Summit
    Books.
Stodolsky, S. (1988) *The subject matters.* Chicago: University of Chicago Press.
Strauss, S. (1993) Theories of learning and development for academics and educators.
    Educational Psychologist, 28(3), 191–203.
Thelen, H. (1954) *The dynamics of groups at work.* Chicago: University of Chicago Press.
Thelen, H. (1981) *The classroom society.* London: Croom Helm.
Thomas, G. (1997) What's the use of theory. *Harvard Educational Review*, 67(1), 75–
    104.
Thomson, S. (Ed.) (1993) *Principals for our changing schools.* Fairfax, VA: National
    Policy Board for Educational Administration.
Thorndike, E. L. (1914) *Educational psychology.* New York: Teachers College Press.
Tonnies, F. ([1887] 1957) *Community and society (Gemeinschaft und gesellschaft).* Trans-
    lated by C. Loomis. New York: HarperCollins.
Tyack, D. and Tobin, W. (1994) The "grammar" of schooling: Why has it been so hard
    to change? *American Educational Research Journal*, 31, 453–479.
von Bertalanffy, L. (1956) General systems theory. *General Systems*, 1, 1–10.
von Bertalanffy, L. (1968) *General systems theory.* New York: George Braziller.
Vygotsky, L. S. (1978) *Mind in society: The development of higher psychological proc-
    ess.* Cambridge, MA: Harvard University Press.
Waldrop, M. M. (1992) *Complexity: The emerging science at the edge of order and
    chaos.* New York: Simon and Schuster.
Watson, G. (Ed.) (1967) *Change in school systems.* Washington, DC: National Training
    Laboratories, National Education Association.
Wehlage, G., Rutter, R., Smith, G., Lesko, N. and Fernandez, R. (1989) *Reducing the
    risk: Schools as communities of support.* Philadelphia: Falmer Press.
Weick, K. (1969) *The social psychology of organizing.* Reading, MA: Addison-Wesley.
Weick, K. (1976) Educational organizations as loosely coupled systems. *Administrative
    Science Quarterly*, 21, 1–19.
Wertch J. V. and Sohmer R. (1995) Vygotsky on learning and development. *Human
    Development*, 38, 332–337.
Wertheimer, M. (1959) *Productive thinking.* New York: Harper.
Westbury, I. (1992) Comparing American and Japanese achievement: Is the United States
    really a low achiever? *Educational Researcher*, 21(5), 18–24.
Wiggins, G. (1995) Curricular coherence and assessment: Making sure that the effect
    matches the intent. In J. A. Beane (Ed.), *Toward a coherent curriculum.* Yearbook
    of the Association for Supervision and Curriculum Development (ASCD). Alex-
    andria, VA: ASCD, 101–119.
Wilson, B., Herriot, R. and Firestone, W. (1988) Explaining differences between ele-
    mentary and secondary schools: Individual, organizational and institutional per-

spectives. In P. Thurston and P. Zodhiates (Eds.), *Advances in educational administration*, 2. New York: JAI Press, 163–200.

Wilson, K. and Daviss, B. (1994) *Redesigning education*. New York: Henry Holt.

Wolf, D., Bixby, J., Glenn, J. and Gardner, H. (1991) To use their minds well: Investigating new forms of student assessment. *Review of Research in Education*, 17, 31–73.

Young, M. (1971) An approach to the study of curricula as socially organized knowledge. In M. Young (Ed.), *Knowledge and control: New directions for the sociology of education*. London: Collier Macmillan, 19–46.

Zander, A. (1982) *Making groups effective*. San Francisco: Jossey-Bass.

Zerubavel, E. (1981) *Hidden rhythms: Schedules and calendars in social life*. Chicago: University of Chicago Press.

Zerubavel, E. (1985) *The seven day circle*. New York: Free Press.

Author Index

Subject Index

Action plans: as part of the school's policy, 82, 86–87; primary components of, 87

Authority: delegated to schools to make changes, 156; hierarchy of, 45, 47, 125, 134; principal as, for teachers, 29

Behavioral objectives: are not the school's mission, 84; too mechanistic for education, 84

Bureacucracy, bureaucratic: approach is replaced by use of collaborative teams, 44; critical features of, 19–21; and documentation of events, 14; dominant role of is shrinking, 37; the essence of the bureaucratic school, 81; as image of organization, 1, 77; and methods of classroom teaching, 4; as oldest of three models of organization, 1; overhaul by restructured school, 77; and the separation of disciplines and teachers, 6; and today's schools, 25; as the traditional form of organization, 2

Carroll, Joseph, 156–157: author of the Copernican Plan, 156–159; main goal is to foster deep reflection and in-depth learning, 157

Centralization, of decision-making power, 4–5

Change: agents, 151–152 (*see also* Consultants); cannot proceed in a mechanistic fashion, 75; critical elements of, 75; duration of change project, 98; and experiential workshops, 98, 100–101; genuine (must encompass all of the school's subsystems), 96; impeded by schools' contradictory messages of required norms versus stated goals, 64; to limit bureaucracy in schools, 6; Miles' classic work on, 102; must be adopted as a part of school policy, 62; need for, 23–25, 115; needed in how schools use time, 149; has occurred in schools less than in other institutions, 96; at one level involves other levels, 35, 44, 48; pragmatic approach to, 25; and relation to in-service teacher training, 59; and resistance to, 6, 64, 67, 110, 154; and restructuring of time, 151–152; in secondary schools is slow in making an appearance, 60; is still accomplished on a school-by-school basis, 96; stages of school change, 65ff.; three main arenas of, in schools, 96–97; too few comprehend how much

About the Authors

SHLOMO SHARAN is Professor of Educational Psychology at Tel-Aviv University–Israel, where he has been involved in school improvement by applying systems theory and small group dynamics to staff organization and classroom instruction. He has been a visiting professor and/or research fellow at Stanford, Yale, Johns Hopkins, and Helsinki (Finland) University. He has authored and edited numerous research studies and books, including *Expanding Cooperative Learning through Group Investigation* (1992) and *Handbook of Cooperative Learning Methods* (Greenwood, 1994).

HANNA SHACHAR is Senior Lecturer in the School of Education at Bar-Ilan University, Ramat Gan, Israel. For many years she chaired the division of consultation to secondary schools in the Institute for the Promotion of Social Integration in the Schools, also at Bar-Ilan University, where she directed citywide intervention projects to introduce participative management in school organization and cooperative learning in classroom instruction. She is co-author, with Shlomo Sharan, of *Organization and Team Management in Schools* (1990) and *Language and Learning in the Cooperative Classroom* (1988).

TAMAR LEVINE is Associate Professor of Education and Chair of the Department of Curriculum and Instruction in the School of Education at Tel-Aviv University. She teaches graduate courses on interdisciplinary and transdisciplinary curriculum development and evaluation. Her major fields of interest and research include the design of effective and constructivist-based instructional strategies, students' and teachers' thinking, the uses of computers to enhance school learning, and gender differences in science and mathematics.

ISBN 0-89789-630-0

HARDCOVER BAR CODE